ROUTLEDGE

GENERAL   EDITC

C000170624

WILFRED OWEN
Selected Poetry and Prose

ROUTLEDGE · ENGLISH · TEXTS
GENERAL EDITOR · JOHN DRAKAKIS

WILFRED OWEN

Selected Poetry and Prose

Edited by
Jennifer Breen

LONDON AND NEW YORK

First published in 1988 by
Routledge
11 New Fetter Lane
London EC4P 4EE

29 West 35th Street
New York, NY 10001

Reprinted 1992

Typeset in Hong Kong by
Best-Set Typesetter Ltd
Printed in England by
Clays Ltd, St Ives plc

British Library Cataloguing in
Publication Data

Owen, Wilfred, 1893–1918
  Wilfred Owen: selected poetry and
  prose. –
  (Routledge English Texts).
  1. English literature, 1900–1945 –
  Texts
  I. Title II. Breen, Jennifer
  828'.91209

  ISBN 0-415 00733 X

Library of Congress Cataloging in
Publication Data

Owen, Wilfred, 1893–1918.
  Wilfred Owen: selected poetry and
  prose.
  Bibliography: p.
  I. Breen, Jennifer. II. Title.
  PR6029.W4A6   1988
  821'.912   87-36954

  ISBN 0-415-00733 X

Contents

Acknowledgements

I am grateful to John Drakakis and Jane Armstrong for their editorial help. I also wish to thank R. W. Noble for his literary advice; John Bell, a literary executor of the Owen Estate, and Gwen Hampshire, at the English Faculty Library, for facilitating my research; and Sharron Livingston for her word-processing.

Acknowledgements are also due to the following copyright holders: the Owen Estate and Chatto & Windus for all poems still in copyright; Wilfred Owen, *Collected Poems*, copyright © 1963 by Chatto & Windus, reprinted by permission of New Directions Publishing Corporation; for Owen's letters © Oxford University Press, reprinted from *Wilfred Owen: Collected Letters* edited by Harold Owen and John Bell (1967) by permission of Oxford University Press (for letters to Siegfried Sassoon also the owners, the Rare Book and Manuscript Library, Columbia University: Wilfred Owen Papers); and Siegfried Sassoon's 'The general' by permission of George Sassoon and Viking Penguin Inc., New York.

Introduction

What is the appeal today of Wilfred Owen's poetry? His main subject – his exposure of the inhumanity of mechanized warfare – is part of it. And the way in which he wrote is equally salient: he radically remodelled traditional poetics by means of technical and colloquial innovation in his sequence of war poems beginning with 'The dead-beat' in August 1917 and ending with 'Smile, smile, smile' in September 1918. Previously, Owen's imitative poetic exercises, in which he had flattered the ghosts of Romantic poets from Keats to Shelley to Swinburne and Wilde, gave little promise of this poetry about war, although his pre-1917 prose – that is, his account of himself in letters addressed mostly to his mother – has occasional passages of impressionistic vigour. It was in the winter months of early 1917 on the Western Front that Owen began to write some entire epistolary sketches which described his truthful impressions of war, thereby transforming both the Keatsian poseur and 'Your very ownest Wilfred'.

To some extent, most of the later accounts of Owen are subjective impressions that are appended to or derived from the poet's own letters. Harold Owen presented a full account of his older brother, Wilfred, in his autobiography, *Journey from Obscurity* (1963–5), but this family memoir is coloured by sentiment and is partly fictionalized, since he relied mainly on memory

1

and not written sources.[1] Other descriptions of Owen at first hand, such as the chapters in Siegfried Sassoon's *Siegfried's Journey* (1945)[2] and Osbert Sitwell's *Noble Essences*, volume 5 (1950),[3] are instances of poets interacting with another poet. The same might be said to a lesser extent about Jon Stallworthy's full-length critical biography, *Wilfred Owen* (1974),[4] in which he distils Owen's letters and Harold Owen's memoir into his own stylized picture of the poet. So we have several vibrant portraits of Owen as a son, a brother, and a poet's poet. Dominic Hibberd's semi-biographical critique, *Owen the Poet* (1986),[5] promises more objectivity in its reassessment of the available sources, especially in relation to the reliability of Harold Owen's memoir, but he salts his re-evaluation of those documents with several major undocumented rumours from, for instance, Robert Graves and Charles Scott Moncrieff.

My brief introductory sketch is an attempt to demythologize the life of 'Owen the poet'. Wilfred Owen was born in 1893. Probably the most important person in his brief 25-year span was his mother, Susan Shaw. She introduced him to the arts – especially music and painting – that she had learnt as a child from her governess, as well as offering him the empathy on which his artistic yearnings thrived. In his letters, long after the actual event, he referred to the formative holiday that he had spent with his mother at Broxton when he was 10: 'Still, was there not Broxton Hill for my uplifting, whose bluebells it may be, more than Greek iambics, fitted me for my job [of writing poetry]' (21 February 1918). What is striking about their mother–son relationship is not so much Susan Owen's concern and love for Wilfred, but his reverence for the maternal, which he celebrated again and again in his letters.

His father, Tom Owen, who was employed as a clerk by the Great Western Railway in Oswestry where Susan Shaw lived, met her there in the late 1870s, but the couple were not married until 1891, when Tom Owen had returned from his subsequent post on the Great Indian Peninsular Railway. Wilfred Owen tried to get along with his conventional father, but their views and interests diverged. The poet was more in touch with the worlds of his two younger brothers, Harold and Colin, and his sister, Mary, despite his conscious attempts to take on an elder brother's role of adviser.

The Owens first lived in the spacious Shaw family home – Plas Wilmot – with Susan's father, Edward Shaw, once Mayor of Oswestry. But in these latter years of her father's life his capital, which had already been diminished by a gambling son who had disappeared to America, was dissipated on the improvidently lavish upkeep of Plas Wilmot. At his death in 1897, the family home was sold. Wilfred Owen consequently enjoyed few social or economic privileges after the age of 4. The Owens moved from the comparative luxury of Plas Wilmot to genteel poverty in the slums of Birkenhead, Liverpool, where Wilfred Owen attended the Birkenhead Institute, a minor fee-paying school which encouraged his interest in language and literature.

When Wilfred was 13, the family moved to Shrewsbury, where Tom Owen had been promoted to the post of assistant superintendent on the Great Western and London and North-Eastern Railways (Western Region). In Shrewsbury, Wilfred finished his schooling at the Shrewsbury Technical School, then became a pupil-teacher at the Wyle Cop School in 1911. He studied for his University of London matriculation examination, but, although he had invested great hopes in this, he gained only a pass, and could not obtain the university scholarship that he longed for in order to enjoy the higher education that his father could not finance for him.

In October 1911 Owen therefore took up the post of unsalaried assistant to the Reverend Wigan, Vicar of Dunsden, near Reading, on the understanding that he would thus establish whether he had a vocation for the Anglican priesthood or not. His two years of religious and social work at Dunsden left him disillusioned with both the clerical life and the evangelical type of Christianity as practised by the Reverend Wigan. In January 1913 Owen left there in a ferment of disaffection. He fell ill, perhaps partly from the trauma of his failure at Dunsden, but by September that year he began working in Bordeaux, France, as an English-language instructor at the Berlitz School. He supplemented his income with private tutoring. The outbreak of the war in August 1914 found him in the Pyrenees happily holidaying with as well as tutoring one of his private pupils, Madame Léger, and her 11-year-old daughter, Nénette.

From early adolescence, especially during his period at Dunsden vicarage, Owen had engaged intermittently in writing poetry. By the age of 18, he had produced a Georgianesque sonnet about his favourite poet, 'Written at Teignmouth, on a pilgrimage to Keats's house'. At 19 he had written the narrative poems, 'Little Claus and Big Claus' and 'The little mermaid', which are based on two of Hans Christian Andersen's fairy-tales. As well as these two long poems, Owen had also sent his mother various other verses, including 'Lines written on my nineteenth birthday'. A few imitative Keatsian sonnets, such as 'On my songs', also stem from his Dunsden period.

Whatever the demerits of his position as lay assistant at Dunsden vicarage, he had more leisure to write poetry there than at Bordeaux. At the Berlitz School he complained about having no time to write poetry, and he claimed that he needed at least 'two *free months*' to prove to himself and the 'impatient world' that he could become a poet (letter to Susan Owen, 24 May 1914). Only a few poems, but again a continuation of his attempts to re-do poetry in the so-called Romantic tradition from Keats to Swinburne, can be ascribed to his two civilian years in France. So did he require the experience of warfare to shake him out of his conformity with the status quo in art if not also in life?

OWEN AND WAR

Only after he had experienced warfare did Owen decisively alter his views about the nature of literary art. In his draft preface to a volume that would have consisted mainly of his major war poems, Owen wrote, 'Above all I am not concerned with Poetry. My subject is War, and the pity of War. The Poetry is in the pity .... All a poet can do today is warn. That is why the true Poets must be truthful.' He had begun in January 1917 to write this 'poetry ... in the pity' in his first letters from the Western Front, before he began doing so in various poetic forms in August 1917. In a letter to his sister, Mary Owen, he compared his early 1917 war letters to some of Siegfried Sassoon's poems, especially 'The redeemer' and 'The death-bed': 'My dear, except in one or two of my letters (ahem!) you will find nothing so perfectly truthfully descriptive of war' (29 August 1917).

In declaring that he was not concerned with 'Poetry', Owen was rejecting the kind of literature which embodied an aesthetically agreeable experience but which did not upset or expose the status quo in detail. Here he was not only repudiating the effete contemporary 'Georgians', such as those whom Edward Marsh anthologized[6] – Walter de la Mare, W. H. Davies, James Stephens, and so on – but also the 1890s' 'aesthetes', such as Wilde and Dowson, who had just had their day. He seemed here to have included in this anathema the neo-Romantic writings of contemporaries such as W. B. Yeats. In effect, Owen here rejected the poems and trends which he himself had tried to emulate in his own poems up to 1917, and which he was not entirely able to shake off in every piece of his writing after that.

By 'pity', Owen meant not compassion but rather the pity which is invoked in the reading and comprehending of tragedy in poetry and other literature. Owen's main concern in his poetry and indeed in his epistolary prose about the war was therefore to reveal its tragic quality, while simultaneously subverting the ideologies of militarism and patriarchy by being truthful about these sets of assumptions which underlie European society. Thus, despite his desire to measure himself as an officer against the values of a militaristic and patriarchal environment, he grappled in both his poetry and his prose with the problems inherent in militarism and patriarchalism, problems which are still with us today.

How did Owen's experiences of militarism relate to his responses to it which are expressed in his poetry and in his epistolary prose? Owen, in trying to be a 'truthful' poet, had one advantage over fellow officers who had attended major public schools: he had not been indoctrinated in the 'mimic warfare' that most of the great public schools at the turn of the century went in for. The pacifist writers, Ogden and Florence, recorded in 1915 that, immediately prior to the 1914–18 war, 'English public schools . . . turn out an imperial race, a race of warriors, and it is not without significance that they are constructed on the barracks system, and that their sport is all mimic warfare'. Moreover, they observed that, at the turn of the century in state elementary schools, children were drilled into 'passive obedience'.[7]

At Shrewsbury Technical School, according to Harold Owen, his brother's teachers did not adopt the usual method of inculcating disciplined behaviour and a physically aggressive spirit

through competitive sport: 'The school ... was quite unconcerned with games or sport of any kind, but outside interests of
educational value were much encouraged and were even woven
into the curriculum itself when sufficient interest was obvious.'[8]
Harold Owen had no reason to idealize this memory. Owen
therefore had not been thoroughly schooled in either the 'warrior'
spirit of the more typical public school product or the unques-
tioning 'obedience' of the state-taught elementary schoolboy.
Between August 1914 and July 1915, unlike many young men
in England, Owen expressed contradictory views about whether
he would enlist or not. On 28 August 1914 he wrote,

> I feel my own life all the more precious and more dear in the
> presence of this deflowering of Europe. While it is true that
> the guns will effect a little useful weeding, I am furious with
> chagrin to think that the Minds which were to have excelled
> the civilization of ten thousand years, are being annihilated –
> and bodies, the product of aeons of Natural Selection, melted
> down to pay for political statues.

Owen's ironic phrase, 'political statues', indicates his subversive
attitude to warlike statesmen who are more interested in their
own power and glory than in the resulting deaths of soldiers.
But his phrase, 'useful weeding', has a chilling Darwinian ring
to it that contradicts his earlier sympathies for the worst-off in
the parish of Dunsden.

Throughout late 1914 Owen remained convinced that artists
should remain non-combatants, and on 2 December he wrote,

> The *Daily Mail* speaks very movingly about the 'duties
> shirked' by English young men. I suffer a good deal of shame.
> But while those ten thousand lusty louts go on playing foot-
> ball I shall go on playing with my little axiom: – that my life is
> worth more than my death to Englishmen. Do you know
> what would hold me together on a battlefield?: The sense that
> I was perpetuating the language in which Keats and the rest of
> them wrote!

Owen is not here expressing any general pacifist argument
against joining up to fight. His assertion of his own confidence
in his talent and of his right to preserve it in the face of war seems

cold-blooded, even if it is true. On the other hand, he here encapsulates the egomania of a dedicated artist.

But by 9 December 1914 he shows that he has become more aware of the brutality of war, which he describes characteristically in terms of the New Testament and the death of his favourite poet, Keats:

> I thought of the thousand redeemers by whose blood my life is being redeemed. To read the Casualty List is like the twenty-first chapter of St Luke [Christ's prophecy of the destruction of Jerusalem] or the last passages of Severn's *Journal* [which describes the death of Keats]; neither readable without tears.

In this passage, Owen no longer distinguishes between the worthy and unworthy, nor between the aristocracy of the sensitive and the lumpenproletariat of cannon-fodder.

It was only in 1915, when he was visiting London to execute a commission for a Bordeaux businessman, Monsieur Peyronnet, that Owen finally decided to enlist. His decision seemed to have been precipitated partly by romantic daydreams after he had noticed 'in London an announcement that any gentleman (fit, etc.) *returning to England from abroad* will be given a Commission – in the "Artists' Rifles" ' (letter to Susan Owen, [*c.*20] June 1915). Owen was sworn in on 21 October 1915 and declared, 'I am the British Army!' Owen's omission of 'in' might have been a slip of the pen, and not a humorous hyperbole, but this entire letter is imbued with exuberance not only about having committed himself to the war but also about having embarked on becoming an officer and a gentleman.

Why did Owen accept patriarchal demands and inducements to join up and fight? That at this stage he submitted wholeheartedly to the social pressures on him to enlist is clear from a letter to his cousin, Leslie Gunston: 'now I don't imagine that the German War will be affected by my joining in, but I know my own future Peace will be' (25 July 1915). Initially, too, Owen was attracted, as the authorities intended, by the romantic idea of soldiering with other 'artists', although he actually met few in that regiment. Moreover, becoming an officer carried with it the rewards of a secure middle-class status. Parental, or at least paternal, pressures might also have been exerted, since once he had begun training in Romford, Essex, he told his mother, 'On the whole, I am fortunate to be where I am, and happy sometimes, as when I think it is a life pleasing to you and Father and the Fatherland' (18 March [1916]). Owen's ironic use of 'Fatherland' for England suggests that he is aware of how war increases the androcentric nature of a society which usually refers to its home-land as the motherland.

Throughout his training, Owen, according to his letters, seemed to have determined to adopt and enjoy the lifestyle of an officer, without much recognition of the destructive con-sequences of this way of life; for example, he was pleased when he scored enough points to be considered a '1st Class shot' (16 August 1916). On 4 June 1916 Owen was commissioned as a sub-lieutenant into the 5th Battalion of the Manchester Regi-ment, and after leave he was sent on 18 June to 3/5th (Reserve) Battalion of the Manchester Regiment, which was then stationed at Witley. The 5th (Reserve) Battalion was a reporting centre for newly commissioned officers, as well as for new recruits, and for men who had recovered from wounds and were awaiting drafts. Because of the great loss of men during the Somme offen-sive in July–November 1916, the Regular Army Manchester Regiment 1st and 2nd Battalions had to be brought up to strength as quickly as possible. Consequently Owen, among others in a draft that was separated from the 5th Battalion, was sent to France in January 1917, where he was attached to the 2nd Battalion. Officially he was listed as 5th Battalion Manchester Regiment, attached to the 2nd Battalion.[9]

Owen seemed not to have questioned the patriarchal ordering of society as exemplified in the army until, at the front in early January 1917, he was shocked into observing the effects of ex-perience of combat: 'On all the officers' faces there is a harassed look that I have never seen before, and which in England, never will be seen – out of jails. The men are just as Bairnsfather has them – expressionless lumps.' But are the officers gaolers or prisoners?

When Owen first fought in France, his battalion was deployed near Beaumont Hamel in order to prepare for an offensive – the Battles of Arras in April 1917. Cyril Falls, an official war his-torian, describes this Allied strategy as if it were part of a ritu-alistic chess game:

Having shown their weakness by making peace proposals on the 12th December 1916, and their desperation by their resort to unrestricted submarine warfare which was most likely to bring the United States into the war as an active participant, the Germans throughout the whole year 1917 were compelled to stand on the defensive on the Western Front.

He also outlined how conditions for the British forces during the winter of 1916–17 in the valley of the Ancre where Beaumont Hamel was situated were worse than formidable:

> in a wilderness of mud, holding water-logged trenches or shell-hole posts, accessible only by night, the infantry abode in conditions which might be likened to those of earth-worms rather than those of human kind.[10]

And it was into those extreme conditions that Owen was precipitated.

During January 1917 the Allied tactic was to capture observation points in preparation for the forthcoming large offensive in April.[11] Owen spent from 4 to 12 January in reconnoitring the part of the line that he and his platoon were to occupy. Subsequently he was thrust into his first dangerous fighting, and his platoon successfully captured and held an advanced post. In this incident, one of Owen's sentries, whom he had placed 'half way down the stairs' of the dug-out, was 'blinded'. In his letter to his mother, Owen was concerned to stress the strength of his nerves, and he emphasized that, despite wishing to escape the shelling by letting himself drown in the flooded dug-out, he behaved with courage. In contrast with himself, Owen's two fellow officers who occupied and commanded adjacent posts could not endure the strain – one was 'completely prostrated' and the other was court-martialled for leaving his guns behind.

Owen's second engagement with the enemy was in an offensive which took place between 20 January and 3 February 1917. By then a 'hard frost' had commenced, and on 25 January 'the thermometer dropped ... to 15 degrees Fahrenheit (−9°C)'.[12] Owen's 'Platoon had no Dug-outs, but had to lie in the snow under the deadly wind' (letter of 4 February 1917). Owen was delighted when he was given a month's respite from the front line and sent on a course to learn the duties of transport officer.

Subsequently, after a couple of relatively safe weeks of digging trenches, Owen suffered concussion from a fall into a cellar and was sent on 18 March (his birthday) for medical treatment at the 13th Casualty Clearing Station. On 4 April he rejoined the 2nd Battalion at the front, commenting, 'My long rest has shaken my nerve.' At the beginning of April, the battles to capture Arras had commenced. The Germans had entrenched themselves behind the new, reinforced, Hindenburg Line, and enjoyed considerable comfort in comparison with the Allies.[13] On his return, Owen immediately became engaged in his battalion's attempts to drive back the German line from Savy Wood to Saint-Quentin, and again he and his men were forced to lie out under German shell-fire in the snow. Owen was by then habitually questioning the wisdom and authority of patriarchal leaders: 'I think that the terribly long time we stayed unrelieved was unavoidable; yet it makes us feel bitterly towards those in England who might relieve us, and will not' (letter to Susan Owen, 25 April 1917). In the context of this letter, Owen meant that the political leaders should 'relieve' them by seeking peace.

Owen's letters in 1917 show a man who on the one hand is trying to conform to the demands of patriarchal and militaristic leadership, and on the other is beginning to see the falseness of his position as a soldier who is engaged in killing and who is afraid of being killed. Also, although he wants to prove how he can fulfil all the requirements of a courageous warrior, he actually relies, in times of stress and danger, on his life-giving relationships with women. On 4 February 1917 he wrote to his mother,

> my Platoon had no Dug-outs, but had to lie in the snow under the deadly wind . . . . I was kept warm by the ardour of Life within me. I forgot hunger in the hunger for Life. The intensity of your Love reached me and kept me living. I thought of you and Mary without a break all the time.

Militaristic policies are reliant on the hardening of men in order that they experience no conflict in their role of killing or being killed. It's not surprising, considering the intensity of conflict within Owen's feelings, that he was sent again to the 13th Casualty Clearing Station for treatment for his 'nerves' or 'shell-shock'. He had been blown off an embankment by high-explosive shells at the same time as his fellow officer, Lieutenant Gaukroger, had been blown to pieces around him.

Once he began to receive treatment from a sympathetic medical officer, the neurologist Captain William Brown, and later Dr Arthur Brock, Owen was able to formulate a more cogent and clearsighted criticism of both militarism and institutionalized religion in relation to his experience of warfare. It is ironic that both Captain Brown and Dr Brock, in curing Owen's 'neurasthenia' by rebuilding his confidence, were also preparing him again for the fulfilment of the patriarchal demand of killing others or being killed in a war of, to say the least, doubtful justification. Both Captain Brown and Dr Brock, whatever their humanitarian aims in peacetime, were part of a military establishment in that they were employed solely to get soldiers ready to fight again as soon as possible.

A War Office committee of inquiry into 'shell-shock' – as many kinds of neurotic terror or abhorrence of warfare were then called – showed that the main aim of nascent psychiatric treatment was to send formerly mentally ill soldiers back to the front as soon as possible. What might appear to be a humane therapeutic regime – that is, nursing and treating soldiers who showed symptoms of fear or abhorrence, instead of court-martialling them – was just another patriarchal policy for ensuring sufficient men to push forward the front line. The report of this committee explains that special centres for the treatment of nervous disorders

> were established in the Army areas in France during the winter of 1916–17 in order to avoid sending large numbers of men suffering from functional nervous disorders to England, as great difficulty was experienced in returning them to their units. Moreover, the French had obtained much success by treating their cases of shell-shock in special centres in the forward areas.[14]

Owen was treated by Captain Brown at one of these centres, but, when he continued to have tremors and nightmares about war, he was transferred in June 1917 to the Craiglockhart War

Hospital which specialized in treating officers who had mental and emotional disorders.

At Craiglockhart, Owen's psychiatrist, Dr Brock, encouraged him to write poetry, edit the residents' magazine *The Hydra*, learn German, teach at a boys' school, participate in amateur dramatics, and join with women volunteers in their social-welfare visits to people in the slums of Edinburgh. These activities renewed Owen's self-confidence. But the most important relationship for Owen at Craiglockhart was to come from meeting there his fellow officer-poet, Siegfried Sassoon. Sassoon had already published *The Old Huntsman and Other Poems* (1917), and Owen was inspired by this contact to begin in August 1917 to write satires, beginning with 'The dead-beat' which he said was 'in Sassoon's style'. But the poems that Owen wrote in the next few months surpassed anything of Sassoon's in both lyrical range and complexity of meaning.

As an army officer in 1916 who was coincidentally recognized as a talented poet by Sassoon in mid-1917, Owen began to move from his precarious lower-middle-class provincial origins into the cosmopolitan middle- or upper-middle-class circle that seemed to dominate the London literary scene. Coincidentally too, through Sassoon's introduction of him to Robert Ross, a patron of young male authors and former friend of Oscar Wilde, Owen got to know Osbert and Edith Sitwell, Charles Scott Moncrieff, and other homosexuals such as Philip Bainbrigge from Shrewsbury. Through Ross and Sassoon, Owen also met Robert Graves as well as H. W. Massingham, who was editor of *The Nation*, and H. G. Wells and Arnold Bennett, who were the two most popular novelists of the day.

What did Owen make of this predominantly male literary circle, with its variety of sexual orientations, ranging from the rampant heterosexuality of H. G. Wells to Sassoon's obsessive bisexuality and Moncrieff's homosexual behaviour? From the evidence of his extant letters to these literary figures and others, we can only conclude that Owen's main concern appeared to be that of getting on friendly terms with them as fellow literary people and discovering what these writers thought of his poetry, not whether any of them evinced any sexual attraction towards him. His central aim was to achieve publication, which seemed to him to depend on his being accepted by this literary circle. Indeed, he was concerned about whether they thought him a poet at all, since he was gratified to hear himself introduced at Robert Graves's wedding on 23 January 1918 as 'Mr Owen, Poet' or even 'Owen, the Poet', on the strength of the circulation of a few of his manuscripts, and Massingham's acceptance of 'Miners', which was to appear in *The Nation* three days later.

At the close of 1917, in his New Year letter to his mother, Owen summarized his life:

> Bouts of awful labour at Shrewsbury & Bordeaux; bouts of amazing pleasure in the Pyrenees, and play at Craiglockhart; bouts of religion at Dunsden; bouts of horrible danger on the Somme; bouts of poetry always; of your affection always; of sympathy for the oppressed always.

If it was the 'bouts of poetry always' which were of most significance, why did Owen return to face death a second time, especially when influential new friends such as Charles Scott Moncrieff had been trying to get him a posting at home?

On 2 October 1917 Owen told his mother, 'I hate washy pacifists as temperamentally as I hate whiskied prussianists. Therefore I feel that I must first get some reputation of gallantry before I could successfully and usefully declare my principles.' For Owen, expediency countermanded logic: only a gallant fighter could be a gallant pacifist – or a truthful poet. Such was (and is) the strength of the belief that a fit man must be willing to fight, or else be labelled a coward, that Owen, who had reputedly suffered from 'loss of nerve' in 1917 at the front, decided in September 1918 to give up toying with the possibility of obtaining a home posting.[15] He returned to France where, in a military offensive on 2 October 1918, he proved his courage by winning the Military Cross. He was killed while helping his men to cross the Sambre Canal under shell-fire on 4 November 1918 – a week before the Armistice.

OWEN'S RECEPTION BY POETS AND CRITICS

Throughout this century, Owen has continued to attract the attention of poets. Edith Sitwell, a minor poet and belletrist, published seven of his war poems posthumously in *Wheels: Fourth Cycle* (1919). Most of the editors of the subsequent collections of his poetry are also poets – Edith Sitwell and Siegfried Sassoon (1920), Edmund Blunden (1931), C. Day Lewis (1963), and Jon Stallworthy (1983) – all of whom admired his work. The poets of the 1930s, according to the dismissive Yeats, adopted Owen as 'a revered sandwich-board man of the revolution' (letter to Dorothy Wellesley, 21 December 1936).[16] Certainly Stephen Spender cited Owen's poetry as an example for young English poets who wrote about the Spanish Civil War while fighting in the Communist-dominated International Brigade.[17] Several of the 1940s' war poets, most notably Keith Douglas, thought that Owen and his fellow soldier–poets had already said all that could be said about modern technological warfare: 'hell cannot be let loose twice: it was let loose in the Great War and it is the same old hell now . . . . Almost all that a modern poet on active service is inspired to write would be tautological.'[18]

Not only supposedly revolutionary or war poets read Owen's poetry: both W. H. Auden and Dylan Thomas helped to establish Owen as an influential figure in twentieth-century poetry. Ironically, some of the 1960s' American Vietnam War poets have come to regard the First World War poets, especially Owen, as having become tamed by the English Literature industry; for example, W. D. Ehrhart, whose early Vietnam poems encapsulate the brutalizing effects of killing others, implies that Owen's poetry is a stereotype in the public's response to war.[19] But Owen's writing survived Yeats's exclusionist tactics and gibes, and it is just as likely to survive the levelling process of academic inclusion.

Various critical approaches of the traditional kind have been tried out on Owen's writing. Initially, Owen was categorized by critics such as F. R. Leavis as a 'poet of the Great War', which suggests that his work was only of historical significance. On the other hand, exponents of various kinds of practical criticism, such as Desmond Graham in *The Truth of War: Owen, Blunden and Rosenberg* (1984), provide detailed *explication de texte* without much consideration of historical milieu. But the most well-travelled track up till now has been that of the biographical bloodhound. The two major exponents of this kind of criticism, which reads the poet's life in the work of art and vice versa, are

Jon Stallworthy and Dominic Hibberd. Although their writings on Owen are often temperate and informative, their method, especially when taken up by others less astute than themselves, gives scope for some confusion between Owen the man and Owen's literary masks. After a somewhat acrimonious exchange in *Stand* between Jon Silkin, another poet, and Dominic Hibberd about their respective methods of 'political' and 'biographical' criticism,[20] Jon Glover argued subsequently in the same journal that appreciation of Owen requires both more and less than a biographical reading of his poetry and prose.[21]

What a new reading must include is some consideration of how readers today, whose world-views have been reoriented by the women's movement and the peace movement, might comprehend Owen's subversion of militarism and patriarchalism. And, if we must structure literature in terms of traditions, schools, and groups, how can we best appreciate his exposure, through his inversions of themes and language, of many of the destructive assumptions implicit in the central poetic tradition of the nineteenth century – Romanticism – to which he himself was once devoted? Even Owen's apparently technical innovation – his sustained and patterned half-rhymes – can be shown as overturning conventional expectations and implying the discord of his exposure of the status quo.

Yet Owen felt paradoxically that his poetry and prose depended upon his intimate experience of that organized violence which he deplored. For, as he wrote just before he returned to the front in September 1918, he had, in order to gain what Stephen Crane called 'the red badge of courage', to experience battle directly again: 'I am much gladder to be going out again than afraid. I shall be better able to cry my outcry, playing my part.' Could his poetry flourish only through his engagement with that which he subverted?

A NOTE ON THE TEXT

My editorial policy has been to print complete poems in chronological order by first date of composition. I have mostly printed complete letters, which I have selected both for their literary merit and the interest of their content.

Owen's poetry, apart from five poems, was not published

15

until after his death in November 1918. Because many of his manuscripts are in an incomplete state, editors have progressively corrected earlier misreadings. Nevertheless, editors still at times disagree about Owen's preferred words when he has left alternatives or has deleted words and not substituted others. Any major disagreement with previous editors is indicated in my Notes to the poems.

My texts for Owen's poems are taken mainly from BL Add. MSS 43720 and 43721, as well as from other manuscripts in the Oxford English Faculty Library, Columbia University Library, and Mr Reresby Sitwell's collection. For the texts of Owen's letters I have consulted microfiche copies of Owen's manuscript letters to his family at the Humanities Research Center, University of Texas at Austin, photocopies of manuscript letters to Siegfried Sassoon at Columbia University Library, as well as manuscript letters at the English Faculty Library in Oxford.

NOTES TO THE INTRODUCTION

1 Harold Owen, *Journey from Obscurity: Wilfred Owen 1893–1918*, 3 vols, Oxford, OUP, 1963–5.
2 Siegfried Sassoon, *Siegfried's Journey, 1916–20*, London, Faber, 1945.
3 Osbert Sitwell, *Noble Essences or Courteous Revelations: An Autobiography*, vol. 5, London, Macmillan, 1950.
4 Jon Stallworthy, *Wilfred Owen: A Biography*, London, OUP and Chatto & Windus, 1974.
5 Dominic Hibberd, *Owen the Poet*, London, Macmillan, 1986.
6 Edward Marsh edited five anthologies of Georgian poetry. Owen had a copy of *Georgian Poetry 1916–17*, London, Poetry Bookshop, November 1917.
7 C. K. Ogden and Mary Sargant Florence, 'Militarism versus feminism: an enquiry and a policy demonstrating that militarism involves the subjection of women' (1915); repr. in Margaret Kamester and Jo Vellacott (eds), *Militarism versus Feminism: Writings on Women and War*, London, Virago, 1987, pp. 121–2.
8 Harold Owen, op. cit., vol. 1, p. 138.
9 Mr George Derbyshire, historian of the 5th Battalion of the

Manchester Regiment, kindly gave me this information.

10 Cyril Falls (comp.), *History of the Great War Based on Official Documents: Military Operations France and Belgium, 1917: The German Retreat to the Hindenburg Line and the Battles of Arras*, London, Macmillan, 1940, Preface, p. vii, and pp. 65–6.
11 ibid., p. 73.
12 ibid., p. 69.
13 ibid., p. 161.
14 *Report of the War Office Committee of Inquiry into 'Shell-Shock'*, London, HMSO, 1922, p. 122.
15 In 1920 Charles Scott Moncrieff said that, when he had enquired in 1918 about obtaining a posting in the War Office for Owen, he had been told that any officer who had suffered a loss of morale as Owen had done could not be given a home posting (Hibberd, op. cit., pp. 76 and 162). But one of Owen's letters shows that he had decided to return to the front and rejoin the ordinary soldiers in their suffering because he thought that it would give credibility to his views as he felt it had done with Sassoon, who had been invalided home in late July 1918 ([*c.*] 30 July 1918).
16 *The Letters of W. B. Yeats*, ed. Allan Wade, London, Rupert Hart-Davis, 1954, p. 874.
17 'Introduction', *Poems for Spain*, ed. Stephen Spender and John Lehmann, London, Hogarth Press, 1939, p. 8.
18 Keith Douglas, 'Poets in this war', *The Times Literary Supplement* (May 1943); 23 April 1971, p. 478.
19 W. D. Ehrhart, *To Those Who Have Gone Home Tired: New and Selected Poems*, Chicago, Thunder's Mouth Press, 1984.
20 Dominic Hibberd, 'Silkin on Owen: some other war', and Jon Silkin, 'Owen: elegist, satirist, or neither; a reply to Dominic Hibberd', *Stand*, 21, 3 (1980), pp. 29–36.
21 Jon Glover, 'Whose Owen?', *Stand*, 22, 3 (1981), pp. 29–31.

List of abbreviations

Owen family

WO	Wilfred Owen
SO	Susan Owen (mother)
HO	Harold Owen (younger brother)
MO	Mary Owen (younger sister)
CO	Colin Owen (youngest brother)
ELG	E. Leslie Gunston (cousin)

Manuscripts

BL 43720	British Library Additional MSS 43720
BL 43721	British Library Additional MSS 43721
OEF	MSS in English Faculty Library, Oxford
OS	MSS presented to Osbert Sitwell; now owned by Mr Reresby Sitwell

Editions in chronological order

Wheels	Edith Sitwell (ed.), *Wheels: Fourth Cycle* (Oxford, Blackwell, 1919), published seven of Owen's war poems
SS/ES	Siegfried Sassoon and Edith Sitwell (eds), *Wilfred Owen: Poems*, London, Chatto & Windus, 1920
EB	Edmund Blunden (ed.), *The Poems of Wilfred Owen*,

London, Chatto & Windus, 1931

CDL   C. Day Lewis (ed.), *The Collected Poems of Wilfred Owen*, London, Chatto & Windus, 1963

DH   Dominic Hibberd (ed.), *Wilfred Owen: War Poems and Others*, London, Chatto & Windus, 1973

JS   Jon Stallworthy (ed.), *Wilfred Owen: The Complete Poems and Fragments*, London, Chatto & Windus/The Hogarth Press and OUP, 1983

Other references

CL   Harold Owen and John Bell (eds), *Wilfred Owen: Collected Letters*, OUP, 1967 (see also John Bell, *Wilfred Owen: Selected Letters*, OUP, 1985, which has some amended notes)

DSRW   Dennis S. R. Welland, *Wilfred Owen: A Critical Study* (London, Chatto & Windus, 1960; repr. with 'Postscript' 1978)

OUP   Oxford University Press

Note: In the case of other works on Owen by any of these authors and editors, details are given in full after the author's or editor's initials.

WILFRED OWEN

Selected Poetry and Prose

SONNET
WRITTEN AT TEIGNMOUTH, ON A PILGRIMAGE TO
KEATS'S HOUSE

Three colours have I known the Deep to wear;
'Tis well today that Purple grandeurs gloom,
Veiling the Emerald sheen and Sky-blue glare.
Well, too, that lowly-brooding clouds now loom
In sable majesty around, fringed fair
With ermine-white of surf: to me they bear
Watery memorials of His mystic doom
Whose Name was writ in Water (saith his tomb).

Eternally may sad waves wail his death,
Choke in their grief 'mongst rocks where he has lain, 10
Or heave in silence, yearning with hushed breath,
While mournfully trail the slow-moved mists and rain,
And softly the small drops slide from weeping trees,
Quivering in anguish to the sobbing breeze.

April 1911   JS, 1983

IMPRESSIONIST

Although his speech ran suavely as a valse
His empty heart gave hollow echoes, false
As ring the vacant city's, late at night.
His narrow eyelids shot suspicious light:

As might the shutters of an evil house.
The more 'good taste' might scavenge, scrub and souse
The alleys of his mind to disembarrass:
The more it left them stony-stark, – like Paris.

And as the erections of his life grew high
And new ambitions piled up fast and thick 10
So narrower was his knowledge of the sky
So denser was his air with dust of brick.

---

* Numbers in square brackets refer to pages on which notes may be found

He valued every man at market price:
Large public parks laid out by legislature
Were his idea and cognisance of Nature.
Neat cemeteries his garden of paradise.

November 1911–May 1912   JS, 1983

LITTLE CLAUS AND BIG CLAUS

There dwelled within a village, once, two men,
Whose names alike were Claus. Four stalwart mares
Had one; the other but a single nag.
Wherefore the richer wight *Big Claus* was called,
While men, if e'er they stayed to speak of him,
Would style his neighbour *Little Claus*. Now hark,
And you shall hear how fared it with them both,
For some do say my story is the truth.

All week, poor Little Claus would plough for Big,
Lending his only horse; and then, in turn,   10
Big Claus would help one day in seven, with all
His team at work. Oh, proudly Little Claus
Curled the lithe whip over the horses five
On Sundays. Were they not his, that day?
And, when the morning sun was warm, and mist
Rose from the fresh furrows like the horses' steam,
While bells out-clamoured hungrily for folk
To fill the void and cavernous church, his heart
Would swell with pride to see the passers-by
Watching his labour; and he smacked his whip   20
And cried out 'Gee ho, my five horses.' 'Nay,'
Quoth Big Claus. 'That ye must not say, for one
Alone is thine.' Alas, no sooner came
Another well-clad churchman by, than Claus
Forgot the prohibition and its giver,
Forgot to guide the ploughshare even, and sang,
Not to the team but to the onlooker,
'Gee ho! my five horses!'
                                'Say it again,'

24

Growled Big Claus, menacing, and nodding slow
His head, much like the toiling nag itself,   30
'And I will knock thy beast upon the pate,
And make an end of it.' Then Little Claus
Ploughed on in silence; till a company
Of pleasant friends crossed o'er the fields, and called
Good-morrow to the tiller at his toil.
Pride set his thoughtless face once more aflush;
Full grandly he replied, and as they passed,
Briskly he clacked his whip. 'Gee ho!' he sang.
'Gee ho! my five horses.' Not a word
Spoke Big Claus, but he snatched a hammer up   40
And smote the hapless creature sudden-dead.
Oh, pitifully Little Claus did weep
To see his one horse dead, and reck his loss.
But afterwards he stripped away the hide
And dried it, till it stiffened in the wind;
Then packed it, slung the bag upon his back
And set foot to a neighbouring town to sell.
The afternoon o'ertook him on his way,
And with it, curdling storm clouds. 'Mid deep brakes
The tempest trapped him; and he wandered wide   50
Below dark sky and darker woods. At length
Firm shadows and a bar of yellow light,
Shining atop of shutters, beckoned him
Towards a farm. His knocking brought the Wife
To door; but 'No!' said she, an unknown man
She could not lodge, the Farmer being from home.
Claus turned round slowly from the sharp-slammed door,
And crept upon a thatch-roofed shed close by;
Whence, as he lay, and twisted him about,
He saw, above the scanty shutters, full   60
Into the kitchen; saw a table spread
With meats and fish and wine; and one there sat –
A Sexton – plying merrily his fork,
The whiles the Woman kept his glass abrim.
Claus watched, lamenting loud, and scarcely heard
The clatter of a heavy horse below.
This, the Farmer's horse, returning. He

Was a worthy man, but long he nursed
A curious prejudice against all Sextons,
Till the bare sight of one would make him mad.	70
So therefore did the Wife regale this one,
The Farmer absent; therefore, too, she now,
At his return, hustled the graveyard-man
Into an empty chest, and thrust the meats
Into the oven, the wines behind the stove.
'Alack,' moaned Little Claus, when all the feast
So vanished. 'Who's above?' the Farmer cried.
'Why liest thou there? Come, rather, in with me.'
Then Claus begged leave to spend the night with him.
'Yea, that thou shalt do; but first we must eat,'	80
Said he; and blithely 'gan to sup a dish
Of gruel, which the Woman set before them.
But Claus still hungered tigerishly for all
Those gravied savouries; and relished ill
The milky groats. So now he placed his foot
Upon his bag, which lay beneath the board;
Making it squeak; and when it squeaked, said 'Hush!'
But saying so, trod harder, and called forth
Still louder noise. 'Hulloa!' said his host.
'What hast thou, in thy bag?'
                  'A wizard dwells	90
In this my bag,' said Claus; 'and wot ye now
What he is saying? Why that we should not
Be spooning gruel, when he's conjured up
Roast meat and pastries hot, inside thy oven there.'
'Zounds!' said the Farmer, peering in the stove.
Mutely the Woman drew her cooking forth
And so they ate. Again the enchanter spoke
In voice of chirping leather; telling now
Of three full wine jars, conjured by the stove.
Tongue-tied and fidgeting, the Wife fetched out	100
Her hidden bottles; so, the Farmer drank,
And was right merry. Presently, he said,
'And can thy mage bring up the Evil One?
I have a mind to see the Infernal sight,
Being in merry mood.' 'He can!' quoth Claus.

'Listen; he answers "Yes"; and he should do't
Only the sight is passing ugly.' 'Pooh!
I have no fear. What form, though, would he take?'
'Oh, he would have the image of a Sexton.'
'Nay, that's ugly indeed; for you must know   110
I cannot tolerate a Sexton. Still,
As I shall know it is the Evil One
The sight will be much easier to be borne.
Proceed, I'm ready; only – not too near!'
They sat awhile in silence, while the bag
Gave forth strange sounds. These Claus interpreted
As meaning that the Demon might be found
Cowering inside the oaken chest, all fear.
Full cautiously they stepped towards the thing;
Slowly and slightly raised they up the lid.   120
The Farmer peeped with eyes half-closed for dread,
Suddenly saw the quaking man, and sprang
Stammering away. 'Oh! Now, I've seen him. Ugh!
Exactly like our Sexton – shocking sight!'
So thereupon he needs must drink again,
And on they drank, till night was far advanced.
But when dawn brake, the Farmer rose and said,
'See, you must sell to me your Conjuror.'
'I cannot, – nay – I cannot; only think
Of all the benefit he is to me.'   130
Long Claus held out against entreaty thus;
Until, as if quick-touched with gratitude
To a kindly host, he parted with his bag
For a bushelful of money, measured fair.
'Moreover,' said the host, 'have thou the Chest;
'Who knows what ill may lurk within it yet?'
And bade the traveller, being well pleased withal,
Take a large barrow for removing it.
'Farewell!' quoth Claus, and pushed forth on his way.
A broad, but bridge-spanned river rolled athwart   140
The forest road; and when Claus gained the bridge
He stopped, hard breathing, questioning thus aloud:
'What if I rid me of this lurdane chest?
Heavy it is as it were filled with stone.

I'll trundle it no more. Belike the flood
Will bear it home; if not – then I care not.'
With that, he dragged and tilted it about
As if to heave it o'er the waterside.
'Hi!' shrieked the Sexton. 'Hi! man, leave it be!
Let me out first!' 'Ha! Zooks!' quoth Little Claus,   150
Feigning a fright. 'And is he still inside?
I'll haste and fling him in, so he may drown.'
'Oh no! No! No! A bushel of my wealth
Shall be your own, and you will set me free!'
At once the frolic knave undid the lock;
And out the Sexton crept, on cramped knees.
Then, after gladly throwing the empty chest
Over the bridge, led Claus back to his house,
Meted the dole, and sent him home behind
A barrow now nigh full of shining coin.   160
To be assured of perfect measure, Claus
Dispatched a lad to Big Claus, craving for
The use of his best bushel. He, brain-teased
To know the cause of such a need, smeared tar
Upon the bottom of the vase; and lo!
The thing, returned, bore three new shillings, fast
Against the tar, bright moons in ebon sky.
Whence comes all this? thought he; and running straight
To Little Claus, was told it was the price
Of his dead horse's skin. 'A goodly price!'   170
Quoth he; and hastened home and smote his team
All dead; and hurried with their skins to town,
To make a mighty bargain. 'Who'll buy skins!'
He cried through all the streets; 'Skins! Skins!'
So brought the cobblers and the tanners out;
But they, being answered that his charge for each
Was a bushelful of money, thought he mocked,
And mocked again; until his senseless cries
Chafed them to wrath. 'Thou crazy loon!' yelled they,
'Thinkest we measure coin in bushels? Fie!   180
I'll warrant that we'll tan *thy* skin for thee
To colours black and blue'; and that they did,
With stirrups, belts and thongs and apron-bands.

28

So flailed him home, skin-seared with murderous stripes,
And burning hot with murderous thoughts within.
'The Knave shall pay for this; shall pay for this;
I'll kill him for his pains.' And, sure, that night,
He crept round to the house of Little Claus,
Stole to his bed, tho' scarcely seeing aught,
And struck the still, prone figure, dastardly   190
With pointed hatchet on the head; and left.
'The wicked man!' chirped Little Claus's voice
From out a corner. 'Tried to kill me! Oh!
Lucky for my grandame she was dead.'
For Little Claus's grandmother had died
That eve; and he, albeit her rancid tongue
Had vexed him oft, out-laid her in his bed,
Hoping the warmth might charm her life-warmth back.
He in a large chair dozed. From which he watched
Big Claus's deed. But soon as Claus was gone,   200
He dressed the dame in holiday attire,
Placed her upon the back seat of his cart,
And drove her, with a borrowed horse, towards town.
By sunrise, they had stopped outside an inn,
Whereof the landlord was a wealthy man,
And good; only as passionate as if
Composed of snuff and pepper. Of this man
Claus asked refreshment; answ'ring to his greeting,
'Yea, host, I stir betimes today; for I
Am taking my old grandame to the town.   210
She's in the cart: I cannot bring her in.
Perhaps, mine host, ye'll take her a glass of mead?
Speak loud; she's somewhat hard of hearing.' . . . 'Hem!'
The landlord cried, at the beldame's side,
Who sat up in the cart as if alive,
'Here is a glass of mead from your grandson, dame!'
Bolt upright sat the dame, nor moved an inch.
'Here is a glass of mead from your grandson, dame!'
Stark stared the dame, nor uttered she a word.
'Do ye not hear? Receive this glass of mead!'   220
Then, when he'd bawled the same a few times more,
As she ne'er stirred, he flew into a rage,

29

And flung the beaker full across her face.
At once she fell stiff backward to the ground.
'Hullo!' cried Little Claus, now rushing out,
And seizing on the landlord. 'What is this?
You've killed my grandmother! D'ye see this hole
Deep in her forehead?' 'Miserable me!
What a misfortune here! And all this comes
Of my too hasty temper!' Loud he moaned,   230
Wringing his hands. Then, 'Little Claus,' he said,
'Dear Little Claus, I'll have thy grandmother
Buried as if she were mine own; and you –
Shall have a bushel of my money, if
You speak no word of what has happened here.
For were it known, my head were not my own.'
So Little Claus took home another load
Of money, and the host inearthed the dame.

A second time, a lad rapped Big Claus' door,
Praying him lend a bushel to his friend.   240
In wide astonishment, he took the thing
Himself to Little Claus; who, smiling, said,
'You killed my grandmother instead of me!
I sold her for this bushelful of coin!'
Not long the elder stayed on hearing this;
But posted home to where his own shrunk gammer
Ever a-knitting sat, and ruthlessly
He struck her feeble spark of life extinct,
Like one that strikes with sudden iron the coals
And makes the low flame vanish into air.   250
This done, he drove to an apothecary
Off'ring to sell to him a defunct corse.
'Whose is it? And how came you by the same?'
'My grandmother's; I struck her dead to get
A bushel of thy money in exchange.'
'Lord help us!' said the man. 'Thou'rt surely mad!
If not, I vow your head's in jeopardy!'
And then he pointed out the heinousness
Of such a deed; the awful wickedness,
And punishment thereof; all which so scared   260

Big Claus, that, like a hounded hare,
He bolted from the shop, leapt on his cart,
And lashed his horses to a maniac's pace.
But maniac all thought the man; and so
They let him go wherever he might please.
Now, after reaching home, he knew one place,
One house, from which no man could turn his step
And that was Little Claus's .... When he stood
Facing that small deceiver, suddenly
He cast a roomy bag o'er all his length,   270
Tied it; and had him safe. He took his fill
Of wordy taunts and vaunts and promises
Of speedy drowning. Then to riverwards
He bore his prey to wreak the act itself.
None of the lightest was his cumbrous load;
Long, very long his way; and, passing by
A Church whence organ-tones were pealing forth,
Big Claus bethought him he would rest therein,
And hear a psalm before he further trudged.
Meantime, because he knew the strings were strong,   280
And thought the people must be all in Church,
He left the bag outside the open door.
'Heigh-ho!' sighed Little Claus, a-squirming round
And thrusting out his prison-sides, as if
Some monstrous ferret poked about its sack.
But never a cord could he unloose; so lay
Quite still again and thought. Ere long a herd
Of cows came pattering by upon the dust;
And when the pattering passed, he heard the slow
Tap-tapping of an ancient drover's staff.   290
'Heigh-ho!' sighed Little Claus, 'I'm very young
To be already bound for heavenly lands.'
'And I,' the answer came, 'who am so old,
Have never found the way to reach them yet.'
'Open the bag; creep in, instead of me,
And thou shalt go to heaven in a trice.'
'Then take my cattle, friend, and feed them well,'
Said he; and Claus soon closed the bag o'er him
And off he drove his thirty lusty cows.

31

The dust had scarcely settled in their rear, 300
When Big Claus stepped into the sun again,
And took his bag. 'How light it seems,' thought he.
'That comes of hearing holy psalms, I ween!'
So, easily he reached the river's banks,
And flung the bag a-gurgling to the deep.
'There lie! I'll smart from no more tricks of thine.'
But, walking home, at the forking of the roads,
Who should he meet but Little Claus himself,
Yelping at stubborn cattle. 'Mercy me!
How's this! Did I not drown thee!' gasped Big Claus. 310
'Oh aye!' said he, as he thwacked a backward beast,
'Oh aye! You threw me in the river there,
Some half an hour ago.' Big Claus was dumb,
And followed lamely on behind the herd.
At length he spoke: 'Where got ye all this kine?'
Said Little Claus: 'Sea-cattle is this herd.
I'll tell thee all the story; thanking thee
For having drowned me; since, escaping thus,
I'm very wealthy. Fearful was the fall
Into the waters; down I sank at once, 320
But lighted on a bed of softest grass.
A moment afterward, the bag was loosed;
The loveliest girl imaginable, dressed
In snowy robes, and wreathed with dripping green,
Gave me her gentle hand, and said, "O Claus,
There is some cattle for thee; if thou go
A mile along the Road, another herd
Thou'lt find; go, take it; as a gift from me."
I now perceived the river is a Road –
The sea-folk's high road; there they walked and drove, 330
Passing from ocean far into the land.
How beautiful it was! How fresh the grass!
The fishes darted past my ear like birds,
And Oh the cattle grazing on the dykes!'
'Hum,' the other said. 'I marvel much
That ye return so soon from such a place.'
'Why! 'tis a piece of policy, my friend!
I cross the fields towards my promised herd,

32

Because the River Road winds round about;
And so I save much time.' ... 'Thou lucky man!   340
Could I obtain sea-cows as thou hast done?'
'No doubt thou could'st! If thou but walk with me,
Towards the banks, then get inside the bag,
I'd throw thee in with all the pleasure in life!'
'Thanks!' said Big Claus. 'But if I get no cows,
I'll beat you famously when I return.'
'Nay, do not be so hard!' And so they went.
Now, as the drove of thirsty cows caught sight
Of running water, on they lumbered fast
Towards it, tossing horns and lowing loud.   350
'Look, look!' cried Little Claus. 'What haste they show!
How they do long to be below again!'
No sooner saw Big Claus that sudden rush
Than furious he waxed to be cast in.
'Give me a stone, for fear I should not sink!'
He cried. 'No fear of that,' the other said.
Still, in the bag he put a stone. Then pushed,
And, plump! into the river fell Big Claus.
'I fear he will not find the cattle, though,'
Said Little Claus. And away he drove his own.   360

March–May 1912   JS, 1983

LINES WRITTEN ON MY NINETEENTH BIRTHDAY:
MARCH 18, 1912

Two Spirits woke me from my sleep this morn;
Both most unwelcome were; for they have torn
Away from me the shady screens of ease
And unreflecting, unself-scanning Peace
Wherein I used to hide me from annoy
In years which found and left me still a boy.
The First rose solemn, with a Voice of stern
Monition; and it said, 'Look back! and learn
To number life by moments, not by years;
Know that thy youth to its completion nears.   10
This night the final minute hath been laid

33

Upon thy nineteen Springs. Aye, be dismayed
To see the Fourth Part of thy utmost span
Now spent! What then? Affrighted dost thou plan
To crowd the rest with action, every whit?
Ev'n so essay; but know thou canst not knit
Thy web of hours so close as to regain
E'en one lost stitch! For ever gaps remain!'
Hereat it ceased; for now a second Shade
Caught all my senses to't; no sound it made;   20
No form it had; but quietly it drew
Its tightening band of pain through every thew
Of my frail body .... Pain? – Why Pain today?
Sure, not a taste of what this tingling clay
Shall suffer through the year? And yet, if so,
'Twill be but my most rightful share, I trow,
Scarce worse than the keen hunger-pinch that racks
Numberless wretches all their life. Pain slacks
Its hold on one, only to grasp another;
And why should I be spared, and not my brother?   30

So thinking, quickly I pass the day. And lo!
What kindnesses the friends around me show!
How many eyes in warm solicitude
Have smiled upon me! Tongues that have been rude
Are gentle now ... Yet still, how do I miss
Thine eyes, *thy* voice, my Mother! Oft I kiss
Thy portrait, and I clutch thy letter dear
As if it were thy hand.
                         At this, fresh cheer
Comes over me; and now upon my couch
Of ruby velvet, o'er the fire I crouch   40
In full content. I only pause from reading
To scribble these few lines; or, scarcely heeding
The dismal damp abroad, to mock the rain
Shooting its sleety balls at me in vain.
– Ho, thus, methinks, hereafter, when the weak
Creations of a mental mist shall seek
To quench my soul, I'll thwart them by the shield
Of crystal hope!

34

For there have been revealed
Heart-secrets since the coming of this day,
Making me thankful for its thorn-paved way.   50
Among them this: 'No joy is comparable
Unto the *melting* – soft and gradual –
Of torture's needles in the flesh. To sail
Smoothly from out the abysmal anguish-jail
And tread the placid plains of *normal ease*
Is sweeter far, I deem, than all the glees
Which we may catch by mounting higher still
Into the dangerous air where actual bliss doth thrill.'

18 March 1912   JS, 1983

EVE OF ST MARK

And as a peach-fruit, hard as stone
Between twelve Autumn eves and morns
Will soften to the ripest pulp;
So, in twelve instants which to him
Were long outdrawn as balmy autumn eves,
Her beauty melted suddenly.
His broad lips trembled o'er her cheek
Like the long peach leaves afluttering round their fruit.

April–May 1912   JS, 1983

THE UNRETURNING

Suddenly night crushed out the day and hurled
Her remnants over cloud-peaks, thunder-walled.
Then fell a stillness such as harks appalled
When far-gone dead return upon the world.

There watched I for the Dead; but no ghost woke.
Each one whom Life exiled I named and called.
But they were all too far, or dumbed, or thralled,
And never one fared back to me or spoke.

35

Then peered the indefinite unshapen dawn
With vacant gloaming, sad as half-lit minds,   10
The weak-limned hour when sick men's sighs are drained.
And while I wondered on their being withdrawn,
Gagged by the smothering Wing which none unbinds,
I dreaded even a heaven with doors so chained.

1912–13 to January 1918   EB, 1931

STUNNED BY THEIR LIFE'S EXPLOSION INTO LOVE

Stunned by their life's explosion into love
Some men stay deaf and dizzy ever after,
And blindly through the press they grope or shove,
Nor heed they more of sorrowing or laughter.

And others, having fixed their hope above,
Chastened and maimed by bitter chastity,
Grow to forget spring flowers, and why the dove
Makes music with her fellow, endlessly.

Ah! pity these were told not that their thirsts
Are slaked not by priest's wine nor lust's outbursts,   10
But Poesy. They, knowing Verse to be
God's soothest answer to all passion's plea,
And loving beauties writ and wrought of art,
Might yet have kept a whole and splendid heart.

?1913–January 1918   JS, 1983

THE SLEEPING BEAUTY

Sojourning through a southern realm in youth,
I came upon a house by happy chance
Where bode a marvellous Beauty. There, romance
Flew faerily until I lit on truth –
For lo, the fair Child slumbered. Though, forsooth,
She lay not blanketed in drowsy trance,
But leapt alert of limb and keen of glance,

36

From sun to shower; from gaiety to ruth;
Yet breathed her loveliness asleep in her:
For, when I kissed, her eyelids knew no stir.　　　10
So back I drew tiptoe from that Princess,
Because it was too soon, and not my part,
To start voluptuous pulses in her heart,
And kiss her to the world of Consciousness.

1914–January 1918　　CDL, 1963

1914

War broke: and now the Winter of the world
With perishing great darkness closes in.
The foul tornado, centred at Berlin,
Is over all the width of Europe whirled,
Rending the sails of progress. Rent or furled
Are all Art's ensigns. Verse wails. Now begin
Famines of thought and feeling. Love's wine's thin.
The grain of human Autumn rots, down-hurled.

For after Spring had bloomed in early Greece,
And Summer blazed her glory out with Rome,　　　10
An Autumn softly fell, a harvest home,
A slow grand age, and rich with all increase.
But now, for us, wild Winter, and the need
Of sowings for new Spring, and blood for seed.

1914–January 1918　　CDL, 1963

MAUNDY THURSDAY

Between the brown hands of a server-lad
The silver cross was offered to be kissed.
The men came up, lugubrious, but not sad,
And knelt reluctantly, half-prejudiced.
(And kissing, kissed the emblem of a creed.)
Then mourning women knelt; meek mouths they had,
(And kissed the body of the Christ indeed.)

37

Young children came, with eager lips and glad.
(These kissed a silver doll, immensely bright.)
Then I, too, knelt before that acolyte.   10
Above the crucifix I bent my head:
The Christ was thin, and cold, and very dead:
And yet I bowed, yea, kissed – my lips did cling.
(I kissed the warm live hand that held the thing.)

May 1915–January 1918   CDL, 1963

NOCTURNE

Now, as the warm approach of honied slumber blurs
    my sense,
Before I yield me to th'enchantment of my bed,
God rest all souls in toil and turbulence,
All men a-weary seeking bread;
God rest them all tonight!
Let sleep expunge
The day's monotonous vistas from their sight;
And let them plunge
Deep down the dusky firmament of reverie
And drowse of dreams with me.   10

Ah! I should drowse away the night most peacefully
But that there toil too many bodies unreposed
Who fain would fall on lethargy;
Too many leaden eyes unclosed;
And aching hands amove
Interminably,
Beneath the light that night will not remove;
Too many brains that rave in dust and steam!
They rave, but cannot dream!

June–August 1915   JS, 1983

SONNET AUTUMNAL

If it be very strange and sorrowful
To scent the first night-frost in autumntide;

38

If, on the sombre day when Summer died,
Men shuddered, awed to hear her burial;
And if the dissolution of one rose,
Whereof the future holds abundant store,
Engender human tears, – ah! how much more
Sorrows and suffers he whose sense foreknows
The weakening and the withering of a love,
The dying of a love that had been dear;   10
Who feels upon a hand, but lately-warm,
A hardness of indifference, like a glove;
And in her hollow calm of voice may hear
The menace of a drear and mighty storm.

1915–January 1918   CDL, 1963

THE ONE REMAINS

I sometimes think of those pale perfect faces
My wonder has not looked upon, as yet.
And of those others never to be met;
And often pore I on the secret traces
Left in my heart, of countenances seen
And lost as soon as seen, – but which mine eye
Remembers as my old home, or the lie
Of landscapes whereupon my windows lean.

And as for those long known and worshipped long,
But now, alas! no longer, and the song   10
Of voices that have said, 'Adieu, we part',
Their reminiscences would cease my heart,
Except I still hoped find, some time, some place,
All beauty, once for ever, in one face.

c.1915–January 1918   CDL, 1963

ON A DREAM

I leaned, blank-eyed, in lonely thoughtless thought,
Upon the night, athwart my threshold stone;
When there came One with hurried, frightened moan,

With tear-drained eyes, wild hair, and hands distraught,
Who fell about my knees, and swift besought
Help and my love, for she was all alone
For love of me; and from her world out-thrown.
I knew that lovely head; her hands I caught;

For hours I felt her lips warm on my cheek,
As through the vast void of the dark we fled.   10
For precious hours her limbs in mine were curled,
Until with utter joy I tried to speak:
And lo! I raved with fever on my bed,
And melancholy dawn bestirred the world.

?1915–January 1918   JS, 1983

WHEREAS MOST WOMEN LIVE
THIS DIFFICULT LIFE

Whereas most women live this difficult life
Merely in order not to die the death
And take experience as they take their breath,
Accepting backyards, travail, crusts, all naif;
And nothing greatly love, and nothing loathe –
Others there are who seemingly forget
That men build walls to shelter from the wet,
For sustenance take meals, for comfort clothe.

These must embellish every act with grace;
These eat for savours; dress to show their lace;   10
Suppose the earth for gardens; hands for nard.
Now which you hold as higher than the other
Depends, in fine, on whether you regard
The poetess as nobler than the Mother.

?1915   JS, 1983

FROM MY DIARY, JULY 1914

Leaves
   Murmuring by myriads in the shimmering trees.

Lives
  Wakening with wonder in the Pyrenees.
Birds
  Cheerily chirping in the early day.
Bards
  Singing of summer, scything through the hay.
Bees
  Shaking the heavy dews from bloom and frond.   10
Boys
  Bursting the surface of the ebony pond.
Flashes
  Of swimmers carving through the sparkling cold.
Fleshes
  Gleaming with wetness to the morning gold.
A mead
  Bordered about with warbling water brooks.
A maid
  Laughing the love-laugh with me; proud of looks.   20
The heat
  Throbbing between the upland and the peak.
Her heart
  Quivering with passion to my pressed cheek.
Braiding
  Of floating flames across the mountain brow.
Brooding
  Of stillness; and a sighing of the bough.
Stirs
  Of leaflets in the gloom; soft petal-showers.   30
Stars
  Expanding with the starr'd nocturnal flowers.

?1915–January 1918   EB, 1931

TO EROS

In that I loved you, Love, I worshipped you.
In that I worshipped well, I sacrificed.
All of most worth I bound and burnt and slew:
Old peaceful lives; frail flowers; firm friends; and Christ.

41

I slew all falser loves; I slew all true,
That I might nothing love but your truth, Boy.
Fair fame I cast away as bridegrooms do
Their wedding garments in their haste of joy.

But when I fell upon your sandalled feet,
You laughed; you loosed away my lips; you rose. 10
I heard the singing of your wings' retreat;
Far-flown, I watched you flush the Olympian snows,
Beyond my hoping. Starkly I returned
To stare upon the ash of all I burned.

1916–January 1918   EB, 1931

TO —

Three rompers run together, hand in hand.
The middle boy stops short, the others hurtle:
What bumps, what shrieks, what laughter turning turtle.
Love, racing between us two, has planned
A sudden mischief: shortly he will stand
And we shall shock. We cannot help but fall;
What matter? Why, it will not hurt at all,
Our youth is supple, and the world is sand.

Better our lips should bruise our eyes, than He,
Rude Love, out-run our breath; you pant, and I, 10
I cannot run much farther; mind that we
Both laugh with Love; and having tumbled, try
To go forever children, hand in hand.
The sea is rising ... and the world is sand.

10 May 1916   CDL, 1963

THE END

After the blast of lightning from the east,
The flourish of loud clouds; the Chariot Throne,
After the drums of time have rolled and ceased.
And by the bronze west long retreat is blown,

– Shall Life renew these bodies? Of a truth
All death will he annul, all tears assuage?
Or fill these void veins full again with youth,
And wash, with an immortal water, age?

When I do ask white Age, he saith not so;
  'My head hangs weighed with snow.'   10
And when I hearken to the Earth, she saith:
  'My fiery heart shrinks, aching. It is death.
Mine ancient scars shall not be glorified,
  Nor my titanic tears, the seas, be dried.'

September 1916–May 1918   SS/ES, 1921 (reissue)

STORM

His face was charged with beauty as a cloud
  With glimmering lightning. When it shadowed me,
  I shook, and was uneasy as a tree
That draws the brilliant danger, tremulous, bowed.

So must I tempt that face to loose its lightning.
  Great gods, whose beauty is death, will laugh above,
  Who made his beauty lovelier than love.
I shall be bright with their unearthly brightening.

And happier were it if my sap consume;
Glorious will shine the opening of my heart;   10
The land shall freshen that was under gloom;
What matter if all men cry aloud and start,
And women hide bleak faces in their shawl,
At those hilarious thunders of my fall?

October 1916–October 1917   EB, 1931

HAPPINESS

Ever again to breathe pure happiness,
So happy that we gave away our toy?
We smiled at nothings, needing no caress?

Have we not laughed too often since with Joy?
Have we not stolen too strange and sorrowful wrongs
For her hands' pardoning? The sun may cleanse,
And time, and starlight. Life will sing great songs,
And god will show us pleasures more than men's.

Yet Heaven looks smaller than the old dolls-home,
No nestling place is left in bluebell bloom,   10
And the wide arms of trees have lost their scope.
The former happiness is unreturning:
Boys' griefs are not so grievous as youth's yearning;
Boys have no sadness sadder than our hope.

February–August 1917   EB, 1931

WITH AN IDENTITY DISC

If ever I had dreamed of my dead Name
High in the heart of London, unsurpassed
By Time forever, and the Fugitive, Fame,
There taking a long sanctuary at last,

I better that; and recollect with shame
How once I longed to hide it from life's heats
Under those holy cypresses, the same
That keep in shade the quiet place of Keats.

Now rather, thank I God there is no risk
Of gravers scoring it with florid screed,   10
Let my inscription be this soldier's disc.
Wear it, sweet friend. Inscribe no date nor deed.
But may thy heartbeat kiss it, night and day
Until the name grow blurred and wear away.

March–October 1917   EB, 1931

THE FATES

They watch me, those informers to the Fates
Called Fortune, Chance, Necessity, or Death:

Time, in disguise as one who serves and waits,
Eternity as girls of fragrant breath.
I know them. Men and Boys are in their pay
And those I hold trustiest friends may prove
Agents of Theirs to take me if I stray
From fatal ordnance. If I move they move, –

Escape? There is one unwatched way: your eyes,
O Beauty! Keep me good that secret gate!   10
And when the cordon tightens of the spies
Let the close iris of your eyes grow great,
So I'll evade the vice and rack of age
And miss the march of lifetime, stage by stage.

June–July 1917   *EB, 1931*

SONG OF SONGS

Sing me at dawn but only with your laugh;
   Like sprightly Spring that laugheth into leaf;
   Like Love, that cannot flute for smiling at Life.

Sing to me only with your speech all day,
   As voluble leaflets do. Let viols die.
   The least word of your lips is melody.

Sing me at dusk, but only with your sigh;
   Like lifting seas it solaceth: breathe so,
   All voicelessly, the sense that no songs say.

Sing me at midnight with your murmurous heart;   10
   And let its moaning like a chord be heard
   Surging through you and sobbing unsubdued.

June–August 1917   The Hydra, *1 September 1917*

SIX O'CLOCK IN PRINCES STREET

In twos and threes, they have not far to roam
   Crowds that thread eastward, gay of eyes;

Those seek no further than their quiet home,
  Wives, walking westward, slow and wise.

Neither should I go fooling over clouds,
  Following gleams unsafe, untrue,
And tiring after beauty through star-crowds,
  Dared I go side by side with you.

Or be you in the gutter where you stand,
  Pale rain-flawed phantom of the place,   10
With news of all the nations in your hand,
  And all their sorrows in your face.

June–October 1917   EB, 1931

THE DEAD-BEAT

He dropped, – more sullenly than wearily
Lay stupid like a cod, heavy like meat,
And none of us could kick him to his feet;
– Just blinked at my revolver, blearily;
– Didn't appear to know a war was on,
Or see the blasted trench at which he stared.
'I'll do 'em in,' he whined. 'If this hand's spared,
I'll murder them, I will.'

            ★ ★ ★

           A low voice said,
'It's Blighty, p'raps, he sees: his pluck's all gone,
Dreaming of all the valiant, that *aren't* dead: 10
Bold uncles, smiling ministerially;
Maybe his brave, young wife, getting her fun
In some new home, improved materially.
It's not these stiffs have crazed him; nor the Hun.'

            ★ ★ ★

We sent him down at last, out of the way.
Unwounded; – stout lad, too, before that strafe.
Malingering? Stretcher bearers winked, 'Not half!'

            ★ ★ ★

Next day I heard the Doc's well-whiskied laugh:
'That scum you sent down last night soon died. Hooray!'

August 1917–May 1918   Wheels, *1919*

AT A CALVARY NEAR THE ANCRE

One ever hangs where shelled roads part.
   In this war He too lost a limb,
But His disciples hide apart;
   And now the Soldiers bear with Him.

Near Golgotha strolls many a priest,
   And in their faces there is pride
That they were flesh-marked by the Beast
   By whom the gentle Christ's denied.

The scribes on all the people shove
   And bawl allegiance to the state,   10
But they who love the greater love
   Lay down their life; they do not hate.

After August 1917   EB, *1931*

INSPECTION

'You! What d'you mean by this?' I rapped.
'You dare to come on parade like this?'
'Please, sir, it's –' ''Old yer mouth,' the sergeant snapped.
'I takes 'is name, sir?' – 'Please, and then dismiss.'

Some days 'confined to camp' he got,
For being 'dirty on parade'.
He told me, afterwards, the damnèd spot
Was blood, his own. 'Well, blood is dirt,' I said.

'Blood's dirt,' he laughed, looking away,
Far off to where his wound had bled   10
And almost merged for ever into clay.
'The world is washing out its stains,' he said.

47

'It doesn't like our cheeks so red:
Young blood's its great objection,
But when we're duly white-washed, being dead,
The race will bear Field Marshal God's inspection.'

August–October 1917   EB, 1931

MY SHY HAND

My shy hand shades a hermitage apart, –
   O large enough for thee, and thy brief hours.
Life there is sweeter held than in God's heart,
   Stiller than in the heavens of hollow flowers.

The wine is gladder there than in gold bowls.
   And Time shall not drain thence, nor trouble spill.
Sources between my fingers feed all souls,
   Where thou mayest cool thy lips, and draw thy fill.

Five cushions hath my hand, for reveries;
   And one deep pillow for thy brow's fatigues;   10
Languor of June all winterlong, and ease
   For ever from the vain untravelled leagues.

Thither your years may gather in from storm,
And Love, that sleepeth there, will keep thee warm.

August 1917–February 1918   EB, 1931

ANTHEM FOR DOOMED YOUTH

What passing-bells for these who die as cattle?
   – Only the monstrous anger of the guns.
   Only the stuttering rifles' rapid rattle
Can patter out their hasty orisons.
No mockeries now for them; no prayers nor bells,
   Nor any voice of mourning save the choirs, –
The shrill, demented choirs of wailing shells;
   And bugles calling for them from sad shires.

48

What candles may be held to speed them all?
   Not in the hands of boys, but in their eyes
Shall shine the holy glimmers of goodbyes.
   The pallor of girls' brows shall be their pall;
Their flowers the tenderness of patient minds,
And each slow dusk a drawing-down of blinds.

September–October 1917   *SS/ES, 1920*

THE NEXT WAR

War's a joke for me and you,
While we know such dreams are true.
                              Siegfried Sassoon

Out there, we've walked quite friendly up to Death, –
   Sat down and eaten with him, cool and bland, –
   Pardoned his spilling mess-tins in our hand.
We've sniffed the green thick odour of his breath, –
Our eyes wept, but our courage didn't writhe.
   He's spat at us with bullets and he's coughed
   Shrapnel. We chorused when he sang aloft,
We whistled while he shaved us with his scythe.

Oh, Death was never enemy of ours!
   We laughed at him, we leagued with him, old chum.
No soldier's paid to kick against his powers.
   We laughed, knowing that better men would come,
And greater wars; when each proud fighter brags
He wars on Death – for Life; not men – for flags.

September 1917   The Hydra, *29 September 1917*

WINTER SONG

The browns, the olives, and the yellows died,
And were swept up to heaven; where they glowed
Each dawn and set of sun till Christmastide.
And when the land lay pale for them, pale snowed,
Fell back, and down the snowdrifts flamed and flowed.

From off your face, into the winds of winter,
The sun-brown and the summer-gold are blowing;
But they shall gleam again with spiritual glinter
When paler beauty on your brows falls snowing,
And through those snows my looks shall be soft-going.　　10

18 October 1917　　EB, 1931

DULCE ET DECORUM EST

Bent double, like old beggars under sacks,
Knock-kneed, coughing like hags, we cursed through
　　sludge,
Till on the haunting flares we turned our backs
And towards our distant rest began the trudge.
Men marched asleep. Many had lost their boots
But limped on, blood-shod. All went lame; all blind;
Drunk with fatigue; deaf even to the hoots
Of tired, outstripped Five-Nines that dropped behind.

Gas! GAS! Quick, boys! – An ecstasy of fumbling,
Fitting the clumsy helmets just in time;　　10
But someone still was yelling out and stumbling,
And flound'ring like a man in fire or lime ...
Dim, through the misty panes and thick green light,
As under a green sea, I saw him drowning.

In all my dreams, before my helpless sight,
He plunges at me, guttering, choking, drowning.

If in some smothering dreams you too could pace
Behind the wagon that we flung him in,
And watch the white eyes writhing in his face,
His hanging face, like a devil's sick of sin;　　20
If you could hear, at every jolt, the blood
Come gargling from the froth-corrupted lungs,
Obscene as cancer, bitter as the cud
Of vile, incurable sores on innocent tongues,
My friend, you would not tell with such high zest,

To children ardent for some desperate glory,
The old Lie: Dulce et decorum est
Pro patria mori.

October 1917–February 1918   *SS/ES, 1920*

DISABLED

He sat in a wheeled chair, waiting for dark
And shivered in his ghastly suit of grey,
Legless, sewn short at elbow. Through the park
Voices of boys rang saddening like a hymn,
Voices of play and pleasure after day,
Till gathering sleep had mothered them from him.

    ★   ★   ★

About this time Town used to swing so gay
When glow-lamps budded in the light blue trees,
And girls glanced lovelier as the air grew dim, –
In the old times, before he threw away his knees.   10
Now he will never feel again how slim
Girls' waists are, or how warm their subtle hands.
All of them touch him like some queer disease.

    ★   ★   ★

There was an artist silly for his face,
For it was younger than his youth, last year.
Now, he is old; his back will never brace;
He's lost his colour very far from here,
Poured it down shell-holes till the veins ran dry,
And half his lifetime lapsed in the hot race
And leap of purple spurted from his thigh.   20

    ★   ★   ★

One time he liked a bloodsmear down his leg,
After the matches, carried shoulder-high.
It was after football, when he'd drunk a peg,
He thought he'd better join. – He wonders why.
Someone had said he'd look a god in kilts.

51

That's why; and maybe, too, to please his Meg,
Aye, that was it, to please the giddy jilts
He asked to join. He didn't have to beg;
Smiling they wrote his lie; aged nineteen years.
Germans he scarcely thought of; all their guilt   30
And Austria's, did not move him. And no fears
Of Fear came yet. He thought of jewelled hilts
For daggers in plaid socks; of smart salutes;
And care of arms; and leave, and pay arrears;
Esprit de corps; and hints for young recruits.
And soon, he was drafted out with drums and cheers.

★ ★ ★

Some cheered him home, but not as crowds cheer Goal.
Only a solemn man who brought him fruits
Thanked him; and then enquired about his soul.

★ ★ ★

Now, he will spend a few sick years in institutes,   40
And do what things the rules consider wise,
And take whatever pity they may dole.
Tonight he noticed how the women's eyes
Passed from him to the strong men that were whole.
How cold and late it is! Why don't they come
And put him to bed? Why don't they come?

October 1917–July 1918   Wheels, *1919*

THE SENTRY

We'd found an old Boche dug-out, and he knew,
And gave us hell, for shell on frantic shell
Hammered on top, but never quite burst through.
Rain, guttering down in water-falls of slime
Kept slush waist-high, and rising hour by hour,
And choked the steps too thick with clay to climb.
What murk of air remained stank old, and sour
With fumes of whizzbangs, and the smell of men
Who'd lived there years, and left their curse in the den,

If not their corpses ...
There we herded from the blast   10

Of whizzbangs, but one found our door at last,
Buffeting eyes and breath, snuffing the candles,
And thud! flump! thud! down the steep steps came
   thumping
And sploshing in the flood, deluging muck –
The sentry's body; then his rifle, handles
Of old Boche bombs, and mud in ruck on ruck.
We dredged him up, for killed, until he whined
'O sir, my eyes – I'm blind, – I'm blind, I'm blind!'
Coaxing, I held a flame against his lids
And said if he could see the least blurred light   20
He was not blind; in time he'd get all right.
'I can't,' he sobbed. Eyeballs, huge-bulged like squids',
Watch my dreams still; but I forgot him there
In posting Next for duty, and sending a scout
To beg a stretcher somewhere, and flound'ring about
To other posts under the shrieking air.

★ ★ ★

Those other wretches, how they bled and spewed,
And one who would have drowned himself for good,
I try not to remember these things now.
Let dread hark back for one word only: how   30
Half-listening to that sentry's moans and jumps,
And the wild chattering of his broken teeth,
Renewed most horribly whenever crumps
Pummelled the roof and slogged the air beneath –
Through the dense din, I say, we heard him shout
'I see your lights!' But ours had long died out.

October 1917–September 1918   Wheels, *1919*

THE CHANCES

I mind as how the night before that show
Us five got talkin'; we was in the know.

53

'Ah well,' says Jimmy, and he's seen some scrappin',
'There ain't no more than five things as can happen, –
You get knocked out; else wounded, bad or cushy;
Scuppered; or nowt except you're feelin' mushy.'

* * *

One of us got the knock-out, blown to chops;
One lad was hurt, like, losin' both his props;
And one, – to use the word of hypocrites, –
Had the misfortune to be took by Fritz.   10
Now me, I wasn't scratched, praise God Almighty,
Though next time please I'll thank Him for a blighty.
But poor old Jim, he's livin' and he's not;
He reckoned he'd five chances, and he had;
He's wounded, killed and pris'ner, all the lot,
The flamin' lot all rolled in one. Jim's mad.

October 1917–July 1918   Wheels, *1919*

SOLDIER'S DREAM

I dreamed kind Jesus fouled the big-gun gears;
And caused a permanent stoppage in all bolts;
And buckled with a smile Mausers and Colts;
And rusted every bayonet with His tears.

And there were no more bombs of ours or Theirs,
Not even an old flint-lock, nor even a pikel.
But God was vexed, and gave all power to Michael;
And when I woke he'd seen to our repairs.

October 1917–January 1918   CDL, *1963*

GREATER LOVE

Red lips are not so red
    As the stained stones kissed by the English dead.
Kindness of wooed and wooer

54

Seems shame to their love pure,
O Love, your eyes lose lure
    When I behold eyes blinded in my stead!

Your slender attitude
    Trembles not exquisite like limbs knife-skewed,
Rolling and rolling there
Where God seems not to care   10
Till the fierce love they bear
    Cramps them in death's extreme decrepitude.

Your voice sings not so soft, –
    Though even as wind murmuring through raftered
        loft, –
Your dear voice is not dear,
Gentle, and evening clear
As theirs whom none now hear,
    Now earth has stopped their piteous mouths that
        coughed.

Heart, you were never hot
    Nor large, nor full like hearts made great with shot;   20
And though your hand be pale,
Paler are all which trail
Your cross through flame and hail, –
    Weep, you may weep, for you may touch them not.

October 1917–July 1918   SS/ES, 1920

CONSCIOUS

His fingers wake, and flutter up the bed.
His eyes come open with a pull of will,
Helped by the yellow mayflowers by his head.
The blind-cord drawls across the window-sill ...
What a smooth floor the ward has! What a rug!
Who is that talking somewhere out of sight?
Three flies are creeping round the shiny jug ...
'Nurse! Doctor!' – 'Yes, all right, all right.'

But sudden evening blurs and fogs the air.
There seems no time to want a drink of water.   10
Nurse looks so far away. And here and there
Music and roses burst through crimson slaughter.
He can't remember where he saw blue sky ...
The trench seems narrower. Cold, he's cold; yet hot –
And there's no light to see the voices by ...
There is no time to ask ... he knows not what.

November 1917–February 1918   *SS/ES, 1920*

THE SHOW

*We have fallen in the dreams the ever-living
Breathe on the tarnished mirror of the world,
And then smooth out with ivory hands and sigh.*
                                                W. B. Yeats

My soul looked down from a vague height, with Death,
As unremembering how I rose or why,
And saw a sad land, weak with sweats of dearth,
Grey, cratered like the moon with hollow woe,
And pitted with great pocks and scabs of plagues.

Across its beard, that horror of harsh wire,
There moved thin caterpillars, slowly uncoiled.
It seemed they pushed themselves to be as plugs
Of ditches, where they writhed and shrivelled, killed.

By them had slimy paths been trailed and scraped   10
Round myriad warts that might be little hills.

From gloom's last dregs these long-strung creatures crept,
And vanished out of dawn down hidden holes.

(And smell came up from those foul openings
As out of mouths, or deep wounds deepening.)

On dithering feet upgathered, more and more,

Brown strings, towards strings of grey, with bristling
  spines,
All migrants from green fields, intent on mire.

Those that were grey, of more abundant spawns,
Ramped on the rest and ate them and were eaten.   20

I saw their bitten backs curve, loop, and straighten.
I watched those agonies curl, lift and flatten.

Whereat, in terror what that sight might mean,
I reeled and shivered earthward like a feather.

And Death fell with me, like a deepening moan.

And He, picking a manner of worm, which half had hid
Its bruises in the earth, but crawled no further,
Showed me its feet, the feet of many men,
And the fresh-severed head of it, my head.

November 1917–May 1918   Wheels, *1919*

ASLEEP

Under his helmet, up against his pack,
After the many days of work and waking,
Sleep took him by the brow and laid him back.
And in the happy no-time of his sleeping,
Death took him by the heart. There was a quaking
Of the aborted life within him leaping,
Then chest and sleepy arms once more fell slack,
And soon the slow stray blood came creeping
From the intrusive lead, like ants on track.

     ★ ★ ★

Whether his deeper sleep lie shaded by the shaking   10
Of great wings, and the thoughts that hung the stars,
High-pillowed on calm pillows of God's making
Above these clouds, these rains, these sleets of lead,

And these winds' scimitars;
Or whether yet his thin and sodden head
Confuses more and more with the low mould,
His hair being one with the grey grass,
And finished fields of autumn that are old,
Who knows? Who hopes? Who troubles? Let it pass.
He sleeps. He sleeps less tremulous, less cold   20
Than we who must awake, and waking, say alas!

November 1917–May 1918   Squire, *November 1921*

APOLOGIA PRO POEMATE MEO

I, too, saw God through mud, –
    The mud that cracked on cheeks when wretches smiled.
    War brought more glory to their eyes than blood,
    And gave their laughs more glee than shakes a child.

Merry it was to laugh there –
    Where death becomes absurd and life absurder.
    For power was on us as we slashed bones bare
    Not to feel sickness or remorse of murder.

I, too, have dropped off Fear –
    Behind the barrage, dead as my platoon,   10
    And sailed my spirit surging light and clear
    Past the entanglement where hopes lay strewn;

And witnessed exultation –
    Faces that used to curse me, scowl for scowl,
    Shine and lift up with passion of oblation,
    Seraphic for an hour; though they were foul.

I have made fellowships –
    Untold of happy lovers in old song.
    For love is not the binding of fair lips
    With the soft silk of eyes that look and long,   20

By Joy, whose ribbon slips, –

58

But wound with war's hard wire whose stakes are
   strong;
Bound with the bandage of the arm that drips;
Knit in the webbing of the rifle-thong.

I have perceived much beauty
   In the hoarse oaths that kept our courage straight;
   Heard music in the silentness of duty;
   Found peace where shell-storms spouted reddest spate.

Nevertheless, except you share
   With them in hell the sorrowful dark of hell,   30
   Whose world is but the trembling of a flare
   And heaven but as the highway for a shell,

You shall not hear their mirth:
   You shall not come to think them well content
   By any jest of mine. These men are worth
   Your tears. You are not worth their merriment.

November 1917   SS/ES, 1920

I SAW HIS ROUND MOUTH'S CRIMSON DEEPEN
AS IT FELL

I saw his round mouth's crimson deepen as it fell,
   Like a sun, in his last deep hour,
Watched the magnificent recession of farewell,
   Clouding, half gleam, half glower,
And a last splendour burn the heavens of his cheek.
   And in his eyes
The cold stars lighting, very old and bleak,
   In different skies.

November 1917   EB, 1931

LE CHRISTIANISME

So the church Christ was hit and buried

Under its rubbish and its rubble.
In cellars, packed-up saints lie serried,
    Well out of hearing of our trouble.

One Virgin still immaculate
    Smiles on for war to flatter her.
She's halo'd with an old tin hat,
    But a piece of hell will batter her.

November–December 1917   EB, 1931

WHO IS THE GOD OF CANONGATE?

Who is the god of Canongate?
– I, for I trifle with men and fate.

Art thou high in the heart of London?
– Yea, for I do what is done and undone.

What is thy throne thou barefoot god?
– All pavements where my feet have trod.

Where is thy shrine, then, little god?
– Up secret stairs men mount unshod.

Say what libation such men fill?
– There lift their lusts and let them spill.

Why do you smell of the moss in Arden?
– If I told you, Sir, your look would harden.

What are you called, I ask your pardon?
– I am called the Flower of Covent Garden.

What shall I pay for you, lily-lad?
– Not all the gold King Solomon had.

How can I buy you, London Flower?
– Buy me for ever, but not for an hour.

When shall I pay you, Violet Eyes?
– With laughter first, and after with sighs.   20

But you will fade, my delicate bud?
– No, there is too much sap in my blood.

Will you not shrink in my shut room?
– No, there I'll break into fullest bloom.

November 1917–March 1918   JS, 1983

CRAMPED IN THAT FUNNELLED HOLE

Cramped in that funnelled hole, they watched the dawn
Open a jaggged rim around; a yawn
Of death's jaws, which had all but swallowed them
Stuck in the bottom of his throat of phlegm.

They were in one of many mouths of Hell
Not seen of seers in visions; only felt
As teeth of traps; when bones and the dead are smelt
Under the mud-trap which they help to swell,
Mixed with the sour sharp odour of the shell.

November–December 1917   EB, 1931

EXPOSURE

Our brains ache, in the merciless iced east winds that knive
    us . . .
Wearied we keep awake because the night is silent . . .
Low, drooping flares confuse our memory of the salient . . .
Worried by silence, sentries whisper, curious, nervous,
        But nothing happens.

Watching, we hear the mad gusts tugging on the wire,
Like twitching agonies of men among its brambles.
Northward, incessantly, the flickering gunnery rumbles,
Far off, like a dull rumour of some other war.
        What are we doing here?   10

61

The poignant misery of dawn begins to grow ...
We only know war lasts, rain soaks, and clouds sag stormy.
Dawn massing in the east her melancholy army
Attacks once more in ranks on shivering ranks of grey,
    But nothing happens.

Sudden successive flights of bullets streak the silence,
Less deathly than the air that shudders black with snow,
With sidelong flowing flakes that flock, pause, and renew;
We watch them wandering up and down the wind's
   nonchalance,
    But nothing happens.   20

Pale flakes with fingering stealth come feeling for our faces.
We cringe in holes, back on forgotten dreams, and stare,
   snow-dazed,
Deep into grassier ditches. So we drowse, sun-dozed,
Littered with blossoms trickling where the blackbird fusses,
    – Is it that we are dying?

Slowly our ghosts drag home: glimpsing the sunk fires,
   glozed
With crusted dark-red jewels; crickets jingle there;
For hours the innocent mice rejoice: the house is theirs;
Shutters and doors, all closed: on us the doors are closed –
    We turn back to our dying.   30

Since we believe not otherwise can kind fires burn;
Nor ever suns smile true on child, or field, or fruit.
For God's invincible spring our love is made afraid;
Therefore, not loath, we lie out here; therefore were born,
    For love of God seems dying.

Tonight, this frost will fasten on this mud and us,
Shrivelling many hands, puckering foreheads crisp.
The burying party, picks and shovels in shaking grasp,
Pause over half-known faces. All their eyes are ice,
    But nothing happens.   40

November 1917–September 1918   *SS/ES, 1920*

INSENSIBILITY

1

Happy are men who yet before they are killed
Can let their veins run cold.
Whom no compassion fleers
Or makes their feet
Sore on the alleys cobbled with their brothers.
The front line withers.
But they are troops who fade, not flowers,
For poets' tearful fooling:
Men, gaps for filling:
Losses, who might have fought   10
Longer; but no one bothers.

2

And some cease feeling
Even themselves or for themselves.
Dullness best solves
The tease and doubt of shelling,
And Chance's strange arithmetic
Comes simpler than the reckoning of their shilling.
They keep no check on armies' decimation.

3

Happy are these who lose imagination:
They have enough to carry with ammunition.   20
Their spirit drags no pack.
Their old wounds, save with cold, can not more ache.
Having seen all things red,
Their eyes are rid
Of the hurt of the colour of blood for ever.
And terror's first constriction over,
Their hearts remain small-drawn.
Their senses in some scorching cautery of battle
Now long since ironed,
Can laugh among the dying, unconcerned.   30

4

Happy the soldier home, with not a notion
How somewhere, every dawn, some men attack,
And many sighs are drained.
Happy the lad whose mind was never trained:
His days are worth forgetting more than not.
He sings along the march
Which we march taciturn, because of dusk,
The long, forlorn, relentless trend
From larger day to huger night.

5

We wise, who with a thought besmirch   40
Blood over all our soul,
How should we see our task
But through his blunt and lashless eyes?
Alive, he is not vital overmuch;
Dying, not mortal overmuch;
Nor sad, nor proud,
Nor curious at all.
He cannot tell
Old men's placidity from his.

6

But cursed are dullards whom no cannon stuns,   50
That they should be as stones.
Wretched are they, and mean
With paucity that never was simplicity.
By choice they made themselves immune
To pity and whatever moans in man
Before the last sea and the hapless stars;
Whatever mourns when many leave these shores;
Whatever shares the eternal reciprocity of tears.

November 1917–April 1918   *SS/ES, 1920*

STRANGE MEETING

It seemed that out of battle I escaped
Down some profound dull tunnel, long since scooped
Through granites which titanic wars had groined.

Yet also there encumbered sleepers groaned,
Too fast in thought or death to be bestirred.
Then, as I probed them, one sprang up, and stared
With piteous recognition in fixed eyes,
Lifting distressful hands, as if to bless.
And by his smile, I knew that sullen hall –
By his dead smile I knew we stood in Hell.   10

With a thousand pains that vision's face was grained;
Yet no blood reached there from the upper ground,
And no guns thumped, or down the flues made moan.
'Strange friend,' I said, 'here is no cause to mourn.'
'None,' said that other, 'save the undone years,
The hopelessness. Whatever hope is yours,
Was my life also; I went hunting wild
After the wildest beauty in the world,
Which lies not calm in eyes, or braided hair;
But mocks the steady running of the hour,   20
And if it grieves, grieves richlier than here.
For by my glee might many men have laughed,
And of my weeping something had been left,
Which must die now. I mean the truth untold,
The pity of war, the pity war distilled.
Now men will go content with what we spoiled,
Or, discontent, boil bloody, and be spilled.
They will be swift with swiftness of the tigress.
None will break ranks, though nations trek from progress.
Courage was mine, and I had mystery,   30
Wisdom was mine, and I had mastery:
To miss the march of this retreating world
Into vain citadels that are not walled.
Then, when much blood had clogged their chariot-wheels,
I would go up and wash them from sweet wells,

65

Even with truths that lie too deep for taint.
I would have poured my spirit without stint
But not through wounds; not on the cess of war.
Foreheads of men have bled where no wounds were.

I am the enemy you killed, my friend.   40
I knew you in this dark: for so you frowned
Yesterday through me as you jabbed and killed.
I parried; but my hands were loath and cold.
Let us sleep now ...'

November 1917–February 1918   Wheels, *1919*

SONNET
ON SEEING A PIECE OF OUR HEAVY ARTILLERY
BROUGHT INTO ACTION

Be slowly lifted up, thou long black arm,
Great gun towering towards Heaven, about to curse,
Sway steep against them, and for years rehearse
Huge imprecations like a blasting charm!
Reach at that Arrogance which needs thy harm,
And beat it down before its sins grow worse.
Spend our resentment, cannon, – yea, disburse
Our gold in shapes of flame, our breaths in storm.

Yet, for men's sakes whom thy vast malison
Must wither innocent of enmity,   10
Be not withdrawn, dark arm, thy spoilure done,
Safe to the bosom of our prosperity.
But when thy spell be cast complete and whole,
May god curse thee, and cut thee from our soul!

November 1917–May 1918   EB, *1931*

S. I. W.

I will to the King,
And offer him consolation in his trouble,

> *For that man there has set his teeth to die,*
> *And being one that hates obedience,*
> *Discipline, and orderliness of life,*
> *I cannot mourn him.*

W. B. Yeats

1 The prologue

Patting goodbye, doubtless they told the lad
He'd always show the Hun a brave man's face;
Father would sooner him dead than in disgrace, –
Was proud to see him going, aye, and glad.
Perhaps his mother whimpered how she'd fret
Until he got a nice safe wound to nurse.
Sisters would wish girls too could shoot, charge, curse ...
Brothers – would send his favourite cigarette.
Each week, month after month, they wrote the same,
Thinking him sheltered in some YM hut,   10
Because he said so, writing on his butt
Where once an hour a bullet missed its aim.
And misses teased the hunger of his brain.
His eyes grew old with wincing, and his hand
Reckless with ague. Courage leaked, as sand
From the best sandbags after years of rain.
But never leave, wound, fever, trench-foot, shock,
Untrapped the wretch. And death seemed still withheld
For torture of lying machinally shelled,
At the pleasure of this world's Powers who'd run amok.   20
He'd seen men shoot their hands, on night patrol.
Their people never knew. Yet they were vile.
'Death sooner than dishonour, that's the style!'
So Father said.

2 The action

One dawn, our wire patrol
Carried him. This time, Death had not missed.
We could do nothing, but wipe his bleeding cough.

Could it be accident? – Rifles go off ...
Not sniped? No. (Later they found the English ball.)

3 *The poem*

It was the reasoned crisis of his soul
Against more days of inescapable thrall,   30
Against infrangibly wired, insuperable trench wall
Curtained with fire, roofed in with creeping fire,
Slow-grazing fire that would not burn him whole
But kept him for death's promises and scoff,
And life's half-promising, and both their riling.

4 *The epilogue*

With him they buried the muzzle his teeth had kissed,
And truthfully wrote the mother, 'Tim died smiling.'

November 1917–May 1918   *SS/ES, 1920*

HOSPITAL BARGE

Budging the sluggard ripples of the Somme,
A barge round old Cérisy slowly slewed.
Softly her engines down the current screwed,
And chuckled softly with contented hum,
Till fairy tinklings struck their croonings dumb.
The waters rumpling at the stern subdued;
The lock-gate took her bulging amplitude;
Gently from out the gurgling lock she swum.

One reading by that calm bank shaded eyes
To watch her lessening westward quietly.   10
Then, as she neared the bend, her funnel screamed.
And that long lamentation made him wise
How unto Avalon, in agony,
Kings passed in the dark barge which Merlin dreamed.

December 1917   The Nation, *15 June 1918*

A TERRE

(BEING THE PHILOSOPHY OF MANY SOLDIERS)

Sit on the bed. I'm blind and three parts shell.
Be careful; can't shake hands now; never shall.
Both arms have mutinied against me, – brutes.
My fingers fidget like ten idle brats.

I tried to peg out soldierly, – no use!
One dies of war like any old disease.
This bandage feels like pennies on my eyes.
I have my medals? – Discs to make eyes close.
My glorious ribbons? – Ripped from my own back
In scarlet shreds. (That's for your poetry book.)   10

A short life and merry one, my buck!
We used to say we'd hate to live dead-old, –
Yet now ... I'd willingly be puffy, bald,
And patriotic. Buffers catch from boys
At least the jokes hurled at them. I suppose
Little I'd ever teach a son, but hitting,
Shooting, war, hunting, all the arts of hurting.
Well, that's what I learnt, – that, and making money.

Your fifty years ahead seem none too many?
Tell me how long I've got? God! For one year   20
To help myself to nothing more than air!
One Spring! Is one too good to spare, too long?
Spring wind would work its own way to my lung,
And grow me legs as quick as lilac-shoots.
My servant's lamed, but listen how he shouts!
When I'm lugged out, he'll still be good for that.
Here in this mummy-case, you know, I've thought
How well I might have swept his floors for ever.
I'd ask no nights off when the bustle's over,
Enjoying so the dirt. Who's prejudiced   30
Against a grimed hand when his own's quite dust,
Less live than specks that in the sun-shafts turn,

69

Less warm than dust that mixes with arms' tan.
I'd love to be a sweep now, black as Town,
Yes, or a muckman. Must I be his load?

O Life, Life, let me breathe, – a dug-out rat!
Not worse than ours the lives rats lead –
Nosing along at night down some safe rut,
They find a shell-proof home before they rot.
Dead men may envy living mites in cheese,   40
Or good germs even. Microbes have their joys,
And subdivide, and never come to death.
Certainly flowers have the easiest time on earth.
'I shall be one with nature, herb, and stone,'
Shelley would tell me. Shelley would be stunned:
The dullest Tommy hugs that fancy now.
'Pushing up daisies' is their creed, you know.

To grain, then, go my fat, to buds my sap,
For all the usefulness there is in soap.
D'you think the Boche will ever stew man-soup?   50
Some day, no doubt if . . .
                              Friend, be very sure
I shall be better off with plants that share
More peaceably the meadow and the shower.
Soft rains will touch me, – as they could touch once,
And nothing but the sun shall make me ware.
Your guns may crash around me. I'll not hear.
Or, if I wince, I shall not know I wince.

Don't take my soul's poor comfort for your jest.
Soldiers may grow a soul when turned to fronds,
But here the thing's best left at home with friends.   60

My soul's a little grief, grappling your chest,
To climb your throat on sobs; easily chased
On other sighs and wiped by fresher winds.

Carry my crying spirit till it's weaned
To do without what blood remained these wounds.

December 1917–July 1918   Wheels, *1919*

MINERS

There was a whispering in my hearth,
    A sigh of the coal,
Grown wistful of a former earth
    It might recall.

I listened for a tale of leaves
    And smothered ferns;
Frond-forests; and the low, sly lives
    Before the fawns.

My fire might show steam-phantoms simmer
    From Time's old cauldron,
Before the birds made nests in summer,
    Or men had children.

But the coals were murmuring of their mine,
    And moans down there
Of boys that slept wry sleep, and men
    Writhing for air.

And I saw white bones in the cinder-shard,
    Bones without number;
For many hearts with coal are charred,
    And few remember.

I thought of some who worked dark pits
    Of war, and died
Digging the rock where Death reputes
    Peace lies indeed.

Comforted years will sit soft-chaired
    In rooms of amber;
The years will stretch their hands, well-cheered
    By our lives' ember.

The centuries will burn rich loads
    With which we groaned,
Whose warmth shall lull their dreaming lids,
    While songs are crooned.

But they will not dream of us poor lads,
    Lost in the ground.

Mid-January 1918   The Nation, *26 January 1918*

HAVING, WITH BOLD HORATIUS, STAMPED HER FEET

Having, with bold Horatius, stamped her feet
And waved a final swashing arabesque
O'er the brave days of old, she ceased to bleat,
Slapped her Macaulay back upon the desk
Resumed her calm gaze and her lofty seat.

There, while she heard the classic lines repeat,
Once more the teacher's face clenched stern:
For through the window, looking on the street,
Three soldiers hailed her. She made no return.
One was called 'Orace whom she would not greet.   10

January–February 1918   EB, *1931*

THE LETTER

With B.E.F. June 10. Dear Wife,
(Oh blast this pencil. 'Ere, Bill, lend's a knife.)
I'm in the pink at present, dear.
I think the war will end this year.
We don't see much of them square-'eaded 'Uns.
We're out of harm's way, not bad fed.
I'm longing for a taste of your old buns.
(Say, Jimmie, spare's a bite of bread.)
There don't seem much to say just now.
(Yer what? Then don't, yer ruddy cow!   10
And give us back me cigarette!)
I'll soon be 'ome. You mustn't fret.
My feet's improvin', as I told you of,
We're out in rest now. Never fear.
(VRACH! By crumbs, but that was near.)

Mother might spare you half a sov.
Kiss Nell and Bert. When me and you –
(Eh? What the 'ell! Stand to? Stand to!
Jim, give's a hand with pack on, lad.
Guh! Christ! I'm hit. Take 'old. Aye, bad. 20
No, damn your iodine. Jim? 'Ere!
Write my old girl, Jim, there's a dear.)

January–February 1918   CDL, 1963

THE LAST LAUGH

'Oh! Jesus Christ! I'm hit,' he said; and died.
Whether he vainly cursed or prayed indeed,
    The Bullets chirped – In vain, vain, vain!
    Machine-guns chuckled – Tut-tut! Tut-tut!
    And the Big Gun guffawed.

       ★ ★ ★

Another sighed – O Mother, – Mother, – Dad!
Then smiled at nothing, childlike, being dead.
    And the lofty Shrapnel-cloud
    Leisurely gestured, – Fool!
    And the splinters spat, and tittered. 10

       ★ ★ ★

'My Love!' one moaned. Love-languid seemed his mood,
Till slowly lowered his whole face kissed the mud.
    And the Bayonets' long teeth grinned;
    Rabbles of Shells hooted and groaned;
    And the Gas hissed.

January–July 1918   CDL, 1963

THE SEND-OFF

Down the close darkening lanes they sang their way
To the siding-shed,
And lined the train with faces grimly gay.

Their breasts were stuck all white with wreath and spray
As men's are, dead.

Dull porters watched them, and a casual tramp
Stood staring hard,
Sorry to miss them from the upland camp.

Then, unmoved, signals nodded, and a lamp
Winked to the guard.   10

So secretly, like wrongs hushed-up, they went.
They were not ours:
We never heard to which front these were sent.

Nor there if they yet mock what women meant
Who gave them flowers.

Shall they return to beatings of great bells
In wild train-loads?
A few, a few, too few for drums and yells,

May creep back, silent, to village wells,
Up half-known roads.   20

March–July 1918   SS/ES, 1920

ARMS AND THE BOY

Let the boy try along this bayonet-blade
How cold steel is, and keen with hunger of blood;
Blue, with all malice, like a madman's flash;
And thinly drawn with famishing for flesh.

Lend him to stroke these blind, blunt bullet-leads,
Which long to nuzzle in the hearts of lads;
Or give him cartridges whose fine zinc teeth
Are sharp with sharpness of grief and death.

For his teeth seem for laughing round an apple.
There lurk no claws behind his fingers supple;   10

74

And God will grow no talons at his heels,
Nor antlers through the thickness of his curls.

May 1918   SS/ES, 1920

FUTILITY

Move him into the sun –
Gently its touch awoke him once,
At home, whispering of fields half-sown.
Always it woke him, even in France,
Until this morning and this snow.
If anything might rouse him now
The kind old sun will know.

Think how it wakes the seeds, –
Woke, once, the clays of a cold star.
Are limbs, so dear-achieved, are sides   10
Full-nerved, still warm, too hard to stir?
Was it for this the clay grew tall?
– O what made fatuous sunbeams toil
To break earth's sleep at all?

May 1918   The Nation, 15 June 1918

THE CALLS

A dismal fog-hoarse siren howls at dawn.
I watch the man it calls for, pushed and drawn
Backwards and forwards, helpless as a pawn.
    But I'm lazy, and his work's crazy.

Quick treble bells begin at nine o'clock,
Scuttling the schoolboy pulling up his sock,
Scaring the late girl in the inky frock.
    I must be crazy; I learn from the daisy.

Stern bells among the rooks and doves at ten.
I watch the verger close the doors, and when   10
I hear the organ moan the first amen,
    Sing my religion's – same as pigeons'.

A blatant bugle tears my afternoons
Out clump the clumsy Tommies by platoons
Trying to keep in step with rag-time tunes,
    But I sit still; I've done my drill.

Gongs hum and buzz like saucepan lids at dusk.
I see a food-hog whet his gold-filled tusk
To eat less bread, and more luxurious rusk.

Then sometimes late at night my window bumps   20
From gunnery-practice, till my small heart thumps
And listens for the shell-shrieks and the crumps
    But that's not all.

For leaning out last midnight on my sill,
I heard the sighs of men, that have no skill
To speak of their distress, no, nor the will!
    A voice I know. And this time I must go.

May 1918   EB, 1931

TRAINING

Not this week nor this month dare I lie down
In languor under lime trees or smooth smile.
Love must not kiss my face pale that is brown.

My lips, panting, shall drink space, mile by mile;
Strong meats be all my hunger; my renown
Be the clean beauty of speed and pride of style.

Cold winds encountered on the racing Down
Shall thrill my heated bareness, but awhile
None else may meet me till I wear my crown.

June 1918   EB, 1931

MENTAL CASES

Who are these? Why sit they here in twilight?
Wherefore rock they, purgatorial shadows,

76

Drooping tongues from jaws that slob their relish,
Baring teeth that leer like skulls' teeth wicked?
Stroke on stroke of pain, – but what slow panic,
Gouged these chasms round their fretted sockets?
Ever from their hair and through their hands' palms
Misery swelters. Surely we have perished
Sleeping, and walk hell; but who these hellish?

– These are men whose minds the Dead have ravished.   10
Memory fingers in their hair of murders,
Multitudinous murders they once witnessed.
Wading sloughs of flesh these helpless wander, –
Treading blood from lungs that had loved laughter.
Always they must see these things and hear them,
Batter of guns and shatter of flying muscles,
Carnage incomparable, and human squander –
Rucked too thick for these men's extrication.

Therefore still their eyeballs shrink tormented
Back into their brains, because on their sense   20
Sunlight seems a bloodsmear; night comes blood-black;
Dawn breaks open like a wound that bleeds afresh.
– Thus their heads wear this hilarious, hideous,
Awful falseness of set-smiling corpses.
– Thus their hands are plucking at each other; –
Picking at the rope-knouts of their scourging;
Snatching after us who smote them, brother, –
Pawing us who dealt them war and madness.

May–July 1918   SS/ES, 1920

THE PARABLE OF THE OLD MAN AND THE YOUNG

So Abram rose, and clave the wood, and went,
And took the fire with him and a knife.
And as they sojourned both of them together,
Isaac the first-born spake and said, My Father,
Behold the preparations, fire and iron,
But where the lamb for this burnt-offering?
Then Abram bound the youth with belts and straps

And builded parapets and trenches there,
And stretchèd forth the knife to slay his son.
When lo! an Angel called him out of heaven,   10
Saying, Lay not thy hand upon the lad,
Neither do anything to him, thy son.
Behold! Caught in a thicket by its horns
A Ram. Offer the Ram of Pride instead.
But the old man would not so, but slew his son,
And half the seed of Europe, one by one.

Mid-1918   SS/ES, 1920

THE KIND GHOSTS

She sleeps on soft, last breaths; but no ghost looms
Out of the stillness of her palace wall,
Her wall of boys on boys and dooms on dooms.

She dreams of golden gardens and sweet glooms
Not marvelling why her roses never fall
Nor what red mouths were torn to make their blooms.

The shades keep down which well might roam her hall.
Quiet their blood lies in her crimson rooms
And she is not afraid of their footfall.

They move not from her tapestries, their pall,   10
Nor pace her terraces, their hecatombs,
Lest aught she be disturbed, or grieved at all.

30 July 1918   EB, 1931

SPRING OFFENSIVE

Halted against the shade of a last hill,
They fed, and lying easy, were at ease
And on the nearest packs and chests and knees
Carelessly slept. But many there stood still
To face the stark blank sky beyond the ridge
Knowing their feet had come to the end of the world.

Marvelling they stood, and watched the long grass swirled
By the May breeze, murmurous with wasp and midge,
For though the summer oozed into their veins
Like an injected drug for their bodies' pains,   10
Sharp on their souls hung the imminent line of grass,
Fearfully flashed the sky's mysterious glass.

Hour after hour they ponder the warm field, –
And the far valley behind, where the buttercup
Had blessed with gold their slow boots coming up,
Where even the little brambles would not yield
But clutched and clung to them like sorrowing hands.
All their strange day they breathe like trees unstirred.

Till like a cold gust thrills the little word
At which each body and its soul begird   20
And tighten them for battle. No alarms
Of bugles, no high flags, no clamorous haste, –
Only a lift and flare of eyes that faced
The sun, like a friend with whom their love is done.
O larger shone that smile against the sun, –
Mightier than his whose bounty these have spurned.

★   ★   ★

So, soon they topped the hill, and raced together
Over an open stretch of herb and heather
Exposed. And instantly the whole sky burned
With fury against them; earth set sudden cups   30
In thousands for their blood; and the green slope
Chasmed and steepened sheer to infinite space.

★   ★   ★

Of them who running on that last high place
Breasted the surf of bullets, or went up
On the hot blast and fury of hell's upsurge,
Or plunged and fell away past this world's verge,
Some say God caught them even before they fell.

But what say such as from existence' brink
Ventured but drave too swift to sink.

The few who rushed in the body to enter hell,   40
And there outfiending all its fiends and flames
With superhuman inhumanities,
Long-famous glories, immemorial shames –
And crawling slowly back, have by degrees
Regained cool and peaceful air in wonder –
Why speak not they of comrades that went under?

July–September 1918   SS/ES, 1920

SMILE, SMILE, SMILE

Head to limp head, the sunk-eyed wounded scanned
Yesterday's *Mail*; the casualties (typed small)
And (large) Vast Booty from our latest Haul.
Also, they read of cheap Homes, not yet planned,
'For', said the paper, 'when this war is done
The men's first instincts will be making homes.
Meanwhile their foremost need is aerodromes,
It being certain war has but begun.
Peace would do wrong to our undying dead, –
The sons we offered might regret they died   10
If we got nothing lasting in their stead.
We must be solidly indemnified.
Though all be worthy Victory which all bought,
We rulers sitting in this ancient spot
Would wrong our very selves if we forgot
The greatest glory will be theirs who fought,
Who kept this nation in integrity.'
Nation? – The half-limbed readers did not chafe
But smiled at one another curiously
Like secret men who know their secret safe.   20
(This is the thing they know and never speak
That England one by one had fled to France
Not many elsewhere now, save under France.)
Pictures of these broad smiles appear each week,
And people, in whose voice real feeling rings
Say: How they smile! They're happy now, poor things.

23 September 1918   SS/ES, 1920

PREFACE

This book is not about heroes. English Poetry is not yet fit
to speak of them.

Nor is it about deeds, or lands, about glory or honour, nor
anything about any might, majesty, dominion, or power,
except War.

Above all I am not concerned with Poetry.

My subject is War, and the pity of War. The Poetry is in
the pity.

Yet these elegies are to this generation in no sense con-
solatory. They may be to the next. All a poet can do today   10
is warn. That is why the true Poets must be truthful.

If I thought the letter of this book would last, I might
have used proper names; but if the spirit of it survives –
survives Prussia – my ambition and those names will have
achieved themselves fresher fields than Flanders . . .

May–September 1918   SS/ES, 1920

TO SUSAN OWEN

2 April 1911   [*Shrewsbury*]
Dear Mother,

Thank you so much for your letter, and for interviewing
Mr Robson. I am very anxious to know 'what else' he has
found or will find out.

I am not able to get much study done in school yet, but
Mr Edwards is going to approach Mr Lightbourne on the
subject (of allowing me to study when not actually teaching)
as soon as I find out exactly what is done in other schools in
the town where *P.T.*'s are.

Leslie tells me you are often hearing the Nightingale. Is   10
it indeed so enchanting? I crave to hear it, and yet I should
almost be afraid lest it should not be as fine as I imagine it.
At present my soul is in a ferment, and the 'leafy month of
June' promises as many terrors as leaves.

'It is a flaw
In happiness to see beyond our bourne,

It forces us in summer skies to mourn,
And spoils the singing of the nightingale.'

(Keats)

You ought, if you feel so moved, dear Mother, to read the   20
'Ode to the Nightingale' by the same Poet, which you will
find in his Poems, in the bookcase. Furthermore, if you [are]
at a loss at any time for good literature, why not study the
Introduction to this volume?

But let me warn you about believing what it says of Keats'
'*attitude to knowledge*, which cannot be justified, must not be
copied, etc.' I know of something which proves the *contrary*
to this view.

If you could find room for it in your trunk, I should be
obliged by a present of some lumps of soft chalk. And might   30
I ask for some complete specimens of Woodruff from the
wood, *of Mary* (who seems to have dwindled into oblivion
for ought I hear, of or from her, of her doings).

W

18 June 1911   *Alpenrose*
My dearest Mother,

I have been to see Mr Robson this afternoon. He had prepared some notes to aid him in his discourse, which he gave
me in his study, smoking meanwhile .... My pre-eminent
plan is to borrow or become possessed of just £150, with
which sum I can get a degree at College. *If I have* rich relations, I ought to try and get them to lend, repaying in the
process of time at, say, 4%. Failing this, teaching in a secondary school might be tried, studying with a Corresp. College
at the same time, but this is '*killing*' work, he says.   10

Finally, he revealed what he had in his mind as being
'easier' than teaching.

It is: – to become the 'assistant' of some hardworked or
studiously inclined parson, helping in parish work, correspondence etc., and being generally companionable to a lonely country-sequestered bachelor, such as himself. *Not* to
himself actually, however, one reason being – that it would

never do to have one *with relations in the parish!* He had heard, however, that 'Wiggan of Dunsden' wanted help in the parish this winter, and suggested applying to him, especially as his views coincide with ours.

For we must be most careful as to the kind of parson I go to. Some would keep me trotting round the parish all day; some (who have no servant perhaps) would require me to scrub floors. He knows of one priest, moreover, who celebrates Mass daily, and requires some one to say 'amen' in the consecration prayer since it is uncanonical to have *no* congregation.

On the other hand, however, it is a post not easily procured, and they are easily 'snapped up'. About £20 a year might be given, or less than that if *coaching* is required.

Mr Robson would be pleased to frame an advertisement for me in the *Churchman* or some such paper, if we like the proposal.

What do you think?

Parish work would not be by any means uncongenial to me, and as I suppose, far less worrying than teaching. And I could render myself 'companionable' to anyone if at all literary-inclined. But everything depends upon the kind of person the parson is.

Which risk shall I take then – (1) *borrowing money* (supposing such available – from E.Q. Esq. – and why not?) and thus sail with a fair wind to B.A. or (2) put myself at the mercy of a reverend man, who may be exacting, eccentric, intolerant and all that?

I mentioned my scheme of getting a thorough knowledge of French *in* France, and he considered it a very good thing, but far better if a degree be obtained first. A year or two in France after that, and I should be *worth something.*

I am to go to see him again on Wednesday afternoon; and to play tennis with another priest who is staying at the Vicarage – a Mr Thackrah, who, in his purple socks, looks about as *secular* as the 'secularest' of laymen. I was asked to be prepared for tennis today, but it rained. One Allwright, however, was there, helping Rev. Mr Thackrah to pass the afternoon at tennis. So we four bachelors had afternoon tea

in the drawing room. The comfort afforded by the luxurious arm-chairs however, was somewhat impaired by the
fact that we held our cups in our hands and had no plates.
Nevertheless Mr Robson, by his humorous stories, made us   60
so much at home that I remained perfectly placid and im-
perturbable when I dropped a large portion of cake into my
unfortunate tea-cup. No liquid escaped the cup, and I am
firmly convinced that I succeeded in conveying (by degrees)
the soppy blobs of dough into my mouth without my host
suspecting it; and thinking me a bounder. That most or all
elem- teachers are bounders is his unshaken faith. During
our conversation in the study I had asked, 'Am I then to avoid
elem^{ty} *teaching*?' He screwed up his visage, raised his hands,
turned aside his head, and murmured 'AS PITCH!!' Now I have   70
often touched pitch and not been defiled, but too much
handling has always resulted in defilement. Hence in answer
to the question 'Can a man touch *pitch* and not be defiled?' I
reply – 'Certainly, for a certain length of time.'

Moral: If I don't want to be defiled I must *drop* the *pitch*
with all speed.

Another power has sprung up to hold me in Shrewsbury. –
'*Uriconium is to be excavated in the near future*' according to Mr
Colyer.

Awaiting your reply to this budget before Wednesday (if   80
you get it in time), including Father's opinion of course,

I am, Your own Wilfred

TO MARY OWEN

7 November 1911   *Dunsden Vicarage*
My dear Sister,

Mother told me you would like me to write to *you* while
she is here; and I am indeed pleased to cover a few sheets of
this my Tablet for your benefit.

Mother has not been over here yet. Perhaps she is coming
on Friday. But she came to church on Sunday Morning.

I addressed the Children's Service in the Parish Hall on
Sunday Afternoon. I am also booked for the Scripture Union

84

on Thurs. I enjoy speaking very much. I use no notes, and
spend no great time in preparation; but I use no high falutin'   10
words, but try to express myself in simple, straightforward
English. I believe the children are impressed for the time
being. I hope they will really benefit, for, of course, I give
them the Messages, with one Purpose, and not with any idea
of displaying my own bumptiousness.

Yesterday, the vicar took me & Mr Kemp to hear an address by Bishop Ingham, at Earley Court, the fine residence
of some of the Suttons' Seeds people. I was introduced to the
Bishop, and spoke a few words with him. I need hardly say
that the Address more than justified the great praise which I   20
heard of him from you at Shrewsbury. He told the story of
the Tiles of Buddha's Shrine! In addition to his Lordship, I
met about half a dozen clergy at the Meeting. This was at
the afternoon tea which followed (in the immense billiard
room).

From such mansions as these, I pass, next afternoon, to
the wretched hovels of this Parish, and carry myself with
equal ease in the crazy, evil-smelling huts of the poor, as in
the wide, luxurious chambers of the rich.

Numbers of the old people cannot read; those who can   30
seldom do so. Scores of them have passed their whole lives
in the same stone box with a straw lid, which they call their
cottage; and are numbed to all interests beyond it. Those who
have within them the Hope of a Future World are content,
and their old faces are bright with the white radiance of eternity. Those who, like the beasts, have no such Hope, pass
their old age shrouded with an inward gloom, which the
reverses of their history have stamped upon their worn-out
memories, deadening them to all thoughts of delight.

There is one poor creature who cannot be said to live – she   40
exists and no more: She can neither speak, hear, nor see; I
suppose she can taste, smell, and feel. But alas, all her feeling
must be that of pain, for she has a disease of the bone; all her
smell must be the smell of a foul cottage; all her taste, the
taste of bread and of tea. What a life! Why am I telling you
these dreadful things? Simply to let them educate you, as
they are educating me, in the Book of Life, and to make us
rejoice in our own happy state.

I spend my afternoons in going round to these cottages. I
am at my books in the morning; while there is nearly always 50
some meeting to keep me busy in the evening. I have been
so busy, indeed, that I have not been able to finish this letter
till this morning (Friday). Let me hear from you when you
have something to say – (I will not say when you have time – I
know you have time to write me a note). Give my benedic-
tions to the boys, and my love to Father, and take as much
as you like for yourself.

Your loving brother, Wilfred

TO SUSAN OWEN

[*4 January 1913*]   [*Dunsden Vicarage*]
[*First page missing*] The furore [*several words missing*] now
abated in the Vicarage, thank Mnemosyne; but I hope that I,
who 'discovered' him something over a year ago, may [*half
page missing*] but the Vicar's presence (taciturn instead of
wontedly gay) symbolic of my stern Destiny, sat heavy on
my soul the night. I have already braced myself to one important interview; the upshot of which was that he begged
me to spend the next morning upon Tracts! Others will
follow.

Murder will out, and I have murdered my false creed. If a 10
true one exists, I shall find it. If not, adieu to the still falser
creeds that hold the hearts of nearly all my fellow men.

Escape from this hotbed of religion I now long for more
than I could ever have conceived a year and three months
ago. It reminds me of that old grange in *Westward Ho!*
whither the priests would resort and hatch plots for the
salvation of England.

To leave Dunsden will mean a terrible bust-up; but I have
no intention of sneaking away by smuggling my reasons
down the back-stairs. I will vanish in thunder and lightning, 20
if I go at all.

It has just struck me that one of the occult Powers that Be
may have overheard the ancient desire of my heart to be like

the immortals, the immortals of earthly Fame, I mean, and is now on a fair way to granting it. This flight of mine from overbearing elders, if it comes off, will only be my version of running away from College (Shelley, Coleridge). Only where in me is the mighty Power of Verse that covered the multitude of their sins. It is true I still find great comfort in scribbling; but lately I am deadening to all poetic impulses,   30 save those due to the pressure of Problems pushing me to seek relief in unstopping my mouth.

Here is a Sonnet that occurred to me this morning: –

On My Songs

Although on many and many a sacred time	a
Poets have spok'n as if they knew my woe;	b
Though, as it seemed, they fashioned many a rime	a
To be my own soul's cry, easing the flow	b
Of my dumb tears with Language like deep sobs,	c
– Yet there are hours when richest hoards of thought	d 40
Hold nothing for me. No heart throbs my throbs;	c
No brain yet knew the thing wherewith mine's fraught.	d
'Tis then I voice my own dim reveries.	e
Low croonings of a motherless child, in gloom,	f
Who fain must sing himself to sleep, are these.	e
Tonight, if Thou should'st lie in this same Room,	f
Dreading the Dark thou know'st not how to illume,	f
Listen; my songs may haply give thee ease.	e

I need scarcely explain the metaphors of the last lines. If however a conscientious '3rd Reading' fails to make it clear,   50 I will cease talking in parables for ever.

I gave dear old E. W. M.'s pamphlet a conscientious reading. But you know such a course of study is now quite beside the mark for me. Discussions which *take it for granted the reader believes in Adam's getting outside some fruit or other!* and then going off into occult matters of retributive dogma, are not what I want. They are trivial, and annoying, like the

tickings of the clock that so annoyed E. W., you know, that
he shelved it deep in a cupboard. Perhaps there is enough
here for you to digest.   60

Blessings attend you, dear Mother, and the dear kindred,
whose message touched me to the heart.

Wilfred

DRAFT OF A LETTER TO THE REV. WIGAN

[*? February 1913*]   [*? Shrewsbury*]
To Vicar – solely on the grounds of affection. I was a boy
when I first came to you and held you in the doubtful esteem
that a boy has for his Headmaster. It is also true that I was
an old man when I left .... The Christian Life affords no
imagination, physical sensation, aesthetic philosophy. There
is but one dimension in the Christian religion, the strait line
upwards whereas I cannot conceive of less than 3. But all
these considerations [?] are nothing to the conviction that
the philosophy of the whole system as a religion is but a religion and therefore one Interpretation of Life & Scheme of   10
Living among a hundred and that not the most convenient.

TO ALEC PATON

November 1913   *Bordeaux*
My dear Alec,

You will think me a weird bird for not answering your
letter of 2 months ago. But it was natural to postpone writing till I was actually settled in France, and since I have been
here I have been very, very busy. So much so that last week,
just before relief came, I broke down, and had to take some
days rest, which gives me leisure to remember my obliga-
tions to you.

I got a post as Professor of English in the Berlitz School
of Languages, Bordeaux. For some weeks, I have been the   10
only English Professor; but at last a lady, one Miss Hewitt
(of Liverpool or Birkenhead) has arrived to share my work.
I like the work well enough, on the whole. It consists in giv-

88

ing individual lessons to well-educated adults; who may or may not speak English. In the case of the ignorants I am obliged to act on the Berlitz Method, and teach them English without one syllable of explanation in French. This is difficult enough, and I was some time acquiring the method. At night there are Courses, and this is quite the most unpleasant part of the business.   20

I hire a room near the School for only 20 f. per month, but the innumerable extras and the cost of food, contrive to make living less cheap than it is imagined to be in these parts.

Bordeaux is a very fine town, and is of all French cities the one that most resembles Paris. The weather seems to be a regular alternation of powerful sunshine, and equally powerful rain. So far I have been rather lonely in this strange land; and it is my great regret that I scarcely speak any French; but on the contrary more English than ever in my life.

A little time ago my Father came over to see me, and spent   30 a few days in the same house with me. It was very pleasant for both of us.

I hardly dare to ask for news of Mr Paton. If he is capable of remembering me, I should be glad if you would convey to him my sincerest sympathies and regrets, and my thanks for the kindness that was shown to me, in the old days in Wales. And to Mrs Paton let me offer sympathies no less earnest.

I was glad to hear that you thought well of your new post, and that the Authorities are well-inclined towards you. I   40 must thank you very much for suggesting to speak to your Professors. There may yet be a time when I may avail myself of your services. Meanwhile, I am looking forward to spending at least the winter in these parts. I shall envy you at home, sometimes, especially at Christmas. I hope *not without cause*, and that the season may be a happy and prosperous one to you.

Always your sincere friend, *Wilfred Owen*
P.S. I was extremely sorry to miss seeing you, even for only *a few* minutes. Do write to me here: I am almost as lonely an   50 individual as the well-known solitary, A.S.P.

TO SUSAN OWEN

Saturday, 14 February [1914]   *Bordeaux*
My own Mother,

... I rejoice over the photographs and their tale. You are
certainly plumper; but I shall soon have to dispute the state-
ments you make concerning your age, and consider them as
a hoax, invented to hinder us from marrying young as you
must have done. Keep up the game for a few more years, for
I shall be young for many years yet. There is no immediate
reason for Mary (or any of you) to learn French, for the
countess has not yet crossed my path. In fact I was never so
absolutely free of 'heart trouble' within these ten years past.   10
This will no doubt give you immense satisfaction. But it
should not ...

You ought not to discourage too hard.

If you knew what hands have been laid on my arm, in the
night, along the Bordeaux streets, or what eyes play upon
me in the restaurant where I daily eat, methinks you would
wish that the star and adoration of my life had risen; or would
quickly rise.

But never fear: thank Home, and Poetry, and the FORCE
behind both. And rejoice with me that a calmer time has   20
come for me; and that fifty blandishments cannot move me
like ten notes of a violin or a line of Keats.

All women, without exception, *annoy* me, and the mercenaries (which the innocent old pastor thought might allure)
I utterly detest; more indeed than as a charitable being, I
ought.

But I should not like to have seen myself in this town, two
years earlier. And if you have not already spoken to Harold,
I do implore you to muster courage and tell him a [? some-
thing] or two more than you told me, which was nothing.   30
Still, if you never had any revelations to make to me, at
fourteen, I shall have no confessions now I am 21. At least,
none such as must make me blush and weep and you [? grow]
pale.

But I shall perhaps continue my Reminiscences next time,
according to the spirit in which you receive these present.
Mistake not my spirit; if I seem joking I am really grave; (even

as when my writing is most worthless my thoughts are most
worthy). We say strange things in our sleep. I have been par-
tially so for half an hour.   40

The enclosed is for Mary. Her photo is lovely; they are all
precious, yours: though not such works of art as is *Leslie's*;
which is quite a masterpiece, don't you think?

I have met more desirable aquaintances (Univ. Students).
Tomorrow I am again dining with the violin boy.

I must not now depict scenes, pickle juicy bits or pick
tricky characters to pieces to tickle you (witness if my wits
are going) – goodnight! call me at 7 in the morning, no
Sunday – *demain c'est dimanche n'est-ce pas: à 9 heures alors; oui
madame*, language – *mixé* . . . ah! put out the light there – ah!   50
warm, comfortable; pillow – soft, all identity lost – save am
Mother's Son

TO SUSAN OWEN

24 May 1914   *Bordeaux*
My dearest Mother,

. . . You asked me whether I should really like to direct a
Berlitz School, if Uncle Ted would raise the capital. (Perhaps
the personal allusion was not your's.) Certainly. I could be
happy enough for a time in France, Switzerland, or Italy.
And these Schools can always be sold. Compared with the
ordinary teaching-post, whether private proprietor of Boys'
School, or on a government staff, Berlitz Direction is incom-
parably more agreeable. And compared as a business with
other businesses of like capital, such a School is much more   10
profitable.

But I must cultivate more grey hairs before that.

I must study – It is among students that I feel at present
the most unhappy.

Such as I teach at School respect me as a man of mature
learning, and wide experience of letters & science. While
by such students as meet me casually I am supposed to be a
young fellow employed in a Commercial House, and am
often asked which wine-business I serve!

But I am neither of these. When I ask myself *what* I am I   20
finish my interrogations in a *crise de nerfs*. You see these self-
examinations, after a year's rest, begin again. At such times

91

the sensation of the passing of Time sharpens into agony. How much have I advanced in study since the Matriculation 1911? Enormously in some fields, but not along the marked-out high-roads, and through those absurd old toll-gates called examinations.

I sometimes wonder whether my mere Pass in Matriculation disenchanted everybody. But no one has any idea of the crushing disadvantages that I suffered through the Wyle Cop work. It was a thrice-evil system: I did what should on no account ought to be attempted by anyone under 25; I did it precisely at the moment when every precious instant should have been devoted to undivided study, and the care of my frame. And I tried to do Both under the most unfavourable of particular circumstances.

Before that time I fought with my hands free and the result was a first place on the List of my first public examination. Such a result will now never be possible more; or if possible less and less probable; more and more cruelly difficult ... Nothing gave me the creeps more surely than the sight of old Kemp, trying to learn his Latin Conjugations at 24! Is any scene in George Eliot more piercing-sorrowful than Baldassare the Scholar failing to read a paragraph?

But think not it is examination results which attract me, and constrain me to a manner of life much less easy than my present. It is more like the call of an Art, which, morning and evening, makes me unhappy in my unfruitful labour. What Art? – Any! Where lies my happiness, there lies my usefulness! I know when I am happy. We may not know what is good for us; but we know what is good to us. (Alas for the man who deceives himself in that.) I am happy with Art. I believe in *Science* more wholeheartedly than in Art; but what good could I do in that way?

I am only conscious of any satisfaction in Scientific Reading or Thinking when it rounds off into a poetical generality and vagueness. I find purer philosophy in a Poem than in a Conclusion of Geometry, a chemical analysis, or a physical law.

But all the time, you are asking: 'What Art is the fellow driving at?'

Music? If only I dare say Yes! I certainly believe I could

make a better musician than many who profess to be, and
are accepted as such. Mark, I do not for a moment call myself a musician, nor do I suspect I ever shall be; but there! I
love Music, Violin first, Piano next, with such *strength* that
I have to conceal the passion, for fear it be thought weakness. Strange to say, I met last Thursday in the woods of the
Chateau Olivier, one of my pupils, who is a student of the
Conservatoire here, and has the intention of being a soloist   70
on the piano, and of giving concerts, and takes care to remark that he has *no* idea of being a Professor of Music. But
what is chiefly strange is that, though he has had the energy
and endurance to vanquish a Father and wit to escape from a
commercial post, I doubt if he understands Music apart from
Crotchets, Rests, and appoggiaturas. When I asked whether
he thought of Composition, it was clear that he considered it
entirely a matter of Counterpoint Rules.

But if I were a pupil of the Conservatoire . . . I should not
complain of overwork. What a blessed tyranny would be   80
the tyranny of a genius of a Master! If I failed . . . but even
the despised 'Professors of Piano' (if anything above kettle-
drummers) command six and ten francs per lesson in Bordeaux; which compares well with the Profession of Tongues!
But it is as extravagant of me to think of Music now as it
would be for, say, Father to think of training as a sea–captain.
And then a little incident has stuck in my mind like a thorn.
It was quite seven years ago; I had just played one of my
juvenile pieces before a 'Company' and Grandpa was so well
pleased that he said quite gleefully 'He! He! But you'll make   90
your livin' at it yet': which remark was instantly crushed with
a storm of Pooh-Poohs! Grandma, though admitting she
couldn't have done the thing herself, snubbed dear Grandpa
as a mere matter of principle and habit. But everybody else
was sincerely indignant. That indignation I have felt and re-
doubted ever since.

Failing Music, is it Pictures that I hanker to do? I am not
abashed to admit it, when I realize I was never really taught
even to draw: for it was evident that Miss Martin who sat in
our Room during Drawing Lessons, could not draw as well   100
as the majority of the class.

But Heigh ho! If there were anything in me I should, fol-

93

lowing Legend, have covered with spirited fresco say Teece's Shed; or carved the Staircase Knob into a serene Apollo!

Yet wait, wait, O impatient world, give me two years, give me two *free months*, before it is said that I have Nothing to Show for my temperament. Let me now, seriously and shamelessly, work out a Poem. Then shall be seen whether the *Executive Power* needful for at least one Fine Art, be present in me, or be missing. 110

My Temperament I have now no right to doubt. That I believe infallible; though it remains to know which, if any, Music, Painting, Sculpture, or Verse, is the most possible.

Witness, to confirm what I believe of my composition, on one side the Tragedy of Uncle Edward Shaw, torn up by the roots by a perverted appetite; and on my other side, the Comedy of Aunt Emily Owen, who literally palpitates with excess of physical sensation.

These are the natures which, labouring for self-expression, produce Art; and which rolling in retrogression produce 120 Nothing or Crime.

Are you saddened by these declarations of mine? Anyhow, you know that as Parents *You* have, of all the world, the least title to find fault with what I am.

You must not take for granted Bernard Shaw, when he says:

> The true artist will let his wife starve, ... his mother drudge for his living at seventy sooner than work at anything than his art.

Nor will I for my part put any faith in this statement, which 130 I read in the same play;

> When a man who is born a poet, refuses a stool in a stockbroker's office, and lives in a garret, sponging on a poor landlady, or on his friends and relatives sooner than work against his grain ... we make large allowances for him.

The large allowance may in Wordsworthian Years have amounted to as much as £200. Today it takes the form of a large allowance of space between the poet and his father's door.

Here I must take breath. I may find more to say another 140

94

day. Meanwhile I am not in a garret, and have been working for money, since I was sixteen, disguised as the fact is!

Now it is Wednes. and I have had with delight your news. I shall hope to have an important piece of your mind on Sunday.

Your dearly-loving Son

TO SUSAN OWEN

Saturday, 1 August 1914   *Chez Monsieur Léger,*
                                                      Villa Lorenzo
                                    La Gayeste, Bagnères-de-Bigorre,
                                                      Htes Pyrénées

My own dear Mother,

I was cut very short in my letter of Friday. I resume. The Villa is not ideal in plan, but pretty and practical. Only it is in a bad, bad state of repair. One ought to live here three months, says M. Léger, before it is 'anything like'. It is not, you understand, the property of the Légers but of a doctor of Bagnères, who is aged and invalid, hence it is shamefully neglected. There is a largish 'property' around about, consisting of copse, meadows and a farm. There is in the garden the beginning of a Vivier, which I think is called in English   10
'stew' or 'kettle of fish' or something like that. But although two charming rivulets leap across the garden, the work is not finished. Here is a rough plan of the house:

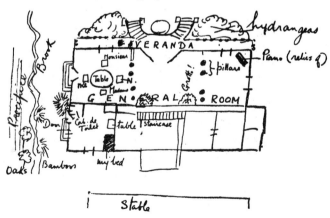

95

The whole front consists of one piece – dining-room, hall,
& drawing-room without separating-walls. The piano is
wicked: absolutely untouchable. O la! la! Mademoiselle
Levallois hasn't arrived yet; comes next week.

There is a second-storey to the villa, which only half-
covers the flat roof.

The view is not vast, being obstructed by a near hill, very   20
like one of the Stretton brotherhood – in fact exactly like.
However, we see beyond and above this, the great Pic-du-
Midi, and the Mont Aigu, on which there is yet snow. I
shall not attempt any arduous climbs, and none at all the
first week.

Now let me speak of my excellent friends. Monsieur
Léger, was educated in a Paris Engineering School, but
'abandoned the Sciences for Dramatic Art' (so saith a short
notice I have read on him). He played Comedies, I think;
and the mere stamp of his countenance is enough to confirm   30
it. He is quite small, but his bearing is notable, and his head
typically dramatic: no hair on top to speak of, deep, dark
eyes under prominent and moustache-like eyebrows, broad
mobile mouth, clean shaven. Head beautifully poised, a little
leaning-back. Voice agreeable – (but I have not yet heard
him recite). There is nothing *stagey* about him, absolutely
nothing in manner of speech, gesture, or idea; and that is
remarkable considering. But the most mysterious thing is
his age. In some lights, whether regarded, entire or in part,
behind, before, or aside, he looks just thirty. At other times   40
he is an old man, a grandfather. As a matter of fact, he is
over fifty.

Madame is much younger. She is elegant rather than *belle*;
has shapely features, luxuriant coiffure, but is much too thin
to be pretty. Probably she has been very pretty indeed. She
is obviously of the same opinion herself. Her toilette, even
for driving in donkey cart, is unimpeachable.

Yesterday she pointedly told me she could not stand plain
people. *Je les déteste* were her words. I felt uncomfortable.
You, who may take the inference in a sense more compli-   50
mentary to myself, may be uncomfortable in another way.
She has even confided to me that she doesn't love her husband

excessively. This is all very amusing for me – and nothing else.

But I am immensely happy to be in the company of Nénette. I am enclosing a picture, with the warning that it is not very like, is not complimentary, and must be seen *through a lens*. Nénette (not a nice name, *tant pis*) is perfectly a child, and, with that, is almost a perfect child. Papa prefers that she should not be educated in a town school, where they learn a great deal, but not of studies. So she goes to school with the peasants, and makes great progress. This is at the sacrifice of her accent, which is an important thing to a father like Mons. Léger. But *that* can be cured. The result of living out here is that Nénette's physique is magnificent. As far as I can judge, she has also more than her share of intellect. Anyhow she began to compose dramas at nine years of age. Some of her writings are astonishing. I said that our piano was atrocious: hence I don't know whether she can play with sense or not; but she goes through her exercises admirably. I made the mistake the other day, of striking the opening bars of *Marche Funèbre*; since when she pesters me daily for more. It is a torture for me, but I do it for the sake of her expression. We walk into Bagnères together sometimes, when we talk chiefly of armaments and what help England is giving to France!

The news of War made great stir in Bagnères. Women were weeping all about; work was suspended. Nearly all the men have already departed. Our household is one in a thousand. Mr Léger, who doesn't look his age, and I, who look French, are objects of mark at present. I had to declare myself, and get a permit to remain here; where I must stay still under penalty of arrest and sentence as a spy – unless I get a special visa for emigrating. I don't know how this state of things will affect my Courses in Bordeaux. Our food is already much dearer, and we are all getting ready to live on bread and maize-soup. If need be, Monsieur & I will undertake the harvest between us. Nobody is very gay.

I don't know whether you will ever receive this letter. I only know everything is horribly upset, in the Post, on the Railway – everywhere. I have got your last letter & Raoul's

97

and feel upset that Father may not get his holiday. I hope
you don't feel the least anxiety about me. I escaped from
Bordeaux in the nick of time. Here I am in the hands of most
amiable friends, away from danger to life, and sure enough of
food. I shouldn't like to be in Germany. Nor yet in Aumont's
shoes. Fancy, he is now at the front; and I airing my fancies
in a charming *villégiature*. I finish in haste. Shall send cards
often. If I find I am a burden to the Légers, I may have to
sneak home. So be prepared.   100

                                    Ever your devoted Wilfred

                          TO HAROLD OWEN

Wednesday, 23 September [*1914*]
                        [*12 rue Blanc Dutrouilh, Bordeaux*]
My dear Harold,

Just a word to say how glad I am that you are safe at
home: and to send you a few belated birthday wishes. One
of them is that I shall see you before you start again: though
this is not really my expectation. I hope anyhow that the
next voyage won't be a long one. I was sorry and annoyed
that you didn't send any pictures by Raoul. You might have
done so without fear of damage or of criticism. Both M. and
Madame Léger are artists. Monsieur had done some oil-
painting, and Madame of course has a genius for Design.   10
She employs three designers for her business, two men and a
young lady. Do you know anything about styles yet? I mean
the way of recognizing and imitating the Louis XV, XVI,
Empire, etc.? Methinks the less you know the better, for I
infinitely prefer the modern manner, and, at any period of
history, the English to the French.

The house where I am is spacious, rather than very large.
It is not furnished as it might be. There are in the drawing-
room two fine oil-paintings representing M. Léger; which
have been hung in the Paris Salon. Also there is a very pretty   20
statuette of Madame L. about six inches high, in sitting pose.
Above all, they have an original bust, by a greatish sculptor,
Escoula, of Mr Léger in his youth. I have seen a fair number
of busts and statues in my time, but I only know of one which
expresses so much energy, and manliness, and feeling, as this;

98

while at the same time it is a marvellously faithful portrait.

The photographs of Nénette are innumerable: Some of them absolute artistic perfections; not a whit below the best work Uncle John ever did. There are also plaster-casts and wood-carvings of this fair child. 30

The business-work of Madame L. is carried on in comparative secrecy: she won't allow me to go into the work-rooms until the articles are completed. Whether it is for fear of my cribbing the *patterns* or whether the *work-girls* I haven't decided. Anyhow I can't inform you about either yet.

I have been living in an admirable fashion, as well in Bordeaux as at Bagnères. My friend Bizardel, who is in the Cabinet of the Prefect of Bordeaux, has two automobiles at his disposition (all the cars are now monopolised by Government). One day he had to make a call on all the French 40 ministers, and he took me in his motor. I didn't see many Ministers, and nor did he; all he did was to leave the Card of the Prefect. But of course we were dressed in *grand chic*: and wore an air of tremendous diplomats. The Minister for War is in the University where I ought to be having my Courses; Minister of Finance, in a school; Minister of Justice in the Law-Courts; Minister of Fine Arts (a friend of Tailhade) in the Theatre; and so on. Poincaré is installed a few steps from my old room. Most Paris newspapers are fixed up around about this street; even money is being coined in Bordeaux. 50 The aspect of the streets has changed a good deal. Fifty thousand extra people are here! It is easy to recognize Parisians. In certain streets pass a dream of fair women. The populace grumbles that *chic* toilets should still be worn; but if not for such gentle ladies, what on earth is the Fighting about? It is the old story of the Lists: the Princess sits in flowers, while the warriors scuffle about in the ring. As a matter of fact, there are already *too many* ladies offering to help with red cross work. This afternoon two friends of Madame Léger, Mlle Levallois (a violinist who has toured all over England, 60 Scotland & Ireland) and another Mlle (once a great singer) have gone out hawking copies of a new patriotic song, to get money for the hospitals.

I went with my friend the Doctor Sauvaître to one of the large hospitals one day last week, where he is operating on

the wounded. The hospital is in the buildings of the Boys'
Lycée and appliances are altogether crude. First I saw a bullet,
like this  cut out of a Zouave's leg. Then we did the
round of the wards; and saw some fifty German wretches:
all more seriously wounded than the French. The Doctor   70
picked out those needing surgical attention; and these were
brought on stretchers to the Operating Room; formerly a
Class room, with the familiar ink-stains on floor, walls, and
ceiling; now a chamber of horrors with blood where the ink
was. Think of it: there were eight men in the room at once,
Germans being treated without the slightest distinction from
the French: one scarcely knew which was which. Considering the lack of appliances – there was only one water-tap in
the room – and the crowding – and the fact that the doctors
were working for nothing – and on Germans too – really   80
good work was done. Only there were no anaesthetics – no
time – no money – no staff for that. So after that scene I need
not fear to see the creepiest operations. One poor devil had
his shin-bone crushed by a gun-carriage-wheel, and the doctor had to twist it about and
push it like a piston to get out
the pus. Another had a hole
right through the knee; and the

doctor passed a bandage thus:

Another had a head into which a ball had entered and come
out again.

100

This is how the bullet lay in the Zouave. Sometimes the feet 90
were covered with a brown scaly, crust – dried blood.

I deliberately tell you all this to educate you to the actualities
of the war.

There were two Englishmen here wounded, last week;
but when Bizardel & I motored out to the Hospital, they had
just moved somewhere else: one having developed scarletina.

I was not much upset by the morning at the hospital; and
this is a striking proof of my health. I understand that you
are likewise 'strapping' and I felicitate you. If you return
from Canada after a month I may just catch you at home. 100
Of course give my dearest love to everybody: I remain here
until the 12th Oct., I think!

Your affectionate, Wilfred

TO SUSAN OWEN

5 March 1915   *Mérignac*
Dearest of Mothers,

My late letters have been writ for the *object* thereof; for
subjects I lacked. But today I have subject enough [*three pages
missing*].

Supposing I underwent the rigours, boredom, disgust,
danger of Barracks or Camp, or saw Action on the Field, I
might have better claim to a subsidy from my Rich Uncle,
which Common Sense, Common Decency, Common Charity are not quite common enough to realize. I say, it is a
matter of Common Sense. Consider; I ask not for a Defence 10
from Life-Troubles or an Excuse for not labouring, but I ask
for a Weapon. I *will* fight through Life; (have I not fought?)
but no headway is to be made without an Arm, whether the
Sword that is called Science, or the Munition, Capital. To
struggle vulgarly with fist and brick-end, I do refuse. I had

101

rather fall back among the Camp Followers of Life and mend potsherds. My present life, as Father points out, is not leading to anywhere in particular; but situated where I was in 1911, I don't think I could have done wiselier than take the steps I did. True, I have not yet struck out in any direction. Since taking Soundings in Deep Waters, finding them fathomless and terrible, and all but losing my breath there, I have looked out from many observation-towers; and I have lifted the curtains from many a human secrecy.

Of the various prospects of the world which I have viewed, I found only one Field in which I could work willingly, and toil without wage. Alas, but we must wait for the waterings of many seasons before hoping to produce therefrom a single acceptable flower!

If I study, it will not be, as writes Father, 'to make a comfortable future'. A comfortable future for myself is to be provided for by other means than study. To some, I seem a fellow without a footing in life. But I have my foothold, bold as any, kept for years. A boy, I guessed that the fullest, largest liveable life was that of a Poet. I *know* it now; but have still to know whether it is the highest and richest: though I begin to think so. Was I born for it? Well, so far, I find myself in possession of a goodly number of birth-certificates to that effect; while I can find only two or three flimsy arguments for the B.A. Craze, and half a dozen sadly unworthy ones for the 'Reverend' pretension. (In measure as I am in darkness, I keep open my ears for the Voice, should it speak. Think not I have stopped my ears to a Call, dear Mother!) But know that my prime object is not to boss a staff of schoolmasters, any more that it is to boom a monster business. There is *one* title I prize, one clear call audible, one Sphere where I may influence for Truth, one workshop whence I may send forth Beauty, one mode of living entirely congenial to me. In proof, I swear I cannot appreciate any other dignity: Headmaster of Eton; Archbishop of Canterbury; King of the English Race. My ambitions are lesser than Macbeth's and greater, not so happy, but much happier.

I said 'in proof'. I should have said 'for evidence'. The real verification is what can I write within say, a year's time?

102

And the crux is this – that *to be able* to write as I *know how to*, study is necessary: a period of study, then of intercourse with kindred spirits, then of isolation. My heart is ready, but my brain unprepared, and my hand untrained. And all, – untested. I quite envisage possibility of non-success.

My hopes rose on a tide of enthusiasm common enough in youths whose Spring is open to the Sun of Sense and Moon of Melancholy. That tide may now be about to ebb. Should it be the Tide that leads to Fortune, miserable me if I take it not at the flood! Shall Poverty leave me unlaunched? Shall my Timidity bar me? Shall my Indolence moor me to the mud?

Pray, dear Mother, that I may be loosed in time. The last two shackles are my own task; and now perhaps I shall forge levers for the First.

One more word: A Captive begs to be set free. Is his Begging contemptible? Is his supplication comparable to the whine of him who begs to eat? Better to beg boldly once, than to beg meanly all the rest of one's days.

So saying, I kiss you my own Mother, and confess I long to see you just as much as I long to see myself as you would have me.

Wilfred

P.S. I like to think you'll keep this letter; as indeed all, not, of course, megalomaniac's reason; but just because I keep no Diary; and the landmarks of one's Thoughts fade away still quicker than Events. You will impart my messages to Father. I never begin 'Dear Mother and Father' because I have the feeling of addressing an audience. P.P.S. I keep unquiet about Harold.

TO SUSAN OWEN

[c.20] *June 1915*   *18 rue Beaubadat. Bx. ler étage*
Dearest Mother,

Notice my address. I have not gone down a floor, but find that an intermediate storey between the ground & mine is not counted as a storey: so, I am for postal purposes on the first floor. A week's stay has now proved that I couldn't have done better than choose this place. I have now 'touched', as they say, the reimbursement of my stay in London, from Peyronnet, amounting to 165 francs, or £6. I was all but penniless after paying my rooms on the first day, and during the day enjoyed the romantic sensation of being absolutely   10 and literally *sans le sou*. Now if you would like me to post back some part of what I have borrowed from you, I can do so. Peyronnet received me very well, and considered I had managed the affair very properly. So he renews his proposition of an Eastern Voyage; to begin in Sept. if possible; but *not* until the Campaign of the Dardanelles be finished. I told him therefore that if the way were still blocked when I return home in Sept. I should try to join the Army. For I noticed in the Hotel in London an announcement that any gentleman (fit, etc.) *returning to England from abroad* will be given a Com-   20 mission – in the 'Artists' Rifles'. Such officers will be sent to the front in 3 months. Thus we shall watch the Dardanelles with a little more interest than before. And, in very sooth, I rather hope things there will last out as long as the war, which will be through the winter. Still more Frenchmen have been mobilised since I left France; and the outlook is not one shade brighter. I don't want the bore of training, I don't want to wear khaki; nor yet to save my honour before inquisitive grand-children fifty years hence. But I *now do* most *intensely want to fight*. In redoubting the exercises during these months   30 of July & August I have perfectly sufficient reason for *not* *'joining' yet*. But when I learnt that Peyronnet prefers me to wait until the East is more settled I felt full of peace – and of war. So the most patriotic thing I can do is to hope for non-success in the Dardanelles! In a month or so from now, forces will be as certainly lacking as munitions are now. So let us hope Lloyd George will have my shooter ready by then. Meanwhile, I lead a really enviable existence. I am adapted to the climate, and re-adapted to the mode of life. I shall play Tennis religiously.   40

When you were writing last Sunday I had just got in the train at the Quai d'Orsay. I shortened the Boulogne–Paris stage, by having dinner on the train; it took 1 hour and a quarter! On the Friday Night before leaving Town I was

seized with a desire to see the Mile End Road, in which I had
not set foot since I wore strap-slippers, at five years old. Although it was dark, I remembered the old spot perfectly;
and Dr Loughrey's name is still up on red-lit glass above the
door. On Sat. being now tired of the West End, I thought a
little ugliness would be refreshing; and striking east from the   50
P.O. walked down Fenchurch St and so into the Whitechapel
High Street, & the Whitechapel Road. Ugliness! I never saw
so much beauty, in two hours, before that Saturday Night.
The Jews are a delightful people, at home, & that night I re-
read some Old Testament with a marvellous great sympathy
& cordiality!

Stay long at Kidmore!

Your own W

Convey every good wish to all good people at Alpenrose & thereabouts & try and convey some photographs to   60
me . . . .

TO SUSAN OWEN

Saturday [postmark 10 July 1915]

[18 rue Beaubadat, Bordeaux]

I have nothing to report to you; if I have many things to hope
for you. I have written to Artists' Rifles without address. If I
don't get an English commission I should like to join the
Italian Army. In any case I shall probably be out of work
here in August, as the boys want an absolute holiday. So
much the better! God save the King! and bless us all, said
Tiny Tim.

Your W.E.O.

TO SUSAN OWEN

Thursday Mng. [21 October 1915]

Les Lilas, 54 Tavistock Square, W.C.

Dearest of Mothers,

I left Alpenrose on Wednesday morning and attacked the
day by going straight to Headquarters. It was found that the
Doctor had not given his signature to my papers so I was

105

examined again – and passed. Three others at the same time were refused. One was mad about it and insisted on knowing why. 'I don't think you *look* a strong man' was the first reply. (But he *did*!) More expostulation.

Dr. 'I shouldn't like to risk you – with those teeth in your head.'

Recruit. 'They can come out.'

Dr. 'Well, if you must know, your heart murmurs sometimes.' And so on with other apparently robust fellows!

I still did not 'swear in'; but spent the afternoon hunting for Rooms. Four hours I passed on this job; and finally I chose on a French Boarding House, where Guests, Conversation, Cooking and everything else is French.

This should be quite valuable to me; but I don't know whether the price is too high – 35s. a week. Bed & Breakfast at other places is 17/6 a week. I scarcely think it would come cheaper, if I took (proper) meals at A.B.C. Moreover there are no A.B.C.s near at hand. I am *two minutes* from the Headquarters. Only 5 minutes from Imperial Hotel, and 5 from Waverley, so I am at home in the region. Tavistock Square is a replica of every other Bloomsbury Square; wadded with fog; skeletons of dismal trees behind the palings; but the usual west-end pervasion of ghostly aristocracy. In London I cannot be unhappy in any surroundings, for what in Manchester would be dismally forlorn, is here Mysterious; What in Liverpool would be detestably sordid, is here romantically free and easy; what elsewhere seems old dinginess is here suggestive Antiquity. (I have a notion that Dickens lived in Tavistock Sq.)

In the middle of this letter I was called to lunch; and then went to 'swear in'. This time it is done: I am the British Army! Three of us had to read the Oath together; the others were horribly nervous! and read the wrong Paragraph until the Captain stopped them! 'Kiss the Book!' says Captain. One gives it a tender little kiss; the other a loud smacking one!!

After that we had to be inoculated for Typhoid. And that is why I am in bed since four o'clock! The delightfully kind, confidence-inspiring doctor gave us full instructions. There were scores of Tommies taking the ordeal before me, and believe me some were as nervous as only fine, healthy animals *can be* before doctors. One fainted before his turn came, merely as a result of the Doctor's description of possible symptoms!

You will be glad to hear, that though it is three hours ago, I have *no* constitutional symptoms whatever! Merely a local   50
soreness! Some will have fever & 'influenza–pains' all night! (My ink is giving out.) I quite expected such myself; but I feel so physically happy that it might have been Morphine injected! We have sick leave until Monday morning. The hours are 9.30 to 5! Jolly reasonable!

The Poetry Bookshop is about 7 mins. walk! There is a Reading this very night!

A Crowd of Belgian Ladies fleeing from Brussels through Holland are staying here today on their way to Paris.

There are just one or two hitches in this pleasant time   60
in bed. First, I have broken the bridge of my specs. and can't read without risk of headache; second, I daren't smoke (Doctor's Orders); third – empty pockets!

You will like me to write again tomorrow mng. This I promise. If only you lived near London!

Fondest Love to *Father, Mary* and the *Dearest of Boys,*
From your lovingest of Boys Wilfred

TO SUSAN OWEN

Saturday [4 March 1916]   *Y.M.C.A.* [*Romford*]
My darling Mother,

Here we are again! The reason of the Remove is that all men with 'Papers in' must go through a six weeks' Training in a School of Instruction before they can be gazetted. The War Office, indeed, has stated that none can have Commissions within 4 months from now. But that is sure to be changed. At the end of the 6 weeks there will be an exam. This is tiresome beyond words (tho' we *have* among ourselves certain words to fit the case).

Our 10 days in Town were so annoying that the departure   10
was made less galling than it might have been. Every day we

'worked', *doing nothing*, well into the evening. On Thursday the Draft left Waterloo for Southampton, and we marched with them thro' London, with *several* Bands, to say Good-bye. Thus we came in for a deal of cheering and staring from the windows & pavements. All day we marched about, and were recalled in the evening for Night Operations on Hampstead Heath, up to which we marched, over which we marched, and back from which we marched. I got in at 9.30!

I thought I should never see Monro; but last night at eleven o'clock, when I had strewn about my goods preparatory to sorting and packing, up comes Monro to my room, with my MSS! So we sit down, and I have the time of my life. For he was 'very struck' with these sonnets. He went over the things in detail and he told me what was fresh and clever, and what was second-hand and banal; and what Keatsian, and what 'modern'.

He summed up their value as far above that of the 'Little Books of Georgian Verse'. The curious part is that he applauded precisely those phrases which Prof. Morley condemned!

So then, I have gained his esteem and a (first) handshake! I need not say that he is a peculiar being; and I doubt whether ever we shall become 'Friends'. For my own part I should prefer a Business Relation, and I believe it possible – when he restarts his Journal *Poetry & Drama*, now checked by the War.

I have quite won the heart of the Swiss Housekeeper, and on two evenings she brought me up Hot Soup etc. out of human kindness. I left this morning without settling my Account, since, luckily, no Bill had been presented to me, and when I left in the early morning nobody was stirring. I have not had your letter. This is my Address now:

Cadet W.E.S. Owen, 4756
W.Co. – Officers' School –
Balgores House,
Gidea Park
Nr. Romford, Essex.

We are crowded into large empty houses, sleeping on the floor, far less comfortable than the Hut. But we have Bat-

men to wash up, and a Mess Room with table-cloths, properly set out. We expect the work to be strenuous.

I am so anxious to hear when Harold arrived, and whether
you have nearly reached your normal *health*(?), and withal
how Mary improves.

Loving wishes for Everyone, Your Wilfred

TO SUSAN OWEN

Tuesday [*15 August 1916*]   *Mytchett Musketry Camp*
Dearest My Mother,

Just a scrap to thank you for your letter just arrived tonight. I was so busy that I scrawled notes over the envelope
before ever I opened it! This Napoleonic Work will stop on
Sat. Meanwhile I have just scraped enough points to be a 1st
Class Shot.

Most of the *men* are 2nd Class and more are 3rd.

But then 9 of them have defective eyesight.

We were caught in Monsoonal Rains this afternoon, and
my poor troops were wet to the bone. (But I had my Trench   10
Coat.) It was the first time I had seen these men *really* cheer-
ful. British troops are beyond my understanding. On a bright
warm day they are as dull and dogged as November.

There is a Rumour that *all* the Manchesters move to New-
haven on the 28th.

Yours ever W.E.O. x

TO SUSAN OWEN

1 January 1917   [*France*]
My own dearest Mother,

1.30 p.m. I have just received Orders to take the train at
Étaples, to join the 2nd Manchesters. This is a Regular Regiment, so I have come off mighty well. The original Party
from the 5th has in the last 2 days got completely dissolved,
and as far as I know I am the only one for this Regt. It is a
huge satisfaction to be going among well-trained troops and
genuine 'real-old' Officers.

I don't pretend it was more than hazard that detailed me
to this Battalion; but it is all very mysterious.   10

I got my Baggage before bed-time.

I have not alas! had any letter from you or anyone.

I *think* 1/2nd Manchester should find me. But don't send any goods yet.

This is a sort of Hotel Camp where none stay more than 2 or 3 days!

I have not been uncomfortable so far, with a tent to my-self, and with a diligent Orderly.

This morning I was hit! We were bombing and a frag-ment from somewhere hit my thumb knuckle. I coaxed out   20
1 drop of blood. Alas! no more!!

There is a fine heroic feeling about being in France, and I am in perfect spirits. A tinge of excitment is about me, but excitement is always necessary to my happiness.

I don't think it is the real front I'm going to.

If on my Field Post Card I cross out 'I am being sent down to the base' with a double one ========= then I shall actually be at the Front.

Can't believe it.

Nor must you.   30

Now I must pack.

Your own Wilfred xx

TO SUSAN OWEN

4 January 1917   *Address. 2nd Manchester Regt. B.E.F.*
My own dear Mother,

I have joined the Regiment, who are just at the end of six weeks' rest.

I will not describe the awful vicissitudes of the journey here. I arrived at Folkestone, and put up at the best hotel. It was a place of luxury – inconceivable now – carpets as deep as the mud here – golden flunkeys; pages who must have been melted into their clothes, and expanded since; even the porters had clean hands. Even the dogs that licked up the crumbs had clean teeth.   10

Since I set foot on Calais quays I have not had dry feet.

No one knew anything about us on this side, and we might have taken weeks to get here, and *must* have, but for fighting our way here.

110

I spent something like a pound in getting my baggage carried from trains to trains.

At the Base, as I said, it was not so bad. We were in the camp of Sir Percy Cunynghame, who had bagged for his Mess the Duke of Connaught's chef.

After those two days, we were let down, gently, into the real thing, Mud.

It has penetrated now into that Sanctuary my sleeping bag, and that holy of holies my pyjamas. For I sleep on a stone floor and the servant squashed mud on all my belongings; I suppose by way of baptism. We are 3 officers in this 'Room', the rest of the house is occupied by servants and the band; the roughest set of knaves I have ever been herded with. Even now their vile language is shaking the flimsy door between the rooms.

I chose a servant for myself yesterday, not for his profile, nor yet his clean hands, but for his excellence in bayonet work. For the servant is always at the side of his officers in the charge and is therefore worth a dozen nurses. Alas, he of the Bayonet is in the Bombing Section and it is against Regulations to employ such as a servant. I makeshift with another.

Everything is makeshift. The English seem to have fallen into the French unhappy-go-lucky non-system. There are scarcely any houses here. The men lie in Barns.

Our Mess Room is also an Ante and Orderly Room. We eat & drink out of old tins, some of which show traces of ancient enamel. We are never dry, and never 'off duty'.

On all the officers' faces there is a harassed look that I have never seen before, and which in England, never will be seen – out of jails. The men are just as Bairnsfather has them – expressionless lumps.

We feel the weight of them hanging on us. I have found not a few of the old Fleetwood Musketry party here. They seemed glad to see me, as far as the set doggedness of their features would admit.

I censored hundreds of letters yesterday, and the hope of peace was in every one. The *Daily Mail* map which appeared about Jan. 2 will be of extreme interest to you.

We were stranded in a certain town one night and I saved

the party of us by collaring an Orderly in the streets and making him take us to a Sergeants Mess. We were famishing, and a mug of beer did me more good than any meal I ever munched. The place was like a bit of Blighty, all hung with English Greetings and Mistletoe.

As I could I collected accoutrement, some here, some   60
there, and almost am complete; Steel Helmets, & Gas; improved Box Respirator, and cetera.

The badge of the Regt. is some red tabs on the shoulder

thus ⬦. I scarcely know any of the officers. The senior

are old regulars. The younger are, several, Artists! In my room is an Artist of the same school as I passed. He is also a fine water-colour sketcher. I may *have* time to write again tomorrow. I have not of course had anything from you.

I am perfectly well and strong, but unthinkably dirty and squalid.   70

I scarcely dare to wash.

Pass on as much of this happy news as may interest people.

The favourite song of the men is

'The Roses round the door
Makes me love Mother more.'

They sing this everlastingly.
I don't disagree.

Your very own W.E.O. x

TO SUSAN OWEN

Sunday, 7 January 1917   [*2nd Manchester Regt. B.E.F.*]
My dear dear Mother,

It is afternoon. We had an inspection to make from 9 to 12 this morning. I have wandered into a village café where they gave me writing paper. We made a redoubtable March yesterday from the last Camp to this. The awful state of the roads and the enormous weight carried, was too much for scores of men. Officers also carried full packs, but I had a horse part of the way.

It was beginning to freeze through the rain when we ar-

rived at our tents. We were at the mercy of the cold, and, 10
being in health, I never suffered so terribly as yesterday afternoon. I am really quite well, but have sensations kindred to
being seriously ill.

As I was making my damp bed, I heard the Guns for the
first time. It was a sound not without a certain sublimity.
They woke me again at 4 o'clock.

We are two in a tent. I am with the Lewis Gun Officer.
We begged stretchers from the doctor to sleep on. Our servant brings our food to us in our tents. This would not be so
bad but for lack of water, and the intense damp cold. 20

I have had to censor letters by the hundreds lately. They
don't make inspiring reading.

This morning I have been reading Trench Standing Orders
to my Platoon. (Verb. Sap.)

Needless to say I show a cheerier face to them than I wear
in writing this letter; but I must not disguise from you the
fact that we are at one of the worst parts of the Line.

I have lost no possessions so far; but have acquired a pair
of boots and a Map Case (presents). And of course my valise
is heavier by much dirt. 30

I want a Compass really more than Field Glasses.

My address is

2nd Manchester Regt.

B.E.F.

I have not a word from England since I left.

I can't tell you any more Facts. I have no Fancies and no
Feelings.

Positively they went numb with my feet.

Love is not quenched, except the unenduring flickerings
thereof. By your love, O Mother, O Home, I am protected 40
from Fatigue of life and the keen spiritual Cold.

Your own W.E.O.

TO SUSAN OWEN

[*9 January 1917*]   [*2nd Manchester Regt. B.E.F.*]
My own dear Mother,

I forget both the day and date. It is about the 9th. We
moved further up yesterday, most of the way on 'Buses.

113

I have just had your long-looked-for letter. It seems wrong that even your dear handwriting should come into such a Gehenna as this. There is a terrific Strafe on. Our artillery are doing a 48 hours' bombardment.

At night it is like a stupendous thunderstorm, for the flashes are quite as bright as lightning.

When we arrived at this deserted Village last night, there 10 had been no billets prepared for the Battalion – owing to misunderstanding. Imagine the confusion!

For my part I discovered, or rather my new chosen and faithful Servant discovered a fine little hut, with a chair in it! A four-legged chair! The Roof is waterproof, and there is a Stove. There is only one slight disadvantage: there is a Howitzer just 70 or 80 yards away, firing over the top every minute or so. I can't tell you how glad I am you got me the ear-defenders. I have to wear them at night. Every time No. 2 (the nearest gun) fires, all my pharmacopoeia, all my 20 boots, candle, and nerves take a smart jump upwards. This phenomenon is immediately followed by a fine rain of particles from the roof. I keep blowing them off the page.

From time to time the Village is shelled but just now nothing is coming over. Anyhow there is a good cellar close to.

I am Orderly Officer today and stamp all the Battalion's letters. This has taken an age, and I have only a minute or two before I must despatch the Post.

I chose to spend an hour today behind the guns (to get 30 used to them). The Major commanding the Battery was very pleasant indeed. He took me to his HQ and gave me a book of Poems to read as if it were the natural thing to do!!

But all night I shall be hearing the fellow's voice:

Number Two – FIRE!

Please send the compass: 2 Manchester Regt. B.E.F. I also need 50 Players Cigarettes & some plain chocolate. There is nothing in all this inferno but mud and thunder.

I am quite incapable of reading anything but your letters; and as you see nearly incapable of writing. Tell me every 40 detail about Colin & Harold that you can; and of course, I

114

long to know everything that happens – or does not happen – at home.

Please tell Leslie & everybody that I really [have] not time nor wits to write to them from under the cannon's mouth.

But it will lull shortly. I am quite well, and have plenty to eat.

I get more and more used to the cold and wet.

Dearest love, my sweet Mother, from your Wilfred
I want a large, soft sleeping helmet and refills for the lamp.   50
s.v.p.

TO SUSAN OWEN

10 January 1917   [*2nd Manchester Regt. B.E.F.*]
My own Mother,

I was censoring letters all afternoon. After tea commenced a big commotion among my friendly neighbours the Howitzers, in the midst of which I wrote a distracted note to Leslie, but the concussion blew out my candle so many times that I lost heart.

I am kept pretty busy, tho' there is only a short 'parade'. The men do practically nothing all day but write letters; but officers have frequent meetings over schemes, maps, instructions, and a thousand cares.   10

Yesterday I took a tour into the Line which we shall occupy. Our little party was shelled going up across the open country. It was not at all frightful and only one 4.7 got anywhere near, falling plump in the road, but quite a minute after we had passed the spot. I tell you these things because *afterwards* they will sound less exciting. If I leave all my exploits for recitation after the war without mentioning them now, they will be appearing bomb-shell-bastic.

Now I am not so uncomfortable as last week, for my new servant who has been a chemist's assistant, has turned out not   20
only clean & smart, but enterprising and inventive. He keeps a jolly fire going; and thieves me wood with much cunning.

My Company Commander (A Company) has been out here since the beginning: 'tis a gentleman *and an original* (!).

Next in command is Heydon, whom I greatly like, and

115

once revered as the assistant Adjutant at Witley & Oswestry.

Then come I, for the remaining subalterns are junior. I chose No. 3 Platoon. I was posted to 2, but one day I took No. 3 in tow when its officer left, because I liked the look of the men.

Even as they prophesied in the Artists, I have to take a close interest in feet, and this very day I knelt down with a candle and watched each man perform his anointment with Whale Oil; praising the clean feet, but not reviling the unclean.

As a matter of fact, my servant and one other, are the only non–verminous bodies in the platoon; not to say Lice-ntious.

Today's letters were rather interesting. The Daddys' letters are specially touching, and the number of xxx to sisters and mothers weigh more in heaven than Victoria Crosses. The Victoria Cross! I covet it not. Is it not *Victorian*? yah! pah!

I am not allowed to send a sketch, but you must know I am transformed now, wearing a steel helmet, buff jerkin of leather, rubber–waders up to the hips, & gauntlets. But for the rifle, we are exactly like Cromwellian Troopers. The waders are of course indispensable. In $2\frac{1}{2}$ miles of trench which I waded yesterday there was not one inch of dry ground. There is a mean depth of 2 feet of water.

It seems an era since Christmas Day, and Goose, Carols, Dickens & Mistletoe.

Assuming the war lasts another year I should get leave twice, or three times, for we get it, or should get it every 3 months.

Be sure to have no Chloride of Lime in the house. Our water is overdosed with it enough to poison us. But in the Mess we can get Perrier fortunately.

You need not ask where I am. I have told you as far as I can. These things I need

    (1) small pair nail scissors
    (2) celluloid hair-pin box from Boots (9d.) with *tightfitting lid*, & containing boracic powder.
    (3) Players Navy Cut
    (4) Ink pellets
    (5) Sweets (!!) (We shall not be in touch with Supplies by day.)

Have no anxiety. I cannot do a better thing or be in a righter place. Yet I am not sainted therefore, and so I beg you to annoy ..., for my wicked pleasure.

W.E.O. xxx

No so bad!

TO SUSAN OWEN

Tues: 16 January 1917   [*2nd Manchester Regt. B.E.F.*]
My own sweet Mother,

I am sorry you have had about 5 days letterless. I hope you had my two letters 'posted' since you wrote your last, which I received tonight. I am bitterly disappointed that I never got one of yours.

I can see no excuse for deceiving you about these last 4 days. I have suffered seventh hell.

I have not been at the front.

I have been in front of it.

I held an advanced post, that is, a 'dug-out' in the middle   10
of No Man's Land.

We had a march of 3 miles over shelled road then nearly 3 along a flooded trench. After that we came to where the trenches had been blown flat out and had to go over the top. It was of course dark, too dark, and the ground was not mud, not sloppy mud, but an octopus of sucking clay, 3, 4, and 5 feet deep, relieved only by craters full of water. Men have been known to drown in them. Many stuck in the mud & only got on by leaving their waders, equipment, and in some cases their clothes.   20

High explosives were dropping all round, and machine guns spluttered every few minutes. But it was so dark that even the German flares did not reveal us.

Three-quarters dead, I mean each of us $\frac{3}{4}$ dead, we reached the dug-out, and relieved the wretches therein. I then had to go forth and find another dug-out for a still more advanced post where I left 18 bombers. I was responsible for other posts on the left but there was a junior officer in charge.

My dug-out held 25 men tight packed. Water filled it to a depth of 1 or 2 feet, leaving say 4 feet of air.   30

117

One entrance had been blown in & blocked.

So far, the other remained.

The Germans knew we were staying there and decided we shouldn't.

Those fifty hours were the agony of my happy life.

Every ten minutes on Sunday afternoon seemed an hour.

I nearly broke down and let myself drown in the water that was now slowly rising over my knees.

Towards 6 o'clock, when, I suppose, you would be going to church, the shelling grew less intense and less accurate: so that I was mercifully helped to do my duty and crawl, wade, climb and flounder over No Man's Land to visit my other post. It took me half an hour to move about 150 yards.

I was chiefly annoyed by our own machine guns from behind. The seeng-seeng-seeng of the bullets reminded me of Mary's canary. On the whole I can support the canary better.

In the Platoon on my left the sentries over the dug-out were blown to nothing. One of these poor fellows was my first servant whom I rejected. If I had kept him he would have lived, for servants don't do Sentry Duty. I kept my own sentries half way down the stairs during the more terrific bombardment. In spite of this one lad was blown down and, I am afraid, blinded.

This was my only casualty.

The officer of the left Platoon has come out completely prostrated and is in hospital.

I am now as well, I suppose, as ever.

I allow myself to tell you all these things because *I am never going back to this awful post*. It is the worst the Manchesters have ever held; and we are going back for a rest.

I hear that the officer who relieved me left his 3 Lewis Guns behind when he came out. (He had only 24 hours in.) He will be court-martialled.

In conclusion, I must say that if there is any power whom the Soldiery execrate more than another it is that of our distinguished countryman. You may pass it on via Owen, Owen.

Don't pass round these sheets but have portions typed for

118

Leslie etc. My previous letter to you has just been returned.
It will be too heavy to include in this.   70

Your very own Wilfred x

TO SUSAN OWEN

Friday, 19 January 1917   [*2nd Manchester Regt. B.E.F.*]
We are now a long way back in a ruined village, all huddled
together in a farm. We all sleep in the same room where we
eat and try to live. My bed is a hammock of rabbit-wire stuck
up beside a great shell hole in the wall. Snow is deep about,
and melts through the gaping roof, on to my blanket. We
are wretched beyond my previous imagination – but safe.

Last night indeed I had to 'go up' with a party. We got
lost in the snow. I went on ahead to scout – foolishly alone –
and when, half a mile away from the party, got overtaken
by   10

G A S

It was only tear-gas from a shell, and I got safely back (to
the party) in my helmet, with nothing worse than a severe
fright! And a few tears, some natural, some unnatural.

Here is an Addition to my List of Wants:

Safety Razor (in my drawer) & Blades
Socks (2 pairs)
6 Handkerchiefs
Celluloid Soap Box (Boots)
Cigarette Holder (Bone, 3d. or 6d.)   20
Paraffin for Hair.

(I can't wash hair, and have taken to washing my face with
snow.)

Coal, water, candles, accommodation, everything is
scarce. We have not always air! When I took my helmet off
last night – O Air it was a heavenly thing!

Please thank Uncle for his letter, and send the Compass. I
scattered abroad some 50 Field Post Cards from the Base,
which should bring forth a good harvest of letters. But
nothing but a daily one from you will keep me up.   30

I think Colin might try a weekly letter. And Father?

We have a Gramophone, and so musical does it seem now that I shall never more disparage one. Indeed I can never disparage anything in Blighty again for a long time except certain parvenus living in a street of the same name as you take to go to the Abbey.

They want to call No Man's Land 'England' because we keep supremacy there.

It is like the eternal place of gnashing of teeth; the Slough of Despond could be contained in one of its crater-holes; the fires of Sodom and Gomorrah could not light a candle to it – to find the way to Babylon the Fallen.

It is pock-marked like a body of foulest disease and its odour is the breath of cancer.

I have not seen any dead. I have done worse. In the dank air I have *perceived* it, and in the darkness, *felt*. Those 'Somme Pictures' are the laughing stock of the army – like the trenches on exhibition in Kensington.

No Man's Land under snow is like the face of the moon chaotic, crater-ridden, uninhabitable, awful, the abode of madness.

To call it 'England'!

I would as soon call my House (!) Krupp Villa, or my child Chlorina-Phosgena.

Now I have let myself tell you more facts than I should, in the exuberance of having already done *'a Bit'*. *It is done*, and we are all going still farther back for a long time. A long time. The people of England needn't hope. They must agitate. But they are not yet agitated even. Let them imagine 50 strong men trembling as with ague for 50 hours!

Dearer & stronger love than ever. W.E.O.

TO SUSAN OWEN

Sunday, 4 February 1917   [*Advanced Horse Transport Depot*]
My own dear Mother,

I am now indeed and in truth very far behind the Line; sent down to this Old Town for a Course in Transport Duties. The Battalion did *not* get out for a rest, and since my last letter I have had another strong dose of the advanced Front Line.

To begin with, I have come out quite unhurt, except for a touch of dysentery, which is now passed, and a severe cold and cough which keep me in bed today.

I have no mind to describe all the horrors of this last Tour. But it was almost wusser than the first, because in this place my Platoon had no Dug-Outs, but had to lie in the snow under the deadly wind. By day it was impossible to stand up or even crawl about because we were behind only a little ridge screening us from the Boches' periscope.

We had 5 Tommy's cookers between the Platoon, but they did not suffice to melt the ice in the water-cans. So we suffered cruelly from thirst.

The marvel is that we did not all die of cold. As a matter of fact, only one of my party actually froze to death before he could be got back, but I am not able to tell how many have ended in hospital. I had no real casualties from shelling, though for 10 minutes every hour whizz-bangs fell a few yards short of us. Showers of soil rained on us, but no fragment of shell could find us.

I had lost my gloves in a dug-out, but I found 1 mitten on the Field; I had my Trench Coat (without lining but with a Jerkin underneath). My feet ached until they could ache no more, and so they temporarily died. I was kept warm by the ardour of Life within me. I forgot hunger in the hunger for Life. The intensity of your Love reached me and kept me living. I thought of you and Mary without a break all the time. I cannot say I felt any fear. We were all half-crazed by the buffeting of the High Explosives. I think the most unpleasant reflection that weighed on me was the impossibility of getting back any wounded, a total impossibility all day, and frightfully difficult by night.

We were marooned on a frozen desert.

There is not a sign of life on the horizon and a thousand signs of death.

Not a blade of grass, not an insect; once or twice a day the shadow of a big hawk, scenting carrion.

By degrees, day by day, we worked back through the

121

reserve, & support lines to the crazy village, where the Battalion takes breath. While in Support we inhabited a vast Boche dug-out (full of all kinds of souvenirs). They are so deep that they seem warm like mines! There we began to thaw. At last I got to the village, & found all your dear precious letters, and the parcel of good and precious things. The Lamp is perfect, your Helmet is perfect, everything was perfect.   50

Then I had the heavenly-dictated order to proceed on a Transport Course. Me in Transports? Aren't *you*? When I departed, the gloom among the rest of the Subs. and even among Captains, was a darkness that could be felt. They can't understand my luck.

It doesn't necessarily mean a job as Transport Officer straight away, but here I am, in a delightful old town billeted in a *house* with a young Scotch Officer.

True, we can get no fuel and the very milk freezes in the   60 jug in a few minutes. True, I am sorely bruised by riding. True, this kind of Life is expensive. But I have not been so full of content since the middle of November last.

Tell Colin how we have to ride all manner of horseflesh in the School, cantering round & round for hours, without stirrups, and folding arms and doing all kinds of circus tricks.

It is very amusing – to watch.

Tomorrow I shall send a P.C. of this Town I must not name in a letter.

Address: R.E. Section   70
        Advanced Horse Transport Depot
        A.P.O. S1.
        B.E.F. France

Hope you had numerous Field P.C.'s which I dropped en route to here.

The Course should last 1 month!!

Alas! I have missed your last letters. It has taken 3 days to get here.

Fondest love to all, & thanks for all their letters,
            Your own Wilfred x   80
P.S. I don't at all deserve the spirited approbation which

122

Father gives me. Though I confess I like to have his kind letters immensely. I shall read them less shame-facedly in dug-outs and trenches, than I do here in this pleasant peaceful town.

Quite 10 years ago I made a study of this town & Cathedral, in the treasury. It is all familiar now!

Auntie Emma fairly hit it when she 'perceived the awful *distaste* underlying' my accounts. Dear Aunt was ever a shrewd Doogie. 90

I suppose I can endure cold, and fatigue, and the face-to-face death, as well as another; but extra for me there is the universal pervasion of *Ugliness*. Hideous landscapes, vile noises, foul language and nothing but foul, even from one's own mouth (for all are devil ridden), everything unnatural, broken, blasted; the distortion of the dead, whose unburiable bodies sit outside the dug-outs all day, all night, the most execrable sights on earth. In poetry we call them the most glorious. But to sit with them all day, all night ... and a week later to come back and find them still sitting there, 100 in motionless groups, THAT is what saps the 'soldierly spirit' ...

Distaste? Distaste, Quotha?

I used to consider Tankerville Street ugly, but now ...

Well, I easily forget the unpleasant, and, look you, I even have to write it down for the sake of future reminders, reminders of how incomparable is an innocent and quiet life, at home, of work creative or humdrum, with books or without books, moneyed or moneyless, in sunshine or fog, but under an inoffensive sky, that does not shriek all night with 110 flights of shells.

Again I have said too much. But let me repeat that I am mighty snug here, and have a goodly prospect before me now.

I am not sorry you keep in bed from time to time, but I do hope you'll soon get some sunny walks. Are you painting?

The Letter from Lancs. was from Bobby. All the brothers are in college there. Miss de la Touche is as Bobby says 'supposed to be boss' of a Belgian Hospital in London.

Again, dearest love to all. W.E.O. 120

123

[? TO SUSAN OWEN]

14 March 1917   *Le Quesnoy-en-Santerre*
... Last night I was going round through pitch darkness
to see a man in a dangerous state of exhaustion. I fell into a
kind of well, only about 15ft, but I caught the back of my
head on the way down. The doctors (not in consultation!)
say I have a slight concussion. Of course I have a vile headache, but I don't feel at all fuddled ... [*The letter is lost.*]

TO SUSAN OWEN

Sunday, [18] *March* [1917]   [*13th Casualty Clearing Station*]
My dearest Mother,
    I am in a hospital bed (for the first time in life).
    After falling into that hole (which I believe was a shell-
hole in a floor, laying open a deep cellar) I felt nothing more
than a headache, for 3 days; and went up to the front in the
usual way – or nearly the usual way, for I felt too weak to
wrestle with the mud, and sneaked along the top, snapping
my fingers at a clumsy sniper. When I got back I developed
a high fever, vomited strenuously, and long, and was seized
with muscular pains. The night before last I was sent to a   10
shanty a bit further back, & yesterday motored on to this
Field Hospital, called Casualty Clearing Station 13. It is nowhere in particular that I know, but I may be evacuated to
Amiens, if my case lasts long enough. For I began to get
right again immediately after getting into these sheets 'that
soon smooth away trouble'. The physician handed me over
to the surgeon. But my head is not broken or even cut in
any way. My temperature etc. *may not* have had any relation
to the knock, and the first doctor said he only hoped it *had*.
Anyhow it was normal yesterday, and below today, and the   20
only abnormal thing about me now is that I don't want a
cigarette. That, then, should not worry you. I have now told
you everything, and I hope, dear Mother, that you are duly
grateful – to me, and concerning the whole circumstance.
    Sometimes a Sister blows in to this ward, and flutes a bit
on a high voice, or pegs around on a high heel, but we are

really attended by orderlies, who are fresh & clean, and much preferable, being not only serener and sensibler, but also private soldiers with no airs of authority about 'em. Rather the other way.

All my kit and belongings have come down with me, including 55 francs, much mud, and Pte. Heath.

Alas! I've had no letter for about 5 days when I had 3 together, and am not likely now to have any for quite a week. I think that for a few days: 2 Man. Regt. with 'Please Forward' will be the best address [*six lines missing*]

ever, Wilfred x

TO SUSAN OWEN

4 April 1917   [*2nd Manchester Regt. B.E.F.*]
Dearest Mother,

Know that I have cut my forefinger with a tin of Lobster, and that is why I write shaky. I have been 4 days caravanning from the CCS, & have just found our HQ. Journeying over the new ground has been most frightfully interesting. The Batt. has just done something great which will find its way into the Communiqué. I am going up to join them in an hour's time. They have lost one officer & many are wounded, Heydon among them. I shall no doubt be in time for the *Counter* Attack. I have bought an automatic pistol in the town (from which I sent a P.P.C.). *By the time you get this we'll be out of the line again.*

Tonight will be over . . . .

My long rest has shaken my nerve. But after all *I hate old age*, and there is only one way to avoid it!

Last night I bedded down with a family of refugees, 3 boys, 2 tiny girls: a good class socially, and of great charm personally. I was treated as a god, and indeed begin to suspect I have a heart as comprehensive as Victor Hugo's, Shakespeare's, or your own. In 24 hours I never took so many hugs & kisses in my life, no, not in the first chapter even. They took reliefs at it. It would have astounded the English mind. – While, just the night before I was in blues as deep as the Prussian Blue – not having heard an affectionate spoken word

125

since I left you – or rather since I left A. I am now in the Pink.

No need to tell you where I am going up to fight. It is *the* town on which the hopes of all England are now turned. I must now dress up in Battle Order.

Your own W.E.O. xxxxx

I find no letters here. Your parcels did not take part in the advance – Too heavy!

Without your Letters I should give in. *What to* I know not, but I 'sorter' feel I should 'give up the unequal contest!' – without a definite object for carrying on. And that object is not my Motherland, which is a good land, nor my Mother tongue, which is a dear language, but for my Mother, of whom I am not worthy to be called

The Son xxx

I hope this bit of paper is not incriminating to send over but it is all I can find. I must write to Colin & send him some small souvenirs tomorrow. Ah my poor angel! He wants to be with me. He would not live three weeks in this sector of Hades.

6 [?8] *April* [*1917*]   [*2nd Manchester Regt. B.E.F.*]
My own dearest Mother,

We are 'in rest'. I arrived at the Battalion a day too late for the stunt: I am therefore not in the 'we' when I say we captured 6 guns, numerous machine guns, and of course, the Position.

But I am still ME.

I am afraid poor Heydon will not live, and other officers, one of my company, fell on the field. It is interdicted to give any figures at all, but a good number of us are (agreeably) wounded.

When I turned up I went back to A Coy., where Captain Green was hanging on with only one officer. We stuck to our line 4 days (and 4 nights) without relief, in the open, and in the snow. Not an hour passed without a shell amongst us. I never went off to sleep for those days, because the others were far more fagged after several days of fighting than I fresh from bed. We lay in wet snow. I kept alive on brandy, the fear of death, and the glorious prospect of the cathedral Town just below us, glittering with the morning. With glasses I could easily make out the general architecture of the cathedral: so I have told you how near we have got. The French are on the skirts of the Town, as I could see. It was unknown where exactly the Boche was lying in front of us. The job of finding out fell upon me. I started out at midnight with 2 corporals & 6 picked men; warning other Regiments on our flanks not to make any mistake about us. It was not very long before the Hun sent up his verilights, but the ground was favourable to us, and I and my Corporal prowled on until we clearly heard voices, and the noises of carrying & digging. When I had seen them quite clearly moving about, and marked the line of their entrenchment it might seem my job was done; but my orders were to discover the force of the enemy. So then I took an inch or two of cover and made a noise like a platoon. Instantly we had at least two machine guns turned on us, and a few odd rifles. Then we made a scramble for 'home'.

Another night I was putting out an Advanced Post when we were seen or heard and greeted with Shrapnel. The man crouching shoulder to shoulder to me gets a beautiful round hole deep in his biceps. I am nothing so fortunate, being only buffeted in the eyes by the shock, and whacked on the calf by a spent fragment, which scarcely tore the puttee.

One day I hung my Trench coat (which you used to button up for me at Southport) on a bush, & had just jumped down into my hole when a splinter ripped a hole through the chest & back. The tears are not big enough to spoil it for Field use.

I found your Parcel waiting for me here, when we got in at 3 in the morning (all half dead with fatigue & some quite, poor lads). It was like a look in at Home to burrow into that lovely big box and examine all the loving presents. I opened it in bed (for I found my blankets ready laid out in this cosy cellar) and before I had opened all the boxes fell fast asleep. I am not awake now properly and my letter may appear disjointed. But then I'm not disjointed. I learned with astonishment that you had measles, and selfishly speaking am glad

127

enough I only know it now you are better of it. O darling
Mother you can't think how you could secure my peace of
mind by being able to tell me you are well. Look at me I am
nearly screwed to death with cold and nerves one night. Two
days later I am in perfect, glowing, brilliant Health.   60

Tell Mary that Captain Crichton Green is immensely complimentary about her gingerbread.

I will write again tomorrow. Just had yours of 27th. Found
Mar. 31st waiting for me. Be sure we shall not go into action
again for a long time. It couldn't be done.

Still, always, and ever your very own

Wilfred xxx

TO SUSAN OWEN

25 April 1917   *A Coy., My Cellar*
My own dearest Mother,

Immediately after I sent my last letter, more than a fortnight ago, we were rushed up into the Line. Twice in one
day we went over the top, gaining both our objectives. Our
A Company led the Attack, and of course lost a certain number of men. I had some extraordinary escapes from shells &
bullets. Fortunately there was no bayonet work, since the
Hun ran before we got up to his trench. You will find mention of our fight in the Communiqué; the place happens to
be the very village which Father named in his last letter!   10
Never before has the Battalion encountered such intense
shelling as rained on us as we advanced in the open. The
Colonel sent round this message the next day: 'I was filled
with admiration at the conduct of the Battalion under the
heavy shell-fire . . . . The leadership of officers was excellent,
and the conduct of the men beyond praise.' The reward we
got for all this was to remain in the Line 12 days. For twelve
days I did not wash my face, nor take off my boots, nor
sleep a deep sleep. For twelve days we lay in holes, where at
any moment a shell might put us out. I think the worst in-   20
cident was one wet night when we lay up against a railway
embankment. A big shell lit on the top of the bank, just 2
yards from my head. Before I awoke, I was blown in the air

128

right away from the bank! I passed most of the following
days in a railway Cutting, in a hole just big enough to lie in,
and covered with corrugated iron. My brother officer of B
Coy., 2/Lt. Gaukroger lay opposite in a similar hole. But he
was covered with earth, and no relief will ever relieve him,
nor will his Rest be a 9 days' Rest. I think that the terribly
long time we stayed unrelieved was unavoidable; yet it makes   30
us feel bitterly towards those in England who might relieve
us, and will not.

We are now doing what is called a Rest, but we rise at
6.15 and work without break until about *10 p.m.* for there is
always a Pow-Wow for officers after dinner. And if I have not
written yesterday, it is because I must have kept hundreds of
letters uncensored, and enquiries about Missing Men un-
answered [*remainder missing*]

TO SUSAN OWEN

2 May 1917   *13th Casualty Clearing Station*
Dearest Mother,

Here again! The Doctor suddenly was moved to forbid
me to go into action next time the Battalion go, which will
be in a day or two. I did not go sick or anything, but he is
nervous about my nerves, and sent me down yesterday –
labelled Neurasthenia. I still of course suffer from the head-
aches traceable to my concussion. This will mean that I shall
stay here and miss the next Action Tour of Front Line; or
even it may mean that I go further down & be employed for
a more considerable time on Base Duty or something of   10
the sort. I shall now try and make my French of some avail
... having satisfied myself that, though in Action I bear a
charmed life, and none of woman born can hurt me, as re-
gards flesh and bone, yet my nerves have not come out
without a scratch. Do not for a moment suppose I have had
a 'breakdown'. I am simply *avoiding* one.

At the first Ambulance I arrived at in the Car, a Corporal
came up to me with a staid air of sleepy dignity that seemed
somehow familiar. And when he began to enter in a Note
Book my name & age, we knew each other. It was old Har-   20

129

top of the Technical! Bystanding Tommies were astounded
at our fraternity. For the Good old Sort brought back in an
instant all the days of study in Shrewsbury, and the years
that were better than these, or any years to come. Although
married, as you may know to one of the girls who acted
with me at the Socials, he has not grown up any more since
the last term at the P.T.C. He was reading the same old books
that we 'did' there. I was jolly glad to see them again, & to
borrow. For he has nothing particular to do but read on his
present job of Pack Store Corporal in the R.A.M.C. Davis   30
also is married. How fortunate is Stanley Webb (not speaking of his engagement, but of his Blighty).

If I haven't got a Blighty in this war, I will take good care
not to get a *Blight*, as many have done, even from this Regiment. I should certainly have got a bullet wound, if I had
not used the utmost caution in wriggling along the ground
on one occasion. There was a party of Germans in a wood
about 200 yds *behind* us, and his trench which we had just
taken was only a foot deep in places, & I was obliged to keep
passing up & down it. As a matter of fact I rather enjoyed   40
the evening after the Stunt, being only a few hundred yds
from the Town, as you knew, and having come through the
fire so miraculously: and being, moreover, well fed on the
Boche's untouched repast!! It was curious and troubling to
pick up his letters where he had left off writing in the middle
of a word! If we had gone down the line next day all would
have been very well, but we were kept up (in another part of
the line) for 9 days after it: under incessant shelling.

I am so glad you got the one Field Card which I was able
to work down from there. Your last Parcel has arrived, and   50
I enjoyed the Munchoc right well. I had some compensation
for lost parcels in being given a parcel sent to an officer who
was wounded the *first day* he joined us. It is a regimental
custom never to send Food Stuffs back after Officers who
go down to Hospital! I shall soon want some more Players.
Nothing else yet! – Don't omit to address C.C.S.13.

I am more glad than I dare say to know that dear Mary is
now all right. I try to imagine that you are really well. How
strange that the fact that I am in Hospital means that all

cause of uneasiness about me is removed from you! Do not   60
hawk this letter about! Nay, I would rather you told no one
I am a Casual again!

Your very own Wilfred

TO COLIN OWEN

14 May 1917   [13th Casualty Clearing Station]
Dearest Colin,

Here is some loot, from a Pocket which I rifled on the Field.
I was thinking of you when I was unbuckling the Bugle from
the equipment, and being then in a particularly noble frame
of mind, meant to present it to you some day. But now I
have got too fond of the thing to part with it!

The sensations of going over the top are about as exhila-
rating as those dreams of falling over a precipice, when you
see the rocks at the bottom surging up to you. I woke up
without being squashed. Some didn't. There was an extra-   10
ordinary exultation in the act of slowly walking forward,
showing ourselves openly.

There was no bugle and no drum for which I was very
sorry. I kept up a kind of chanting sing-song: Keep the Line
straight!

Not so fast on the left!

Steady on the Left!

Not so fast!

Then we were caught in a Tornado of Shells. The various
'waves' were all broken up and we carried on like a crowd   20
moving off a cricket-field. When I looked back and saw the
ground all crawling and wormy with wounded bodies, I felt
no horror at all but only an immense exultation at having
got through the Barrage. We were more than an hour moving over the open and by the time we came to the German
Trench every Boche had fled. But a party of them had remained lying low in a wood close behind us, and they gave
us a very bad time for the next four hours.

When we were marching along a sunken road, we got the
wind up once. We knew we must have passed the German   30
outposts somewhere on our left rear. All at once the cry ran

131

down 'Line the Bank'. There was a tremendous scurry of fix-
ing bayonets, tugging off breach-covers & opening pouches,
but when we peeped over, behold one solitary German,
haring along towards us, with his head down and his arms
stretched in front of him, as if he were going to take a high
dive through the earth (which I have no doubt he would like
to have done). Nobody offered to shoot him, he looked too
funny; that was our only prisoner that day!

Did I tell you that on Easter Sunday evening we brought   40
down a Hun Plane, I took the aviator's handkerchief as a
souvenir! It is not permitted to take anything belonging to
the machine ....

TO SUSAN OWEN

[?26] May 1917   *41st Stationary Hospital*
My own dear Mother,

Just had yours of Sat. Evening and was astonished to ap-
prehend that the Great Shadow is creeping on towards Colin.
What will he be next birthday, seventeen?

I wrote him a wholesome bit of realism in that last letter,
as well as a fantasy in the language of the Auth: Ver: of 1611.
I have changed my mind and see no reason why you should
not have that letter and that fantasia. It was on the model of
Leslie's 'Throw her down. So they threw her down. And
he said Throw her down again. And they threw her down   10
again. And they gathered up of the fragments that remained
etc.'

I did it without reference to the Book, of course; and without any more detraction from reverence, than, say, is the
case when a bishop uses modern slang to relate a biblical
story. I simply employed seventeenth century English, and
was carried away with it.

Incidentally, I think the big number of texts which jogged
up in my mind in half-an-hour bears witness to a goodly
store of them in my being. It is indeed so; and I am more   20
and more Christian as I walk the unchristian ways of Chris-
tendom. Already I have comprehended a light which never
will filter into the dogma of any national church: namely

132

that one of Christ's essential commands was: Passivity at
any price! Suffer dishonour and disgrace; but never resort to
arms. Be bullied, be outraged, be killed; but do not kill. It
may be a chimerical and an ignominious principle, but there
it is. It can only be ignored: and I think pulpit professionals
are ignoring it very skilfully and successfully indeed.

Have you seen what ridiculous figures Frederick & Arthur   30
Wood are cutting? If they made the Great Objection, I should
admire them. They have not the courage.

To begin with I think it was puny of Fritz to deny his name.
They are now getting up a petition, mentioning their 'uni-
que powers', 'invaluable work' and so on, and wish to carry
on their work from *82 Mortimer St. W.* as usual. I do not recollect Christ's office address in Jerusalem, but in any case I
don't think He spent much time there.

St Paul's business premises, if I remember, were somewhat cramped, not to say confined.   40

But I must not malign these Brethren because I do not
know their exact Apologia.

And am I not myself a conscientious objector with a very
seared conscience?

The evangelicals have fled from a few Candles, discreet
incense, serene altars, mysterious music, harmonious ritual
to powerful electric-lighting, overheated atmosphere, palm-
tree platforms, grand pianos, loud and animated music, ex-
tempore ritual; but I cannot see that they are any nearer to
the Kingdom.   50

Christ is literally in no man's land. There men often hear
His voice: Greater love hath no man than this, that a man lay
down his life – for a friend.

Is it spoken in English only and French?

I do not believe so.

Thus you see how pure Christianity will not fit in with
pure patriotism.

I am glad you sent that cutting from Wells' Book. I hope
you understood it. I did not. Not a word of it can I make
sense of. I would rather we did not read this Book. Now   60
The Passionate Friends I found astounding in its realism but
like all the great terrible books it is impossible to 'take sides'.

It is not meant to be a comfortable book; it is discussional; it refuses to ignore the unpleasant.

(This practice of *selective ignorance* is, as I have pointed out, one cause of the War. Christians have deliberately *cut* some of the main teachings of their code.)

At present I am deep in a marvellous work of Hugo's *The Laughing Man*.

By the same post as your letter came two books from 70 Leslie, by O. Henry.

So I am well set up.

I am marked *for the next Evacuation*!!

So glad my Oak Seedlings are growing. How many are there likely to thrive, out of how many acorns? They have been 'dry', you know, for 6 years. Give them every chance.

This countryside is now superb. But from this we are no longer allowed out of the hospital bounds.

Many thanks for *Punch*. Yes Colin has been very good in writing to me. Keep him up to it. It will do *him* good, don't- 80 you-know! And as for me: they bring me Shropshire, even as yours bring me Home.

Expect me – before Christmas.

Your – one and only – Wilfred x

TO LESLIE GUNSTON

Wednesday, [25] July 1917   *Craiglockhart*
Dear L.

Thanks for yours of this morning. I hope you have had my card posted last Monday.

On Mond. next I lecture the 'Field Club' – a Nat. Hist. association, on the lines of our old Society – Geological, (you & me) & Botanical (Vera). Do you remember: you old Black Moth? Well, the days have come when I am one of the founders of a real learned society. My subject has the rather journalese Title of 'Do Plants Think?' – a study of the Response to Stimuli & Devices for Fertilisation, etc. I have no 10 books yet, but I remember a number of useful points from your big Cassell's (I think it was Cassell's) studied in 1911. Meanwhile I'm beastly bothered with our Mag. (herewith)

134

and I'm [to] take German Lessons at the Berlitz, Edin. Last week I wrote (to order) a strong bit of Blank: on *Anteaus v. Heracles*. These are the best lines, methinks: (N.B. Anteaus deriving strength from his Mother Earth nearly licked old Herk.)

> . . . How Earth herself empowered him with her touch,
> Gave him the grip and stringency of winter, 20
> And all the ardour of th'invincible Spring;
> How all the blood of June glutted his heart.
> And all the glow of huge autumnal storms
> Stirred on his face, and flickered from his eyes.

I had seen your Song. May the music be equally happy. You *are* lucky! You shall have my Locke's *Usurper* if you will. It's now at home.

I see Swinburne also wrote a number of replicas of the olde Ballad! Heigh ho!

Ever Your W.E.O. 30

TO SUSAN OWEN

Tues. Night [*7 August 1917*]   [*Craiglockhart*]
Dearest of Mothers,

... Yes, you will like to read Mrs Browning. Having listened so long to her low, sighing voice (which *can* be *heard* often through the page), and having seen her hair, not in a museum case, but palpably in visions, and having received kindness from a boy to whom she was kind (M. Léger – he is still a boy); for these reasons, I say, the Flapper flaps in vain.

The other day I read a Biography of Tennyson, which says he was unhappy, even in the midst of his fame, wealth, and domestic serenity. Divine discontent! I can quite believe 10 he never knew happiness for one moment such as I have – for one or two moments. But as for misery, was he ever frozen alive, with dead men for comforters. Did he hear the moaning at the bar, not at twilight and the evening bell only,

but at dawn, noon, and night, eating and sleeping, walking and working, always the close moaning of the Bar; the
thunder, the hissing and the whining of the Bar?

Tennyson, it seems, was always a great child.
So should I have been, but for Beaumont Hamel.
(Not before January 1917 did I write the *only lines* of mine
that carry the stamp of maturity: these:

But the old happiness is unreturning.
Boys have no grief so grievous as youth's yearning:
Boys have no sadness sadder than our hope.)

Mayes has just been in, and it is now quarter to one on
Wednesday. There is this advantage in being 'one of the ones'
at the Hospital, that nurses cease from troubling the weary
who don't want rest.
I have a sort of suspicion your note was written in bed;
but perhaps it was before nine in the morning.
It is worthy of mention that we have been in mist for 3
days: a gloriously luminous mist at times. I saw Holyrood
on Sunday Afternoon (being alone on Salisbury Crags), a
floating mirage in gold mist. A sight familiar enough in
dreams and poems, but which I never thought possible in
these islands. It was the picture *of* a picture; if you understand. I don't.
It's too late o'night to talk like this. Time I snuggled myself away. Goodnight, dear Mother.

x W.E.O.

TO SUSAN OWEN

Friday Night [*10 August 1917*]   [*Craiglockhart*]
My own dear Mother,
. . . I laughed at your hoping I should learn German during
my stay in Edinburgh. It's a vile language to learn. I'm over-
joyed that you think of making bandages for the wounded.
Leave Black Sambo ignorant of Heaven. White men are in
Hell. Aye, leave him ignorant of the civilization that sends

136

us there, and the religious men that say it is good to be in
that Hell. (Continued, because important) Send an English
Testament to his Grace of Canterbury, and let it consist of
that one sentence, at which he winks his eyes: 10

'Ye have heard that it *hath* been said: An eye for an eye,
and a tooth for a tooth:

But I say that ye resist not evil, but whosoever shall smite
thee on thy right cheek, turn to him the other also.'

And if his reply be 'Most unsuitable for the present dis-
tressing moment, my dear lady! But I trust that in God's good
time ... etc.' – *then there is only one possible conclusion*, that
there are no more Christians at the present moment than
there were at the end of the first century.

While I wear my star and eat my rations, I continue to take   20
care of my Other Cheek; and, thinking of the eyes I have
seen made sightless, and the bleeding lads' cheeks I have
wiped, I say: Vengeance is mine, I, Owen, will repay.

Let my lords turn to the people when they say 'I believe in
... Jesus Christ', and we shall see as dishonest a face as ever
turned to the East, bowing, over the Block at Tyburn.

I fear I've written like a converted Horatio Bottomley.

And to you who need no such words.

That is why I want you not to destroy them; for I write
so because I see clear at this moment. In my eye there is no   30
mote nor beam, when I look through you across the world.

There is a mote in many eyes, often no other than a tear. It
is this: That men are laying down their lives for a friend. I
say it is a mote; a distorted view to hold in a general way.

For that reason, if no other, I won't publish in any way
the 'Kings and Christs'.

Saturday
Have just got the parcel up from Slateford Station by an
Orderly. The Rly. sent me a notification this morning. The
suit is not crushed. Everything in order. Wish *I* were. Shan't   40
wear the ring, or the Emerald!

Have not re-read last night's copy, lest I should cancel it,
and you be without a letter of any sort.

Your own W.E.O. x

137

TO LESLIE GUNSTON

22 August 1917   *Craiglockhart*
My dear Leslie,

   At last I have an event worth a letter. I have beknown myself to Siegfried Sassoon. Went to him last night (my second
call). The first visit was one morning last week. The sun
blazed into his room making his purple dressing suit of a
brilliance – almost matching my sonnet! He is very tall and
stately, with a fine firm chisel'd (how's that?) head, ordinary
short brown hair. The general expression of his face is one
of boredom. Last night when I went in he was struggling to
read a letter from Wells; whose handwriting is not only a   10
slurred *suggestion* of words, but in a dim pink ink! Wells talks
of coming up here to see him and his doctor; not about Sassoon's state of health, but about *God the Invisible King*. After
leaving him, I wrote something in Sassoon's style, which I
may as well send you, since you ask for the latest.

   The Dead-Beat (*True* – in the incidental)
   He dropped, more sullenly, than wearily,
      Became a lump of stench, a clot of meat,
      And none of us could kick him to his feet.
   He blinked at my revolver, blearily.   20

   He didn't seem to know a war was on,
      Or see or smell the bloody trench at all ...
      Perhaps he saw the crowd at Caxton Hall,
   And that is why the fellow's pluck's all gone –

   Not that the Kaiser frowns imperially.
      He sees his wife, how cosily she chats;
      Not his blue pal there, feeding fifty rats.
   Hotels he sees, improved materially:

   Where ministers smile ministerially.
      Sees Punch still grinning at the Belcher bloke;   30
      Bairnsfather, enlarging on his little joke,
   While Belloc prophesies of last year, serially.

These lines are years old!!

> We sent him down at last, he seemed so bad,
>   Although a strongish chap and quite unhurt.
>   Next day I heard the Doc's fat laugh: 'That dirt
> You sent me down last night's just died. So glad!'

Those are the very words! {

Next day

I am going to send you *The Old Huntsman* as a festive gift for the occasion of your First Publication.

'The Death Bed' is the finest poem. I told him my opinion. 40
It is his own. This poem is coming out in the Georgian Anthology. He was struck with the 'Dead Beat', but pointed out that the facetious bit was out of keeping with the first & last stanzas. Thus the piece as a whole is no good. Some of my old Sonnets didn't please him at all. But the 'Antaeus' he applauded fervently; and a short lyric which I don't think you know 'Sing me at morn but only with thy Laugh' he pronounced perfect work, absolutely charming, etc. etc., and begged that I would copy it out for him, to show to the powers that be. 50

So the last thing he said was 'Sweat your guts out writing poetry!' 'Eh?' says I. 'Sweat your guts out, I say!' He also warned me against early publishing: but recommended Martin Secker for a small volume of 10 or 20 poems.

He himself is 30! Looks under 25!

So glad your proofs are done. How long now before I have my cop*ies*? That 'Farley Down' occasional verse did not impress me, I am longing to re-read *The Nymph*, & give it to Sassoon!

Would you mind sending me *all the MSS* verse of mine in 60
your keeping as soon as you can get at them? How I want a confabulation with you in my Room with everything to hand!

Sassoon admires Thos. Hardy more than anybody living. I don't think much of what I've read. Quite potatoey after the meaty *Morals*.

You'll have had enough of Sassoon, what? Just one more tit-bit. Wells said in his last letter: hope you will soon 'devote yourself to the real business of your life, which is poetry only by the way.' Poor Wells! We made some fancy guesses 70

as to what he meant: – Tract-writing? stump-oratory? politics? what?

Cheero! I'm well enough by day, and generally so by
night. A better mode of life than this present I could not
practically manage.

Yours, with affection, ever, W.E.O.

TO TOM OWEN

26 August 1917   [*Craiglockhart*]
My dear Father,

I think this work of Sassoon's will show you to the best
possible advantage the tendencies of Modern Poetry. If you
don't appreciate these then it's Na-poo. There is nothing
better this century can offer you. I've marked the pieces for
first reading, and those underlined are specially good. 'The
Old Huntsman' was put in as a title piece, to catch the
hunting-people, and make 'em read the rest.

'The Death-Bed' is a piece of perfect art.

'Morning Express', page 56 is the kind of thing that makes   10
me despair of myself; everyone says 'I could have done that
myself!'

Only no one ever did.

Please send me your Criticisms.

I am beginning to feel uncomfortably editorial again after
a fortnight's rest. Nobody is willing to write about our last
Concerts, and it looks as if I shall have to fill half the Mag.
myself, between now & tomorrow.

I *am* glad Colin is with you.

Realizing how impossible it is for me to be there has spoilt   20
my holiday here. I was make-believing that I was a free creature here, but it is only that my chain has been let out a little.
I should only hurt myself with tugging at it.

Fondest love to all,

Your W.E.O.

TO MARY OWEN

Thursday, 29 August 1917   *Craiglockhart*
My dear Mary,

I was grieved – almost aggrieved – to hear you had had some bad days at Aberystwyth, and I am still waiting to hear you are all right. This cloud, and a great many other real ones messing about in the heavens and sometimes mooning around the building itself, and generally behaving unbecomingly on the top of us all – and the Russians panicking, and getting out of the war, and ourselves getting deeper and deeper into it, these things, I say, do not make one (eider)-downhearted. So it is not to be wondered at that I was a bit   10
snappy in my Editorial, which you shall have in a day or two.

But a word from Sassoon, though he is not a cheery dog himself, makes me cut capers of pleasure.

My dear, except in one or two of my letters (ahem!) you will find nothing so perfectly truthfully descriptive of war. Cinemas, cartoons, photographs, tales, plays – Na–poo.

Now you see why I have always extolled Poetry.

The 'Redeemer', I have been wishing to write every week for the last three years.   20

Well, it has been done and I have shaken the greater hand that did it.

'The Death-Bed', my dear sister, should be read seven times, and after that, not again, but thought of only.

Here is a very good brooch, a *very* good brooch. Unless you like it much, I shall very likely sneak it again for a model of latter-day design! There is no hint of a Board for me yet! I'm going down to make my Evening Tea now. Just a card will tell me how you & dear Mother are.

Your loving Wilfred   30

TO SUSAN OWEN

7 September 1917   [*Craiglockhart*]
My dearest Mother,

These last two days Thursday and Friday have been the very fullest–happiest of the year – excluding only one or two

141

of the days when you were up here. Went with Mayes to a
perfect little dinner at the Grays' and passed an evening of
extraordinary fellowship in All the Arts. The men are not
of the expansive type – one is a History Honoursman at
Oxford, the other owner of a large Munition Works. The
ladies have more effusiveness, but are genuine. One is really
witty and the other is a sculptor of great power. 10

They showered books upon me on leaving; and on Monday I am to escort Mrs Gray on an expedition into the slums
to see an old Italian – a street singer whom she 'took-up' and
who says he was once an operatic star! He is probably a fraud,
but we shall see that – and we shall see his many children.

Mayes and I crept in at a late hour last night. This is known
to the C.O. but he has said nothing to me. Mayes talked it
over with him this morning. At midnight, however, a nurse
came to me very austerely: 'Dr Brock will see you at once
Mr Owen!' I went: in pyjamas and perspiration. He said a 20
lady in Edinburgh expected me to lunch today to show me
around the Slum Gardens. Goodnight! I retired in stupor.

So I went to lunch at their palatial house with two maiden
sisters. The Misses Wyer. One of them took me over the
Gardens and I gave my opinions and views. (Dr Brock is
trying to get me in touch with the Edinburgh submerged
tenth.) It will never come off while I am in uniform: but I
can't tell him that. I went back to a marvellous pleasant Tea
with the other lady, who has travelled far and wide over the
continents and the literatures. Then in sailed an enormous 30
old lady of the type of old lady I have but once or twice met
– outside Thackeray – intellectual, witty, vigorous: told some
good stories and eat a huge tea; an admirer of Alec Waugh's
book *Loom of Youth*! Waugh wrote this at 18. But more of
this book later. The touches of what I can only call 'kultur'
in its universal sense, not English, French or German but
universal, and the discovery of my own – almost secret –
views of such things as sculpture, state-craft, ethics, etc. etc.,
in these strange beings and places were enough to make the
day memorable in itself. 40

But tonight Sassoon called me in to him; and having condemned some of my poems, amended others, and rejoiced

over a few, he read me his very last works, which are superb beyond anything in his Book. Last night he wrote a piece which is the most exquisitely painful war poem of any language or time. I don't tell him so, or that I am not worthy to light his pipe. I simply sit tight and tell him where I think he goes wrong. He is going to alter one passage of this very poem for me.

No wonder I was happy last night, and that tonight I must   50
get it off my chest before I sleep.

The Field club of 12 members went to the Observatory this afternoon. I forgot I was missing that. But Sassoon as it happens has just asked me to go to tea with the Astronomer Royal tomorrow. So I shall see much more than what I missed! How I shall get a Magazine out this week-end I don't know.

Will you do a sacred task for me? Wrench open the cupboard of my Desk and withdraw from the top-shelf right-hand side, three portfolios – two are khaki, one is Harold's   60
gilt-stencilled velvet blotter. Upon your unimpeachable honour *do not inspect the contents either of the cupboard or of the portfolios*. But promptly pack off the portfolios under *secure wrappings and plain address*. I don't care if you damage the cupboard-door. But don't damage the hinges of your mind by wrenching the secrets of my portfolios. This sounds mysterious; but I am serious. Some of these verses will light my cigarettes, but one or two may light the darkness of the world. It is not a question of wheat and chaff, but of devils and angels   70

I have written to Harold. I hope I am not 'feeding' you with this kind of talk, but I write straight from my experiences and heart.

Do thou likewise.

Your own W.E.O. x

TO SUSAN OWEN

Tuesday [*10*] *September 1917*   [*Craiglockhart*]
My own dear Mother,

Many true thanks for your long letter. I have read it many

times. You also find letter writing a fitter mode of intimate communication than speaking.

The enclosed came out of my Parcel of Portfolios rec'vd this evening, together with a stamped letter addressed to Langley, Worcester, which I have duly posted. They had slipped right inside the parcel! Was it a trick of some urchin of Cleveland Street?

The MSS arrived in perfect order. Did I classify them as Angels & Devils! I meant simply: Live Ones and Duds. I have written *no Barrack Room Ballads*! You may be a little shocked by Sassoon's language. He is of course, with W.E.O. practically the only one in the place who doesn't swear conversationally. He is simply honest about the war.

Your questions concerning him are searching. You will do well to put them on all similar occasions.

For it is very true there are not a few whom I like, say, as a poet only, as an actor only, as a table-companion only, as a trench-mate only, as a servant only, as a statue only, as a marble idol only.

Sassoon I like equally in all the ways you mention, as a man, as a friend, as a poet.

The *man* is tall and noble-looking. Before I knew him I was told this and by this much only I spotted him! I quote from a publication: 'very slim and shy, with eyes which may be blue or brown when you come to examine them closely.'

He is thirty-one. Let it be thoroughly understood that I nourish no admiration for his nose or any other feature whatever.

The *Friend* is intensely sympathetic*, with me about every vital question on the planet or off it. He keeps all effusiveness strictly within his pages. In this he is eminently *English*. It is so restful after the French absurdities, and after Mrs Gray who gushes all over me. But there is no denying to myself that he is already a *closer* friend than, say, Leslie. Just as this assertion is not the result of having been with him so much lately, neither is it derogated by the shortness of our acquaintance-time. We have followed parallel trenches all our lives,

* sym-pathy = feeling with (Greek)

144

and have more friends in common, authors I mean, than most   40
people can boast of in a lifetime.

As for the *Poet* you know my judgement. What's yours? *If*
I ever said anything so ambiguous as 'I wish I had Father's
views' I meant 'I wish I *knew* Father's views' – and had them
before me. By the way S. has written two or three pieces
'around' chance things I have mentioned or related! Thus the
enclosed scribble is a copy of what he wrote after I had read
three Sonnets on 'Beauty' (subject) by E.L.G., O.A.J., and
me . . . . I do think it a pity Leslie is in such a hurry.

I had a jolly afternoon with Mrs Gray on Saturday. We   50
got ourselves admirably stared at in Lower Edinburgh. I
wore a hooligan manner and cap, but unimpeachable gloves,
boots and tie. Mrs Gray wore weird clothes and some price-
less rings. Tomaso was out. We left the macaroni, the toffees
and so on, in the wrong house at first. We thought the stupe-
faction of the good woman 'part of the day's work'. However she discovered our mistake and came after us. We were
then mingling with a crowd following a poor (sober) woman
who was being arrested. Tomaso *was* out, but we found a
suitable object of compassion in his (unmistakably Italian)   60
boy who had impaled his leg on a railing-spike. We did not
inspect the leg. The smell of carbolic was strong enough
under the clothes. Then we rummaged over a delightful dark
and filthy curiosity-shop, and I discovered a real Roman
Vase which I got for a shilling. But Mrs Gray bought a real
bronze, – doubtful Roman – lamp for 1/6 as a present for
me. So I had to give her the vase! For I had another little
dinner with them and came up to the Concert in their taxi.
Mrs Steinthal is a mighty clever sculptress. We had great fun
in Princes St buying a laurel-wreath for Mayes for presenta-   70
tion after the play. Poor Mayes overdid himself and has lost
his speech. Came up to my room and woke me up this morning with appealing eyes and curious gesturations. I thought
he was mad and have yet to get over it! He has been often
seized thus, and will soon get right again.

Surely you have some more MSS – 'Purple' for instance. If

not, many are lost. I hate losing trifles; – and because they
are my only diary, I humbly desire you to keep these letters.

Your very own W.E.O. x

How is Mary? 80

TO SUSAN OWEN

Sunday, 14 October [1917]   *Craiglockhart*
My own dear Mother,

It's getting time I saw you again. Three months without
leave would seem long with a Regiment, longer perhaps than
it does here; where I am kept amused.

This afternoon, after lunching with Miss Wyer, and a
scholastic lady-friend of hers, we went up to Colinton, a
village close to here, to see Mr Blaikie, one of the heads of
Constable's Printers. I was not long discovering that he was
a friend of Stevenson's from boyhood. Stevenson's famous
old nurse was Blaikie's first. So it was an interesting after- 10
noon; tho' old Blaikie affects a contempt for R.L.S. It is a
beautiful thing that children of Tynecastle School, – or of the
Birkenhead Institute are able to get nearer to the romantic
heart of Stevenson, and really know him in a better way,
than this person who played with him before even *Treasure
Island* was dreamed of.

On Friday I went to the Lintotts again. Lintott has reason
to be proud of his work, which he is not – particularly –; and
the beautiful Mrs Lintott has reason to be proud of her boy,
which she is. From there I went to see Mrs Scott, Mrs Gray's 20
mother, and her daughter, who has just given up work in
the War Office. Miss Scott was out.

On Sat. I met Robert Graves (see last poem of *O.H.*) for
Sassoon, whom nothing could keep from his morning's golf;
& took Graves over to the Course when he arrived. He is a
big, rather plain fellow, the last man on earth apparently
capable of the extraordinary, delicate fancies in his books.

No doubt he thought me a slacker sort of sub. S.S. when
they were together showed him my longish war-piece 'Disabled' (you haven't seen it) & it seems Graves was mightily 30
impressed, and considers me a kind of *Find*!! No thanks,
Captain Graves! I'll find myself in due time.

146

I think it a rather precious exhibition of esteem that S.S. lends me the MSS of his next book. On the other hand, when I pointed out a quotation from Shakespeare that I intended for my Frontispiece, he collared it by main force, & copied it out for himself!

I don't think of anything else of interest to tell you – even if the above is so. My next board should be a week next Tuesday. They may cast me out the same day, – or give me another month. Both issues are acceptable. I could do a lot with another month here; but I feel a growing homesickness.

I am no longer neurasthenic, though I may be neurotic.

It is high time you started a special course of *getting fit* so that I may find you all bonny, & so that the exertion of my company may not fatigue you. Time also to get the house swept and garnished, not of dust and cobwebs but of the Webby people that come to spin their yarns there.

Dearest love all round and round

From Wilfred x

40

50

TO SIEGFRIED SASSOON

5 November 1917   *Mahim, Monkmoor Road, Shrewsbury*
My dear Sassoon,

When I had opened your envelope in a quiet corner of the Club Staircase, I sat on the stairs and groaned a little, and then went up and loosed off a gourd, a Gothic vacuum of a letter, which I 'put by' (as you would recommend for such effusions) until I could think over the thing without grame.

I have also waited for this photograph.

Show some rich anger if you will. I thank you; but not on this paper only, or in any writing. You gave – with what Christ, if he had known Latin & dealt in oxymoron, might have called Sinister Dexterity. I imagined you were entrusting me with some holy secret concerning yourself. A secret, however, it shall be until such time as I shall have climbed to the housetops, and you to the minarets of the world.

Smile the penny! This Fact has not intensified my feelings for you by the least – the least *grame*. Know that since mid-September, when you still regarded me as a tiresome little knocker on your door, I held you as Keats + Christ + Elijah

10

147

+ my Colonel + my father-confessor + Amenophis IV in
profile.   20

What's that mathematically?

In effect it is this: that I love you, dispassionately, so much,
so *very* much, dear Fellow, that the blasting little smile you
wear on reading this can't hurt me in the least.

If you consider what the above Names have severally done
for me, you will know what you are doing. And you have
fixed my Life – however short. You did not light me: I was
always a mad comet; but you have fixed me. I spun round
you a satellite for a month, but I shall swing out soon, a dark
star in the orbit where you will blaze. It is some consolation   30
to know that Jupiter himself sometimes swims out of Ken!

To come back to our sheep, as the French *never* say, I have
had a perfect little note from Robt. Ross, and have arranged
a meeting at 12.30 on Nov. 9th. He mentioned staying at
Half Moon St, but the house is full.

I have ordered several copies of *Fairies & Fusiliers*, but
shall not buy all, in order to leave the book exposed on the
Shrewsbury counters! I'm also getting Colvin's new *Life of
Keats*, no price advertised, but damn it, I'm to enjoy my
Leave!   40

I am spending happy enough days with my Mother, but I
can't get sociable with my Father without going back on
myself over ten years of thought.

What I most miss in Edinburgh (not Craiglockhart) is the
conviviality of the Four Boys (L. *vivere* – to live). Someday,
I must tell how we sang, shouted, whistled and danced
through the dark lanes through Colinton; and how we
laughed till the meteors showered around us, and we fell
calm under the winter stars. And some of us saw the path-
way of the spirits for the first time. And seeing it so far   50
above us, and feeling the good road so safe beneath us, we
praised God with louder whistling; and knew we loved one
another as no men love for long.

Which, if the Bridge-players Craig & Lockhart could have
seen, they would have called down the wrath of Jahveh, and
buried us under the fires of the City you wot of.

To which also it is time you committed this letter. I wish

you were less undemonstrative, for I have many adjectives
with which to qualify myself. As it is I can only say I am

Your proud friend, Owen   60

TO SIEGFRIED SASSOON

27 November 1917   *Scarborough*
I sit alone at last, and therefore with you, my dear Siegfried.
For which name, as much as for anything in any envelope of
your sealing, I give thanks and rejoice.

The 5th have taken over a big Hotel, of which I am Major
Domo, which in the vulgar, means Lift Boy. I manage Accommodation, Food, and Service. I boss cooks, housemaids,
charwomen, chamber-maids, mess orderlies and – drummers.

There were 80 officers when I came or 800 grouses daily.

I had a Third Heaven of a time in London, and should   10
have got into a Fourth or Fifth if I had not missed you on
Wednesday. Were you there for a 'Reading'? I know nothing
of it to this day.

After London, I went to Winchester to see my Cousin,
whose fine Book cover with its enclosed pages I dare to send
you herewith. ('Herewith' is the staple of my morning's
letters, *re* this and *per* that.)

In Town, then, R.R. gave me a glorified morning at the
Reform, & evening at Half Moon St. – When he had steered
me to a lunch-table I found beside me an upstart rodent of a   20
man, who looked astonished to find himself there. But dear
Ross sang out with blessed distinctness 'Mister Arnnoldd
Bennnettt'. So I stood up and shook hands. Presently I became aware of a pair of bayonet-coloured eyes, threatening
at me from over, as it were, a brown sandbag. 'H.G. Wells!'
So I stood up and shook hands. I think these men noticed me
because I stood up to them – in two senses. Anyhow I got
A.B. into a corner about you, as I will tell you someday.
And H.G. talked to me exclusively for an hour. I was only
ill at ease with him once, and that was when he tried to make   30
me laugh with him at Bennett's gaudy handkerchief.

What sport for my imagination is the idea of your Meet-

149

ing with R. Nichols. – He is so self-concerned & *vaniteux* in
his verse that I thought he must efface himself in a room:
even as you who write so acid are so – unsoured; and me,
who write so big, am so miniscule.

What is Nichols up to now?

I called at the P. Bookshop the Wednesday you were in
Town. A lady was badgering H. Monro, trying to discover
your age and whereabouts, and so on. Monro proved him-   40
self as reticent as his books. But we exchanged some delicious
winks. R.G.'s book came in during the hour I was there. I
should never stop if I started to rejoice over these poems.

You read many to me: but, wisely, not the best: – or the
most charming.

The 'Legion' is too glorious. I tell you I can *not* believe I
rode in a taxi with the man Gracchus. But I did, and he has
cursed, battered on the table, over a poor word of mine. Oh!
world you are making for me, Sassoon!

I think I liked reading his Letter to you more than yours   50
to him, but for no better reasons than that I like the future
better than the past, and hope you *will* learn the piccolo.

If these tetrameters aren't enough to bring you to your
senses, Mad Jack, what can *my* drivel effect to keep you from
France?

Have you been very sat upon by this Board? Do tell me
quick what your movements are.

I have studied and expanded every sentencience of your
sole letter to me; until I can make no more out of it, and want
some more, please.   60

Concerning Gunston's book: you might, of your charity,
read (1) page 41, because it is the best.

(2) page 49, the sestet, because I asked him to write, on
this subject . . .

(3) page 11. There is a conceit in v. 3, – a poor thing, but
mine own.

My 'Vision' is the result of two hours' leisure yesterday, –
and getting up early this morning! If you have objections to
make, would you return it! If not, pass it on to R.R.

I trust you'll like the 'Soldier's Dream' well enough to pass   70
it on to the *Nation* or Cambridge.

This was the last piece from Craiglockhart.

Winchester Downs gave me 'Asleep'.

As I do no parades, I shall presently be able to make time for seclusion.

There is no one here whose mind is Truth, or whose body Keats's synonym for Truth.

I'll mind my business, I'm a good worm.

Could you get me another portrait for my room here? I framed the one, and could not pack it.   80

But don't make it an excuse for delaying a letter.

I hope you will read through this, twice.

I hope you read Graves's Letter to S.S. twice a day, *till war ends*.

We have had some strong sunshine; and when it strikes anything blue I see you sitting by the bedside as on That Morning in September. You look round, – over my head, which annoys me, so that I go down and rate the kitchen staff of the Hotel, and insult the new subalterns.

> I am Owen; and I am dying   90
> I am Wilfred; and I follow the Gleam

TO SIEGFRIED SASSOON

6 December 1917   *Scarborough*

My friend,

I shall continue to poop off heavy stuff at you, till you get my range at Scarborough, and so silence me, for the time. This 'Wild with all Regrets' was begun & ended two days ago, at one gasp. If simplicity, if imaginativeness, if sympathy, if resonance of vowels, make poetry I have not succeeded. But if you say 'Here is poetry', it will be so for me. What do you think of my Vowel-Rime stunt in this, and 'Vision'? Do you consider the hop from *Flea* to Soul too abrupt?   10

Wouldn't our Theosophist like the Thought Form of this piece? I quite see the origin of Theosophy. It's the same as that of heaven, and Abraham's bosom, and of the baby that sucked Abraham's bosom (supposing he lived long enough ago): desperate desire.

Your W.E.O.

151

TO LESLIE GUNSTON

30 December 1917   *Scarborough*

My dear Leslie,

It is overlong since I wrote; but now, composed by my bedroom fire this Sunday afternoon, my thoughts impel themselves after you, & wish you were here to read a little Swinburne, whom I find particularly fine on Sundays.

Have you yet got Gosse's life of A.C.S.?

I had a longish letter from Sassoon recently, saying he will get Robert Nichols to write to me, for he likes him much. Nichols' *Ardours & Endurances* you know, are in the 3rd or 4th Edition.

Graves also wrote to me, telling me to 'puff out my chest & look big' for I have as much right as most of Them.

Some poems of mine sent him by S.S. he is passing on to Nichols.

They believe in me, these Georgians, and I suffer a temptation to be *satisfied* that they read me; and to remain a poet's poet!

S.S. who has your book (for the letter which he acknowledges, was in it) says *not a word* of the book. He may have unfortunately read the 'Nations' Debt' first, and taken offence. Remember Poetry with him is become a mere vehicle of propaganda.

Already, by now, I believe he is in France.

I have had some good inspirations in Scarboro', but my need is to revise now, rather than keep piling up 'first drafts'. My duties, as you know, are in your Line, and I like 'em. Went to the most atrocious bad play ever witnessed, the other night: low melodrama shocking bad acting.

But there were a dozen girls who danced & sang by way of Interlude; & they being only 14 to 18 had adorable slender bare legs, nude as you could wish. What's more some of them came outside the Hotel next day. I waved and blew kisses from the window, but didn't speak to them. Anyhow it was better than overhearing conversation in a motor-car!

An old Bordeaux friend of mine is now interpreter in the American Y.M.C.A. near Bordeaux. Will write again soon.

                                                  Always your W.E.O.

31 December 1917   *Scarborough*

My own dear Mother,

Just a short note to thank you for the message enclosed with forwarded letters. I guess you saw the Cards, from Johnny & Bobby; characteristic cards: pictures of monkeys & the motto: 'Times change, & we with Time, but not in ways of Friendship.' So they are unchanged – from the old shallow waggery, and the old deep affection. I haven't written to them since my arrival in England.

The other letter was from my *cher ami* in Bordeaux who, unlike Raoul, persists in his expressions of fidelity. What 10 I taught him of English has got him a post as Interpreter to the *American* Y.M.C.A. at Bordeaux (*verb. sap.*). I think Bordeaux is first on my post-war Visiting List. Many & various, strange & multitudinous are the friends that befriend me in this world. Yet I never found one false, or that did not surpass me in some virtue.

Some are very young, and some are already old, but none are middling.

And there are no dogs among my friends.

No dogs, no sorcerers, nor the other abominations on 20 that list. For I have been bitten by the dogs of the world; and I have seen through the sorceries and the scarlet garments.

And so I have come to the true measure of man.

I am not dissatisfied [with] my years. Everything has been done in bouts:

Bouts of awful labour at Shrewsbury & Bordeaux; bouts of amazing pleasure in the Pyrenees, and play at Craiglockhart; bouts of religion at Dunsden; bouts of horrible danger on the Somme; bouts of poetry always; of your affection always; of sympathy for the oppressed always. 30

I go out of this year a Poet, my dear Mother, as which I did not enter it. I am held peer by the Georgians; I am a poet's poet.

I am started. The tugs have left me; I feel the great swelling of the open sea taking my galleon.

Last year, at this time (it is just midnight, and now is the intolerable instant of the Change) last year I lay awake in a

153

windy tent in the middle of a vast, dreadful encampment. It
seemed neither France nor England, but a kind of paddock
where the beasts are kept a few days before the shambles. I   40
heard the revelling of the Scotch troops, who are now dead,
and who knew they would be dead. I thought of this present
night, and whether I should indeed – whether we should
indeed – whether you would indeed – but I thought neither
long nor deeply, for I am a master of elision.

But chiefly I thought of the very strange look on all faces
in that camp; an incomprehensible look, which a man will
never see in England, though wars should be in England;
nor can it be seen in any battle. But only in Étaples.

It was not despair, or terror, it was more terrible than   50
terror, for it was a blindfold look, and without expression,
like a dead rabbit's.

It will never be painted, and no actor will ever seize it. And
to describe it, I think I must go back and be with them.

We are sending seven officers straight out tomorrow.

I have not said what I am thinking this night, but next
December I will surely do so.

I know what you are thinking, and you know me

Wilfred.

TO LESLIE GUNSTON

8 January 1918   [*Scarborough*]
My dear Leslie,

I was glad to find you take up a strong attitude with regard to your poetry & mine.

You ask me if I saw the Reviews of S.S. I have read every
word of them – in his huge book of Press Cuttings. The vast
majority are entirely appreciative. As for Graves, have you
seen *Chamber's Journal* lately, or the Sat. *Westminster*? And
remember the *Edinburgh Review*; fame itself!

But these men are not out for fame.

They simply say what Everyman most needs. And Every-   10
man is glad.

Graves's technique is perfect. Did Poetry ever stand still?
You can hark back if you like, and be deliberately archaic,

but don't make yourself a lagoon, salved from the ebbing tide of the Victorian Age.

The Times is just in what it says. But you have only to go on with your quiet unassuming graceful style, and presently everybody else will so scream themselves hoarse that you will be the only happy voice remaining, then you will be indeed original, and a haven for many.   20

The more I think of your ease & rapidity in writing, the more I hope for an inimitable book next time. But not within five years.

We Georgians are all so old.

Tell me all the Reviews you get.

I am much in doubt whether to put forth any poems next Spring or not.

Someday I'll lend you my *Georgian Poetry* 1917. If you would like it soon I'll send it.

I don't forget I am in debt to you for 3/- isn't it?   30

I've been reading Wells' *What is coming?*,

Hazlitt's *Essays*,

and a glorious book of critical essays by A. K. Thompson, called *The Greek Tradition*.

I read no fiction. Wells' *Wife of Sir Isaac Harman* which I've just finished isn't fiction.

Ever your affectionate Wilfred

TO LESLIE GUNSTON

Saturday Night [*26 January 1918*]   [*Scarborough*]
Dear L.

Great thanks for your letter. I can't identify your 'A. & E.' without applying the method of superposition, co-ordinating the figures each to each, and so on.

Went up to Town for Robert Graves's Wedding last Tuesday, calling Home on the way. Arrived at Padd. on Wed. Mng. I hired a bath room, but had no time to get in the water as the page announced my taxi before I had finished shaving. So I arrived punctually at the Reform to lunch with Robert Ross.   10

Wells was there, but at a different table. But he waved to

me from afar, and we had a few words on going out.

Lord Rhondda sat within reaching distance of me!

To you, Max Beerbohm and George Belcher will be the most interesting people at the Reception. Belcher appeared as a dandy of the 1870 period! – Very long Frock coat, *very* tall dull hat, Cravat, Choker Collar, Side whiskers, and a pole of a walking stick.

Max B. dressed fairly ordinarily, but when he looked at me, I felt my nose tip-tilting in an alarming manner; my legs warped; my chin became a mere pimple on my neck.

Heinemann was there; and Edward Marsh, the Georgian Anthologist tho' I did not know him as such till afterwards. I was introduced as 'Mr Owen, Poet' or even 'Owen, the poet'.

You may feel keen enough to buy this week's *Nation*. I have at last a poem in it, which I sent off on the same evening as writing!!

Don't yet ask Matthews for Keats thanks very much, as Boots Ltd may lend it me. I subscribe for 3 months.

Always your W.E.O.

TO LESLIE GUNSTON

Picture postcard addressed Y.M.C.A. Hazely Down Camp, Near Winchester. The card bears the following verse, as amended by Wilfred:

A Little Health, A Little Wealth, A Little
  House, and Freedom – and at The End,
I'd like a Friend, and Every Cause to Need Him.

[*Postmark 12 February 1918*]   [*Postmark Scarborough*]
Quite as delighted to have your blunt criticism as your first postcard. I suppose I am doing in poetry what the advanced composers are doing in music. I am not satisfied with either. Still I am satisfied with the Two Guineas that half-hour's work brought me. Got the Cheque this m'ng!

Your W.E.O.

156

Tuesday [*postmark 12 March 1918*]   *Officers Command Depot*
32 Lines, Ripon

An awful Camp – huts – dirty blankets – in fact W A R once
more. Farewell Books, Sonnets, Letters, friends, fires, oys-
ters, antique-shops. Training again!

Your W.E.O.

Scroll arrived just in time to see Priestley open it. Thank
you!

TO SUSAN OWEN

Easter Sunday [*13 March 1918*]

The Ante-Room, O.C.D., Ripon

My Mother Dear,

I am writing crouched up in one of the good easy chairs
with which we have stocked our Common Room Hut. We
have also a good piano, which helps to drown the chinkling
of silver on the Bridge Tables. I scarcely have spoken to any
of this crowd of 'gentlemen' except to decline to make a
Four at bridge.

I find myself growing more conventional in the matter
of 'Proper Introductions' as I grow older. There are no less
than five people made aware of my presence in Ripon, by   10
friends who tell me I must go and see them

(1) Mrs A. – done.
(2) A Major, friend of Bainbrigge of Shrewsbury – not
done.
(3) A friend and relation of Priestley's – not done.
(4) A great friend of the Grays of Edinburgh – not done
yet.
(5) Two maiden ladies, benefactresses when he was in
Ripon of the Scottie in Clarence Gardens (who faints
and has undiscoverable parents). These old dears as I   20
had been advised provide a mighty good tea to anything in khaki that strays into their house. They have
also some inklings of breeding, and traces of Accent,

157

having been in the service of the Marchioness of Ripon
for 37 years. I shall go there again the next time there's
a bad lunch in Camp.

Outside my cottage-window children play soldiers so
piercingly that I've moved up into the attic, with only a
skylight. It is a jolly Retreat. There I have tea and contem-
plate the inwardness of war, and behave in an owlish manner   30
generally.

One poem have I written there; and thought another. I
have also realized many defectuosities in older compositions.

The enormity of the present Battle numbs me. Because I
perfectly foresaw these days, it was that I said it would have
been better to make peace in 1916. Or even last Autumn. It
certainly is 'impossible' now.

What did I say about America?

Why did I denounce them?

Fancy the old 13th C.C.S. being in German hands! Even   40
Nesle, a town hospital where I paused 3 days, is occupied.
On Good Friday I believe the most frightful fighting was
round about the Canal where I used to board the barges.

The Mystery Gun of St Gobain Wood is about as romantic an episode as the whole war has provided. Paris, after all,
has so many ugly buildings and unnecessary civilians . . .
160 casualties in a second or two, and that in the heart of the
enemy country, is pretty work.

I wonder how many a *Frau, Fräulein, Knabe und Mädchen*
Colin will kill in his time?   50

Johnny de la Touche leaves school this term, I hear, and
goes to prepare for the Indian Army.

He must be a creature of killable age by now.

God so hated the world that He gave several millions of
English-begotten sons, that whosoever believeth in them
should not perish, but have a comfortable life.

I could face the world-facts better if I could be sure of at least
your health and peacefulness at home. Don't let your fire
burn low; don't leave off winter-clothing; don't eat pickles;
and don't read newspapers. Thus you'll keep well.   60

158

I meant, when I said you must get a servant before I get leave, *that it will be a severe discomfort to me*, – not otherwise than as thus: –

That I will not eat from plates which you must needs wash. The moral discomfort, I say, will drive me to the Crown, aye the Britannia, aye the Oyster Bar, and finally the Cop Fried Fish Shop.

Now you know.

Your lovingest old Wilfred

TO OSBERT SITWELL

July 1918   [*Scarborough*]

Dear Osbert Sitwell,

I rehearsed your very fine epigram upon our Mess President – rather a friend of mine. He did not immediately recognize Jesus. The rest of the Mess would not of course know the name of Monsieur Clemenceau. (To my mind this would be no indication of any man's ignorance of affairs.) May I send 'Ill Winds' to a French youth who might translate and circulate it where it would be appreciated?

Always hoping to find an hour in which to copy out and generally denebulize a few poems acceptable to you either as   10
Editor or – may I not say – friend – I have delayed this letter so long. Tonight there is only time for a tedious brief speech with you before the mind wakes up for its only amusement these days – dreams.

For 14 hours yesterday I was at work – teaching Christ to lift his cross by numbers, and how to adjust his crown; and not to imagine he thirst till after the last halt; I attended his Supper to see that there were no complaints; and inspected his feet to see that they should be worthy of the nails. I see to it that he is dumb and stands to attention before his accusers.   20
With a piece of silver I buy him every day, and with maps I make him familiar with the topography of Golgotha.

Last week I broke out of camp to order *Wheels*, 1917. Canning refused to stock copies. I persisted so long that the Young Lady loudly declared she knew all along that I was 'Osbert himself'. This caused a consternation throughout

159

the crowded shop; but I got the last laugh by – 'No, Madam; the book is by a friend of mine, Miss Sitwell.'

Rigby's people would not order a single copy without deposit!   30

Is the 1918 vol. designed to go on the caterpillar wheels of Siegfried's Music Hall Tank? If so I might help with the ammunition. Would you like some short War Poems, or what? Please give me a final date for submitting them to you.

I very much look forward to meeting you again, and if it be in Scarborough the pleasure will be that of all snatched joys. I am incarcerated more strictly than you imagine. Westborough is now a weekly ambition. The Spa is beyond my hopes. This is the beginning of decadence. As is proved by   40 my Father's message on hearing I was G.S.: 'gratified to know you are normal again.' – Very sympathetically yours,
W.E.S. Owen

TO SUSAN OWEN

Saturday [10 August 1918]   *Scarborough*
Dearest Mother,

Tomorrow I am for a medical inspection with 21 others, to be declared fit for draft. This means we may be sent on draft leave tomorrow, & I may reach you even before this letter! I know not. I am glad. That is I am much gladder to be going out again than afraid. I shall be better able to cry my outcry, playing my part.

The secondary annoyances & discomforts of France behind the line can be no worse than this Battalion. On Friday we were called up at 3 a.m. and had the usual day's work.   10 The adjutant is ill, & Stiebel is ill. I did Stiebel's job on the Stunt, & am still doing it.

These are only mock alarms of course. But this morning at 8.20 we heard a boat torpedoed in the bay about a mile out, they say who saw it. I think only 10 lives were saved. I wish the Boche would have the pluck to come right in & make a clean sweep of the Pleasure Boats, and the promenaders on the Spa, and all the stinking Leeds & Bradford Warprofiteers now reading *John Bull* on Scarborough Sands.

Siegfried is being moved to Berwick on Tweed next week.   20
Am trying to find which day. Imagine what wretched uncertainty I'm in tonight. All I feel sure of is my excellent little servant Jones, who'll pack my stuffs in quarter of an hour, night or day.

Let me thank Mary for her Boat Letter. Hope we'll all have a River Afternoon in spite of my wished-for torpedoes-nearer-home.

I like poor Doris better now I hear she understands *The Old Huntsman* Book.

My mind is a cobweb of lines radiating to Shrewsbury,   30
London, Hastings, Berwick, London, Shrewsbury, Berwick, Edinburgh, Portsmouth ...

Ever, W.E.O.

TO SUSAN OWEN

Sat., 31 August 1918   E.F.C., Officers Rest House and Mess
[*Half page missing*] Arriving at Victoria I had to wheel my own baggage down the platform & through the streets to the Hotel, which was full, but I got a bed (as I [*half page missing*] My last hours in England were brightened by a bathe in the fair green Channel, in company of the best piece of Nation left in England – a Harrow boy, of superb intellect & refinement, intellect because he detests war more than Germans, and refinement because of the way he spoke of my going away; and the way he spoke of the Sun; and of the Sea, and the Air; and everything. In fact the way he spoke.   10

And now I go among cattle to be a cattle-driver ...

I am now fairly and reasonably tired & must go to my tent, without saying the things which you will better understand unsaid.

O my heart,
Be still; you have cried your cry, you have played your part.

Did I ever send you Siegfried's poem which he wrote on the boat:

For the last time I say War is not glorious;   20
Tho' lads march out superb & die victorious,

161

And crowned by peace, the sunlight on their graves;
    You say we crush the Beast; I say we fight
    Because men lost their landmarks in the night,
    And met in gloom to grapple, stab, & kill.
    Yelling the fetish names of Good & Ill
    Which have been shamed in history.
                O my heart,
Be still; you have cried your cry, you have played your
    part!   30

Goodnight, goodnight.
You are at home; yet you *are* home;
Your love is my home, and I cannot feel abroad.

                                Wilfred x

TO SIEGFRIED SASSOON

Sat., 31 August 1918   *E.F.C., Officers Rest House and Mess*
Goodbye –
    dear Siegfried –
I'm much nearer to you here than in Scarborough, and am
by so much happier.
    I have been incoherent ever since I tried to say goodbye on
the steps of Lancaster Gate. But everything is clear now; &
I'm in hasty retreat towards the Front. Battle is easier here;
and therefore you will stay and endure old men & women to
the End, and wage the bitterer war and more hopeless.
    When you write, please address to Mahim,   10
                        Monkmoor Rd.
                        Shrewsbury.
    What more is there to say that you will not better under-
stand unsaid.

                           Your W.E.O.

TO SIEGFRIED SASSOON

Sunday, 1 September 1918
                    A Depot, A.P.O. S.17, B.E.F. France
Dearest of all Friends,
    Here is an address which will serve for a few days.
    The sun is warm, the sky is clear, the waves are dancing

162

fast & bright ... But these are not Lines written in Dejection. Serenity Shelley never dreamed of crowns me. Will it last when I shall have gone into Caverns & Abysmals such as he never reserved for his worst daemons?

Yesterday I went down to Folkestone Beach and into the sea, thinking to go through those stanzas & emotions of Shelley's to the full. But I was too happy, or the Sun was too supreme. Moreover there issued from the sea distraction, in the shape, Shape I say, but lay no stress on that, of a Harrow boy, of superb intellect & refinement; intellect because he hates war more than Germans; refinement because of the way he spoke of my Going, and of the Sun, and of the Sea there; and the way he spoke of Everything. In fact, the way he spoke –

And now I am among the herds again, a Herdsman; and a Shepherd of sheep that do not know my voice.

Tell me how you are.

With great & painful firmness I have not said you goodbye from England. If you had said in the heart or brain you might have stabbed me, but you said only in the leg; so I was afraid.

Perhaps if I 'write' anything in dug-outs or talk in sleep a squad of riflemen will save you the trouble of buying a dagger.

Goodbye W.E.O.

TO SIEGFRIED SASSOON

22 September 1918   *D Coy., 2nd Manchester Regt.*
My dear Siegfried,

Here are a few poems to tempt you to a letter. I begin to think your correspondence must be intercepted somewhere. So I will state merely

I have had no letter from you $\begin{cases} \text{lately} \\ \text{for a long time,} \end{cases}$

and say nothing of my situation, tactical or personal.

You said it would be a good thing for my poetry if I went back.

That is my consolation for feeling a fool. This is what

163

[266]

shells scream at me every time: Haven't you got the wits to
keep out of this?

Did you see what the Minister of Labour said in the *Mail* the
other day? 'The first instincts of the men *after the cessation of*
hostilities will be to return home.' and again – 'All classes
acknowledge their indebtedness to the soldiers & sailors ...'

About the same day, Clemenceau is reported by the *Times*
as saying: '*All* are worthy ... yet we should be untrue to
ourselves if we forgot that the *greatest* glory will be to the   20
splendid poilus, who, etc.'

I began a Postscript to these Confessions, but hope you
will already have lashed yourself (lashed *yourself*!) into
something ...

O Siegfried, make them Stop!

W.E.O.

P.S. My Mother's address is *Mahim*
Monkmoor Rd. Shrewsbury
I know you would try to see her, if —— I failed to see her
again.   30

TO SUSAN OWEN

4 (or 5) October 1918   *In the Field*
Strictly private
My darling Mother,

As you must have known both by my silence and from
the newspapers which mention this Division – and perhaps
by other means & senses – I have been in action for some
days.

I can find no word to qualify my experiences except the
word SHEER. (Curiously enough I find the papers talk about
sheer fighting!) It passed the limits of my Abhorrence. I lost
all my earthly faculties, and fought like an angel.

If I started into detail of our engagment I should disturb   10
the censor and my own Rest.

You will guess what has happened when I say I am now

164

Commanding the Company, and in the line had a boy lance-corporal as my Sergeant-Major.

With this corporal who stuck to me and shadowed me like your prayers, I captured a German Machine Gun and scores of prisoners.

I'll tell you exactly how another time. I only shot one man with my revolver (at about 30 yards!); the rest I took with a smile. The same thing happened with other parties all along 20 the line we entered.

I have been recommended for the Military Cross; and have recommended every single N.C.O. who was with me!

My nerves are in perfect order.

I came out in order to help these boys – directly by leading them as well as an officer can; indirectly, by watching their sufferings that I may speak of them as well as a pleader can. I have done the first.

Of whose blood lies yet crimson on my shoulder where his head was – and where so lately yours was – I must not 30 now write.

It is all over for a long time. We are marching steadily *back*.

Moreover

The War is nearing an end.

Still,

Wilfred and more than Wilfred

TO SIEGFRIED SASSOON

10 October 1918   [*2nd Manchester Regt.*]
Very dear Siegfried,

Your letter reached me at the exact moment it was most needed – when we had come far enough out of the line to feel the misery of billets; and I had been seized with writer's cramp after making out my casualty reports. (I'm O.C. D Coy.)

The Batt. had a sheer time last week. I can find no better epithet: because I cannot say I suffered anything; having let my brain grow dull: That is to say my nerves are in perfect order. 10

It is a strange truth: that your *Counter-Attack* frightened me much more than the real one: though the boy by my side, shot through the head, lay on top of me, soaking my shoulder, for half an hour.

Catalogue? Photograph? Can you photograph the crimson-hot iron as it cools from the smelting? That is what Jones's blood looked like, and felt like. My senses are charred.

I shall feel again as soon as I dare, but now I must not. I don't take the cigarette out of my mouth when I write Deceased over their letters.

But one day I will write Deceased over many books.

I'm glad I've been recommended for M.C., & hope I get it, for the confidence it may give me at home. Full of confidence after having taken a few machine guns (with the help of one seraphic lance corporal), I held a most glorious brief peace talk in a pill box. You would have been '*en pamoisons*'.

I found one of your poems in another L. Cpl's possession! The Theosophist one it was: containing, let me tell you, the one line I resent.

> In bitter safety I awake *unfriended*.
> Please apologise – now.

Yes, there is something you can send me: 2 copies of *C. Attack*, one inscribed. One is for the Adjutant, – who begged a book of Erskine MacD.'s Soldier-Poets which I had with me – because I met one of these amalgamations at the Base. And liked him for his immediate subjugation to my principles and your mastery.

But he is now sending me V.A.D. love poems, so he will remain a private in my section of poets.

Was so interested about Prewett.

At the Base I met O'Riordan (of the Irish theatre, & collaborator with Conrad). A troll of a man; not unlike Robbie for unexpected shocks. It was easy, & as I reflect, inevitable to tell him everything about oneself.

I have nothing to tell you except that I'm rather glad my servant was happily wounded: & so away from me. He had lived in London, a Londoner.

While you are apparently given over to wrens, I have found

brave companionship in a poppy, behind whose stalk I took
cover from five machine-guns and several howitzers.   50

I desire no more *exposed flanks* of any sort for a long time.

Of many who promised to send me literary magazines no
one has succeeded, except the Ed. of *Today* who sent me (by
whose request?) Mais's article & the picture, which I have
at last managed to stick to the corrugated iron wall of my
Tamboo. For mercy's sake send me something to read which
may help to neutralize my present stock of literature. I send
you the choicest of specimens.

Ever your W.E.O.

TO LESLIE GUNSTON

25 October 1918   *2nd Manchester Regt. France*
Dear Leslie,

I rejoice with you over your success with the *Nation*. Certainly that Roundel meant more to me than all the *Nymph*
poems put together. Now you are recognized by Massingham, Sassoon will want to see your work: I'll tell him. He
wrote to me on the 16th a letter which I got yesterday, telling how he was with dear Robbie Ross on the evening before
our inestimable friend suddenly died. Siegfried mentions
that A. Bennett offered him a job under Beaverbrook, but
that S.S. wrote to Beaver's Pte. Sec. saying he had no quali-   10
fications for War Propaganda *except that he had been wounded
in the head*: that repartee deserves eternal fame.

You must not imagine when you hear we are 'resting' that
we lie in bed smoking. We work or are on duty *always*. And
last night my dreams were troubled by fairly close shelling. I
believe only civilians in the village were killed (Thank God).
In this house where I stay five healthy girls died of fright
when our guns shelled the place last fortnight. You & I have
always been open with each other: and therefore I must say
that I feel sorry that you are neither in the flesh with us nor   20
in the spirit against War . . . .

There are two French girls in my billet, daughters of the
Mayor, who (I suppose because of my French) single me
for their joyful gratitude for *La Déliverance*. Naturally I talk

167

to them a good deal; so much so that the jealousy of other
officers resulted in a Subalterns' Court Martial being held on
me! The dramatic irony was too killing, considering certain
other things, not possible to tell in a letter.

Until last night though I have been reading Swinburne, I
had begun to forget what a kiss was 30

I have found in all these villages *no evidence of German atro-
cities*. The girls were treated with perfect respect. All the
material ruin has been wrought by our guns. Do you still
shake your befoozled head over the *Daily Mail* & the *Times*?

Love W.E.O.

P.S. I should be glad of *any literary literature*.

TO SUSAN OWEN

Thurs., 31 October [1918], 6.15 p.m.   [2nd Manchester Regt.]
Dear Mother,

I will call the place from which I'm now writing 'The
Smoky Cellar of the Forester's House'. I write on the first
sheet of the writing pad which came in the parcel yesterday.
Luckily the parcel was small, as it reached me just before we
moved off to the line. Thus only the paraffin was unwelcome in my pack. My servant & I ate the chocolate in the
cold middle of last night, crouched under a draughty Tamboo, roofed with planks. I husband the Malted Milk for
tonight, & tomorrow night. The handkerchief & socks are 10
most opportune, as the ground is marshy, & I have a slight
cold!

So thick is the smoke in this cellar that I can hardly see by
a candle 12 ins. away, and so thick are the inmates that I can
hardly write for pokes, nudges & jolts. On my left the Coy.
Commander snores on a bench: other officers repose on wire
beds behind me. At my right hand, Kellett, a delightful servant of A Coy. in *The Old Days* radiates joy & contentment
from pink cheeks and baby eyes. He laughs with a signaller,
to whose left ear is glued the Receiver; but whose eyes roll- 20
ing with gaiety show that he is listening with his right ear to
a merry corporal, who appears at this distance away (some
three feet) nothing [but] a gleam of white teeth & a wheeze
of jokes.

Splashing my hand, an old soldier with a walrus moustache peels & drops potatoes into the pot. By him, Keyes, my cook, chops wood; another feeds the smoke with the damp wood.

It is a great life. I am more oblivious than alas! yourself, dear Mother, of the ghastly glimmering of the guns outside, 30 & the hollow crashing of the shells.

There is no danger down here, or if any, it will be well over before you read these lines.

I hope you are as warm as I am; as serene in your room as I am here; and that you think of me never in bed as resignedly as I think of you always in bed. Of this I am certain you could not be visited by a band of friends half so fine as surround me here.

Ever Wilfred x

Critical commentary

OWEN AND TRADITION

In 1919 – the same year in which Edith Sitwell published seven of Owen's poems about war in *Wheels: Fourth Cycle* – T. S. Eliot provided the terms of reference for the taming of Owen:

> what happens when a new work of art is created is something that happens simultaneously to all the works of art which preceded it. The existing monuments form an ideal order among themselves, which is modified by the introduction of the new (the really new) work of art among them. The existing order is complete before the new work arrives: for order to persist after the supervention of novelty, the *whole* existing order must be, if ever so slightly, altered.[1]

It's possible now to see how Eliot's influential essay was bad news for any exceptional poet. Owen's major poems, drawing upon his searing experiences of the Great War, comprise a sustained subversion of poetic tradition. In his use of old and new techniques of parody, his ironic inversion of Romantic forms and expression, and his innovatory half-rhyme, he mocks the whole tradition of poesy. And in his content – the anti-romance, the anti-civilization of war in all its detail – he exposes the 'order' from which war had emanated. How could the 'order' be adjusted to include its antithesis?

One ploy has been to scale Owen's poetry down: 'modernism' was in vogue, and where did Owen fit in there? F. R. Leavis suggested that Owen had no part in the 'new start' that the Eliot–Pound revolution in technique gave to British poetry.[2] Since Leavis is using Eliot's assumption about the reordering of tradition, Owen is automatically put aside, since he didn't so much reorder poetic tradition as invert its implicit values. This scaling down of Owen's work is nowhere more elegantly summarized than by A. Alvarez in *The Savage God* (1971): 'there is an anti-heroic force at work in Owen which corresponds to all those elements in his writing which went to make him one of the British fore-runners of modernism.'[3] So Owen made a dummy run rather than actually participating in the race to reorder tradition? 'Modernism', with its breaking up of time sequences, its irrational juxtaposition of discrete images, its stream-of-consciousness techniques, and so on, must have its anticipators, and Owen is conveniently a 'fall guy' here – although Robert Browning or Laurence Sterne would do equally as well.

Another ploy was to attempt to measure Owen against the main non-reorderers of tradition, especially W. B. Yeats. C. K. Stead took this line:

> The particularization of experience in the work of the new war poets was an immense improvement over the generalizing facility of their imperialist predecessors. But their poems still fall short of the yardstick we have taken – Yeats's 'Easter 1916'. The relationship between the poet and his experience of life is now an honest relationship: here is the poet, and here is his experience which he faces without pre-conception.[4]

We might wonder what Stead means by grading 'Easter 1916' as a more honest poem than Owen's most radical war poems such as 'The show', 'Strange meeting' or 'Disabled'. Yeats's poem on the brief and aborted Irish rebellion, which ended in sixteen executions, seems to spring from ideologies of the far right or far left about the necessity for violence. The 'macho' emotion behind it is not masculine, but is rather a perversion of masculinity. Yeats's chorus, 'A terrible beauty is born', generates a glamour which disguises the shabbiness and pettiness of the historical events – remnants of which persist in Ulster's violence today. 'Easter 1916' can be read therefore as a poeticized dream of revolution which was as untruthful in 1916 as it is now. Owen's war poems, by contrast, are nothing if not truthful about violence.

The relegation of Owen's poetry has to do also with the relegation of the category 'war poet', as if this archetypically violent and destructive war were marginal either in history itself or in Owen's vision of it in his poetry. When we consider, apart from anything else, that the Great War of 1914–18 resulted in over 7 million deaths of soldiers on all sides, and at least $11\frac{1}{2}$ million wounded, and that Owen projected a sustained vision of this violence and waste in his poetry, we might wonder why critics like F. R. Leavis see the so-called 'war poet' Owen as a marginal aberration who deals with a marginal aberration. It's as if such critics believe that the history of literature has little to do with the specificity of events. What literary critics such as Leavis and Stead have tried to do with Owen, despite their protestations to the contrary, is to dissociate poetry from experience, whereas poetry is of little significance if it is not a close response to experience, whether actual or an imagined distillation of it.

Critics who up to 1986 have written essays or books on Owen, such as D. S. R. Welland, Jon Stallworthy, Dominic Hibberd, as well as myself, have allowed ourselves *inter alia* to be set this somewhat futile task of assessing what Owen has done or not done to the late Victorian 'Romantic' or the twentieth-century 'modernist' phases of the tradition of writing poetry. This conventional treatment of Owen epitomizes the way in which voices are marginalized in the prevailing status quo that is determined mainly by men, however raffish or ineffectual these literary patriarchs may seem to be to the authoritarian patriarchs who control the economy and the state.

Since the 1970s, women critics and readers, particularly in France, America, and Britain, have begun to reread and rediscover a tradition of women's writing, which, apart from a few authors such as George Eliot, Jane Austen, and the Brontë sisters, has up till now been dismissed from the predominantly male 'canon' of authors in English studies. And it's not only works by women that have been absent or accepted belatedly; the work of any author who is outside the white male hegemony, whether because of race, class, or gender, has often been ignored by the dominant literary establishment. Such writing is either subversive or discomforting because it differs radically in content and/or style from the accepted modes of literary expression; for example, poets as varied as Charlotte Mew, John Clare, Ivor Gurney, and William Blake were in their day neglected by the literary establishment.

Some literary works are of such striking quality, however, that from the start they make an impact that cannot be overlooked. Then the literary establishment finds other ways to deradicalize them; for example, it is only recently that certain of Virginia Woolf's original essays about women's writing in relation to men's have been reprinted. And, as her editor, Michèle Barrett, points out,

> Critics of her novels have consistently emphasized their supposedly 'feminine' and 'domestic' character, and indeed one critic makes for us the link between the novels and the essays. 'I doubt,' writes G. S. Fraser in his study *The Modern Writer and His World* (Penguin, 1970), 'from her own writings, whether Mrs Woolf was any more capable of following an abstract philosophical argument than Clarissa Dalloway.' Such a remark is not so likely to be made of a male writer. Such judgements are perhaps more easily made of a woman who invades not only the arena of creativity (for which there are major precedents in the nineteenth-century novel), but also presumes to enter, as fewer women have done, the sphere of criticism, argument and theory.[5]

As Barrett indicates, male judgements about women writers may be biased partly from envy and partly from outmoded prejudices about the nature of the female intellect. But, more seriously, such judgements pre-empt any consideration of what Woolf as social and literary critic has to say; for example, her extensive critique in *Three Guineas* (1938) of male violence and misogyny has usually until recently been mocked or ignored.

In the case of Owen, critics have marginalized his work by pushing it into the cul-de-sac known as 'war poetry', and then deradicalized it by examining how to attach it to *the* literary tradition somewhere between 'modernism' and 'Georgian' Romanticism. The first question that must therefore be taken up today about Owen's poetry is: what has the literary establishment avoided recognizing in Owen's exposé – in both his prose and his poetry – of the patriarchal society that he lived in and that we have inherited?

'Patriarchalism' might be considered an inelegant term, but this word is suggestive of the inelegant ideology that underpinned the behaviour not only of governments and military high commands on both sides during the First World War, but also of large sections of the populace. By 'ideology', I mean a set of ideas and beliefs, assumptions and prejudices, to which groups or classes of people in any given society subscribe. Kate Millett describes 'patriarchy' thus:

> If one takes patriarchal government to be the institution whereby that half of the populace which is female is controlled by that half which is male, the principles of patriarchy appear to be twofold: male shall dominate female, and elder male shall dominate younger. However, just as within any human institution, there is frequently a distance between the real and the ideal; contradictions and exceptions do exist within the system.[6]

Millett might have listed as some of the exceptions and contradictions the behaviour of both men and women in wartime; for example, women in wartime become more free of patriarchal domination in that they are encouraged to take on what in peacetime is considered male employment. But in wartime many women also support the oppression of young men, just as in peacetime older women collaborate with their oppressors in order to bring young women into line with what they have accepted as their roles in society.

Critics of Owen who accept an ideology of patriarchy have drawn attention to what they see as his criticism of the 'distance between the ideal and the real' in the establishment of patriarchal command, as if patriarchy is the only morally possible ideal. Mark Sinfield, for example, comments that Owen in 'The parable of the old man and the young' is 'using a well-known Scriptural passage ironically to demonstrate the gap between his civilization's ideals and its practices'.[7] But actually Owen, in his 'Parable', rather than postulating an 'ideal' authoritarian figure in the myth of Abraham, is showing us how any authoritarian patriarch is likely to become corrupted by power as well as by pride.

In the Old Testament, Abraham actually prepared Isaac for human sacrifice, but the voice of the divine intervened in order to stop it, thus allegorizing for male theologians and preachers how willingness to kill one's own male offspring is morally good. In his sonnet, Owen is subversively parodying the language of the Bible:

When lo! an Angel called him out of heaven,
Saying, Lay not thy hand upon the lad,
Neither do anything to him, thy son.
Behold! Caught in a thicket by its horns
A Ram. Offer the Ram of Pride instead.
But the old man would not so, but slew his son,
And half the seed of Europe, one by one.

The narrator emphasizes Isaac's innocence in the face of Abraham's perverse behaviour. The patriarchy is caught up in its own pride, however, and divine guidance as voiced through 'an Angel' is ignored.

In wartime, when the traditional upper age limit for war service is 40, subservience from young men is particularly demanded. During the First World War the way in which young men – at first without being conscripted – willingly exposed themselves to death in innumerable battles on the front lines in France is astonishing. The so-called 'war aims' in this enormous conflict were paltry and destructive to the eye of common sense. Yet these young men at first saw it all through an ideological haze of nationalistic slogans about 'serving king and country' and of patriarchal assumptions about 'being a man'. At that time, only the occasional pictorial or literary artist, or committed pacifists such as C. K. Ogden and Mary Sargant Florence, seemed able to reveal to the public the folly of conforming to authoritarian modes of thought and behaviour.

176

Before Owen, Siegfried Sassoon, in poems such as 'The general' (April 1917), had already begun to use poetry to satirize such elements of the war as patriarchal incompetence:

'Good-morning, good-morning!' the General said
When we met him last week on our way to the line.
Now the soldiers he smiled at are most of 'em dead,
And we're cursing his staff for incompetent swine.
'He's a cheery old card,' grunted Harry to Jack
As they slogged up to Arras with rifle and pack.

★ ★ ★

But he did for them both by his plan of attack.

That this poem was thought to be subversive is shown by the fact that it was held back for a year because even the editors of the radical *Cambridge Magazine* feared an angry response to Sassoon's satire about the stupidity of military strategies which not only fail to achieve any objectives but also result in unnecessary deaths. Sassoon sets up the general as a type of patriarch who covers up stupidity with bluff conviviality.

On 22 August 1917 Owen sent Leslie Gunston 'The dead-beat' with the comment, 'I wrote something in Sassoon's style . . .'. Owen had just met Sassoon, and his use of lyric poetry to reveal ironically the causes and conduct of the war began after he had read Sassoon's satires of warfare in *The Old Huntsman and Other Poems* (1917) and later manuscripts. In the two versions of 'The dead-beat', the first of Owen's major war poems, we can see how Owen worked towards particularizing the limitations of the ideologies of his society and its war through specifying details about an individual incident – the death of a soldier through neglect because the doctor assumed he was malingering. In this satire, Owen exposes to ridicule certain well-known stereotypes: the loyal wife at home, the notion of the humane medical doctor, and, above all, the militaristic convention of soldierly courage. The doctor's contempt for the soldier who succumbs to natural feelings of fear is contrasted by the narrator with the doctor's non-combatant role, the stress of which he has to ameliorate with whisky.

In other poems, too, Owen explored the meaning of the two

opposites, courage and cowardice in warfare. So-called cowardice in young men was, of course, deplored by those in authoritarian positions in society, such as the doctor in 'The dead-beat', because, if too many men refused to fight, then no war could be conducted. In 'S.I.W.' the narrator asks the reader to consider the effects of authoritarian men dominating younger men: in this instance, a young soldier who has been demoralized by battle commits suicide. In the phrase, 'Courage leaked, as sand', a stock war image of protective trench sandbags is linked with the feelings of a demoralized soldier: just as the sandbags can't protect even in a limited way without sand, so the soldier is exposed to self-inflicted death by the slow seepage of his courage. In addition, sand carries an allusion to the passage of time – the hourglass – which suggests to the reader that the months spent in the trenches have undone the soldier.

Owen in his poetry not only responded to his experience on the battlefield. He was also alive to contemporary writing, particularly popular verse and journalism, and his poetry is often an ironic comment on the stereotypes about militarism and patriotism that such verse and journalism embodied. What makes for significant art about contemporary events is whether the author has the perception or vision – whatever you choose to call that imaginative force within a writer – to see through the assumptions that form part of current ideologies and then to expose them in original language. What is wrong with popular verse is not just that it's often aesthetically unsatisfying, but that its authors usually have no original perceptions; they merely echo current sentiments and ideas. Thus the plethora of war jingles in the press and books of verse usually reflected the official view that the Great War was necessary and its causes worth fighting and dying for.

Owen reacted ironically to verses like 'The call' by Jessie Pope,[8] who is representative of many jingoistic writers of that period:

> Who'll earn the Empire's thanks –
>   Will you, my laddie?
> Who'll swell the victor's ranks –
>   Will you, my laddie?
> When that procession comes,

Banners and rolling drums –
Who'll stand and bite his thumbs –
    Will you, my laddie?

Pope's highly popular verses were featured regularly in *Punch*,
the *Daily Mail*, and the *Daily Express*, and she collected together
four books of them.

A few less well-known writers, however, such as Helen
Hamilton, rejected jingoistic calls to patriotic sacrifice. Although
Helen Hamilton set out, in *Napoo! A Book of War Bêtes Noires*
(1918), to respond to stereotypes about war, her answers have
more of the tone and rhythm of rhetorical prose than of poetry.
In the following extract from 'The jingo-woman', she is attack-
ing a woman of Jessie Pope's type:

But still the day may come
For you to prove yourself
As sacrificial as upbraiding . . . .
And if and when that dark day dawns,
You'll join up first, of course,
Without waiting to be fetched.
But in the meantime,
Do hold your tongue!
You shame us women.
Can't you see it isn't decent,
To flout and goad men into doing,
    What is not asked of you?[9]

Although Hamilton is exposing the falsity of any woman writer
trying, along with the state and other institutionalized forms of
patriarchy, to coerce men into fighting in a dubious war in which
women themselves are not expected to fight, her sparse, gener-
alizing use of language suggests that she is not writing poetry so
much as anti-propaganda.

In contrast with Hamilton's 'The jingo-woman', Owen's
'Dulce et decorum est' (a draft of which he dedicated satirically
'To Jessie Pope') works by means of original perception and in-
direction: the soldier who is gassed is not described as such, but
the narrator sees him through the pane of his gas-mask as if he
were drowning. The reader is not told that the gassed soldier is

179

dying, but is shown 'the blood / Come gargling from the froth-corrupted lungs'. Thus the narrator builds up an ironic context for his refutation of the patriot's 'Lie': 'It is sweet and meet to die for one's country.' Owen, through his narrator, vividly exposes a patriarchal hegemony which depended upon men believing that to die in war for king and country made them heroes.

According to Owen in his unfinished 'Preface', 'the true poets must be truthful.' In his poetry he therefore broke away from poets whom he formerly admired, so that he could write about what he saw happening in war. Instead of such highly coloured stock images as 'sowings for new Spring, and blood for seed' in his sonnet '1914', Owen began in mid-1917 in 'The dead-beat' to invert Romantic images and use the colloquialisms of ordinary speech to reveal the truth about war. In his subsequent war poetry from 1917 until his death, Owen partly displaced, and partly inverted, the dominant tradition of poetic diction, particularly through his use of consonantal half-rhyme.

But it's not the use of half-rhyme itself which is subversive of poetic tradition, since Owen had used half-rhyme earlier in 'From my diary, July 1914' and 'Song of Songs' to little effect. In his war poems, it's the conjunction of his parodying of both the content *and* forms of 'Romantic' poetry which creates a uniquely challenging effect. In 'The show', the vowel sounds in the half-rhymes – 'Death/dearth', 'why/woe/wire' – echo the discordance of the violence on the battlefield, and the pictorial imagery also parodies the 'Romantic' mythological landscapes of poetic dramas like those of W. B. Yeats. Or, in another war poem, 'Exposure', which partly parodies the language of Keats's 'Ode to a nightingale', the poet also, through sophisticated half-rhymes such as 'knive us/nervous' and 'silent/salient', is slyly mocking Keats's full rhymes: 'pains/drains', 'drunk/sunk' and 'lot/plot'. Although Owen often reverts to full rhyme, in his war poetry he continually inverts the poetic diction of the 'Romantic' tradition from Keats to Brooke. In 'Apologia pro poemate meo', for example, the poet avers that 'love is not the binding of fair lips'; 'beauty' can be found in 'oaths', 'music' in silence, and 'peace' in 'shell-storms'. His anti-lyricism, which is based on parodic diction and half-rhyme, relentlessly links the 'high' culture of a privileged class in a patriarchal society with the violence of a war in which 'death becomes absurd, and life absurder'.

Which genre or form can best evoke modern technological warfare? Whatever form each writer chooses, one might suppose. But John H. Johnston contends that poets who wrote about the First World War, including Owen, were hooked on the lyric, which Johnston thinks was not suitable for delineating mechanized warfare on a large scale:

> In Owen's poetry we have the physical background of war, the sense of hazard and duress, the pathos of suffering, and even a perception of tragic extremity. But these, at best, are but fragmentary aspects of the whole. They appear not as products of a unified and comprehensive poetic vision but as effects of a lyric sensibility vainly attempting to find order and significance on a level of experience where these values could not exist – where, in fact, they had been destroyed.[10]

As if destruction of man and terrain could obliterate a form of poetry.

In relation to increased mechanization, Owen's poems expose man's inability to handle modern technology by showing how, instead of using science in order to work with nature, man has both intensified an attack on his fellow man and corrupted the natural world. In 'Exposure', the power of the natural world and the sinister effects of technologically advanced weaponry become interchangeable: 'Dawn massing in the east her melancholy army' is a personification which alludes both to the opposing force and to the clouds which will bring freezing temperatures and snow; the 'iced east winds ... knive' as if the winds were the enemy; and the machine-gun bullets are 'Less deathly than the air that shudders black with snow'. The ambiguity of the title refers not only to the wartime exposure of men to the malevolent frost and bullets but also to Owen's exposure, through poetry, of the futility of the military action in which they were engaged: 'All their eyes are ice, / But nothing happens.' The narrator reveals how the corruption of the natural world in order to kill men through exposure in freezing temperatures on a battlefield is on a par with men trying to kill each other with machine-guns. Man has abrogated his concern for his fellow man, as well as for the natural world that has been turned against him.

In 'Spring offensive', modern technology is shown to have created a 'whole sky' burning with 'fury', so that such advanced application of scientific knowledge is destroying not only nature but also man's conception of himself as in control, to some extent, of the ability to keep himself alive. Widespread destruction from the 'sky', so to speak, has proliferated throughout this century, but not always through warfare, since the most recent example is the explosion that occurred at Chernobyl in 1986, raining radioactive particles on much of the rest of Europe. The enemy's warning prophecy in 'Strange meeting' – 'None will break ranks, though nations trek from progress' – seems all too true.

The narrator in 'The show' presents us with nature war-deformed, without beauty or possibility of fertility. From above the scene of battle, the technologically shattered earth resembles the cratered surface of the moon, or a human face which is 'pitted with great pocks and scabs of plagues'. Owen had earlier used similar imagery in a letter in order to describe No Man's Land: 'It is pock-marked like a body of foulest disease and its odour is the breath of cancer . . . . No Man's Land under snow is like the face of the moon chaotic, crater-ridden, uninhabitable, awful, the abode of madness' (letter to Susan Owen, 19 January 1917). In his poem, platoons of soldiers are metamorphosed into 'caterpillars' which are creatures of darkness:

> From gloom's last dregs these long-strung creatures crept,
> And vanished out of dawn down hidden holes.

Technological warfare has distorted the contours of the earth into an unrecognizable form, and groups of men have been metaphorically transformed into larvae.

By means of his epigraph to this poem, in which he effectively misquotes Yeats, so that Yeats's 'burnished' mirror becomes 'tarnished', Owen mocks false dreams of beauty in art, which are contrasted ironically with war-torn reality. Owen thus calls into question those ideologies which have assumed nature to be an ever-renewable subject for Romantic art as well as an everlastingly renewable resource for man.

PATRIARCHY AND CHRISTIANITY

Although Owen had already criticized those evangelical practices that he had disliked at Dunsden Parish Church in 1912–13, his poems and letters about his war experiences scathingly criticized the church itself – another patriarchal institution which attempted to ensure that the ordinary citizen behaved in a way that upheld the state. He censured those clergymen who hypocritically supported the war: 'Passivity at any price! Suffer dishonour and disgrace; but never resort to arms. Be bullied, be outraged, be killed; but do not kill . . . . I think pulpit professionals are ignoring it very skilfully and successfully indeed . . . . And am I not myself a conscientious objector with a very seared conscience?' (letter to Susan Owen, [?26] May 1917). Such criticism of clergymen led Owen, the former would-be clergyman, to look at a split between his writings and his actions: the difficulty of reconciling his poetry with his participation in war. By 1918 he concluded that his role in warfare was partly that of observer and recorder: 'I came out in order to help these boys – directly by leading them as well as an officer can; indirectly, by watching their sufferings that I may speak of them as well as a pleader can' (letter to Susan Owen, 4 (or 5) October 1918). Yet, in earlier paragraphs in that same letter, he described how he 'only shot one man' with his 'revolver (at about 30 yards!)' and that, after capturing 'a German Machine Gun and scores of prisoners', he had been 'recommended for the Military Cross'. This pride in having kept his 'nerve' apparently contradicts his early 1917 letters in which he questions the morality of killing in warfare. Judith Kazantis's criticism that Owen and Sassoon 'both stayed submissive to the high-minded macho ethic of the English officer' might, if we judge Owen by his late 1918 letters, seem in part to be true.[11] But she overlooks the paradox – of which Owen was fully aware – that subversive poetry about war had emerged from his participation in that war, and might do so again.

Thus, in 'Exposure', the narrator draws upon the experience

that he has shared with his fellow soldiers, in order to question the nature of that 'love of God' which is supposed to inspire their civilization and justify the war:

> Since we believe not otherwise can kind fires burn;
> Nor ever suns smile true on child, or field, or fruit.
> For God's invincible spring our love is made afraid;
> Therefore, not loath, we lie out here; therefore were born,
>   For love of God seems dying.

At first these soldiers seemingly accept the conventional attitude that, in fighting and conquering the enemy, innocence and goodness will be restored. But is the supposed love of God and man sufficient to bring about rebirth in the natural or spiritual world? The ironic ambiguity of 'For love of God seems dying' encourages an open reading: are the soldiers exposing themselves to death as Christian martyrs for the love of a patriarchal God, or is God's supposed love for them dying? Or are the whole Christian creed and God's love for creation dying? The narrator thus evokes a conflict in the soldiers' minds about the nature of their role and the place of Christian belief, if any, in society.

The more impersonal voice of the third-person narrator in 'Spring offensive' uses symbolism which can be given a Christian or secular reading: 'earth set sudden cups / In thousands for their blood' might metaphorically represent sacrificial chalices of the Christian mass, or might merely describe the slaughter of soldiers who filled the cupped flowers with their blood. A subsequent reference to a Christian allegorical representation of the meaning of death supports a secular reading: 'Some say God caught them even before they fell.' The tone of 'Some say' suggests that the narrator does not expect the reader to believe this comforting myth. Those who survived the hell of those 'superhuman inhumanities' are so stunned by battle that, through the narrator, they are shown as incapable of any platitude. Their silence implies that mythologies about a providential Christian God are pointless for men who are dying in such a hell.

Yet, in 'Greater love', the soldiers 'trail' the 'cross' (the rifle) through a storm of explosions, while God the Father 'seems not to care'. Equally ironically, the soldier-narrator of 'Apologia pro poemate meo' has a vision of God which is distinguished by its divergence from Christian stereotypes: 'I, too, saw God through mud'. The positive aspect of the divine in these poems is reflected in the image of the suffering Christ, in contrast with Jehovah, demander of horrendous sacrifices.

In relation to this distinction between Son and Father, Owen wrote four satires on the church and its clergy. 'Soldier's dream' epitomizes conflict in the Christian religion between two opposites – a kind and loving Jesus who stops the war, and a patriarchal God the Father who sets it going again. In 'At a calvary near the Ancre' the narrator sets up a parallel contrast between the soldier-Christs who 'love the greater love' and the patriarchs who 'hate', that is, who keep the war going. And in 'Inspection' an authoritarian and vengeful God ironically takes on a military rank: 'when we're duly white-washed, being dead, / The race will bear Field Marshal God's inspection.' In a similar vein, the parody of a gun-blessing bishop's prayer in 'Sonnet: On seeing a piece of our heavy artillery brought into action' effectively satirizes the church's hypocrisy and cant. This theme is developed in 'At a calvary near the Ancre', which can be read as an allegory. 'Golgotha', the place where Christ was crucified, represents the place of battle where soldiers are making what used to be known as the 'supreme sacrifice', and the priests are the war chaplains and war-supporting clergy who are now the Antichrist: their flesh-wounds are made by the 'Beast' of war who denies Christ as saviour of mankind. Through the imagined voices of ordinary soldiers, the poet satirizes the professional exponents – invariably male – of the various Christian denominations for their denial of Christ's message of love as well as for their support of a bloodthirsty militarism.

GENDER STEREOTYPES AND WAR

The 1914–18 war temporarily forced men and women to break away from a few stereotypes that were then current about their roles and behaviour, but the war machine ruthlessly enforced many other gender stereotypes. Women during the war had to do what had been considered men's work; yet, at the same time, inured as they were to domestic and public obedience, they on the whole retrogressively fostered the war by actively encouraging young men to enlist. The movement for women's suffrage split into two factions over support or non-support of the Great War, and the pacifist group, despite some well-organized international meetings against war, achieved little.

From early in 1917, Owen in his letters, especially to his mother, did not appear to go along with the conventional assumption that women should be shielded from the 'horrors' of warfare. In his early poems, however, he had attitudinized about women in various ways; for example, in the sonnet 'Whereas most women live this difficult life', the narrator questions the relative importance of the mother and the decorative narcissist. Women might be dedicated mothers or creators of beauty, even artists – those 'who embellish every act with grace' – but not both. In 'Lines written on my nineteenth birthday' the celebration of the maternal, which is a dominant aspect of many of his letters, forms part of its opening; and in 'Happiness' the maternal is central to perceived childhood joys.

In one later fragment, which was probably written after he experienced warfare, Owen again adopted this flat typology of women, this time satirizing women's preoccupation with their appearance:

Men seldom speak of beauty, beauty as such
Not even lovers think about it much.
Women of course consider it for hours
In mirrors . . .

Such a stock jocularity might hold some truth, but Owen in his innovatory parodic mode might have made a more telling point by presenting the reader with men at the mirror.

In Owen's completed war poems, however, he progressively discarded such stereotypes about the 'types' of the feminine; for example, early drafts of 'Greater love' were addressed 'To any Woman', then to 'Beauty', 'To Physical Beauty', 'To any beautiful Woman', and 'To anyone beautiful'. By eliminating all the restrictive references to women and beauty from his title, Owen extended the meaning of his poem in order to mock all the kinds of love that society falsely held up as ideal: romantic love, Christian love, and patriotic love. Any kind of love in a patriarchal society, except perhaps maternal love, is bound to be tarnished, since love itself is built on a false premiss: that man is naturally superior to woman, and that older men have the right to demand the patriotic sacrifice of even the lives of younger men. Perhaps the main import of the poem 'Greater love' is in its demonstration that love in any genuine form, such as platonic comradeship – as against ideological forms – occurs only to the extent that all human beings are equal, even if this equality is based on a common possible fate, that is, death in war. Owen's ironic inversion of stereotyped metaphors about romanticized sexual love should especially attract women readers: his insights into the hollowness of received ideas about the nature of sexual love have become part of our late twentieth-century recognition that 'romance' is a construct which, in its fostering of the false importance of the notions of physical beauty and sexual appeal, has proved self-defeating particularly for women.

Part of the mythology constructed about women is concerned with protecting women from reality, a mythology which Owen satirizes; for example, the schoolteacher in 'Having, with bold Horatius, stamped her feet' can embrace heroism in the rhetorical guise of Macaulay's poetry, but has learned to reject sexual pleasantries from living soldiers. And in 'The letter' the soldier-correspondent pretends to his wife that all is well at the front – until he is suddenly and mortally wounded. Ironically, even at the point of death, any complaint would be considered unmanly.

Thus it is not only in relation to women that ideologies about gender have been constructed: if women at the beginning of this century even more so than now were expected to make themselves look beautiful, and were supposed to enjoy protection from harsh truths if not from harsh experience, men were enjoined to cultivate in themselves an image of exaggerated manliness. Manliness then and now is associated with physical courage and aggression. Willingness and ability to fight, whether or not in defence, and prowess at physical sports including hunting and killing, are mostly still considered to be some of the qualities desired of men.

In several poems, such as 'The dead-beat', Owen has explored some of the more perverse aspects of the cult of manliness. Through the voice of the mutilated officer-narrator in 'A terre' –

187

which the epigraph indicates is 'the philosophy of many soldiers' – he implicitly challenges received ideas about masculinity:

> Shooting, war, hunting, all the arts of hurting.
> Well, that's what I learnt, – that, and making money.

The wounded man continues:

> I'd love to be a sweep now, black as Town,
> Yes, or a muckman. Must I be his load?

The buccaneering male – 'A short life and a merry one, my buck!' – has been changed by war into one who craves any kind of life. The narrator's final resignation towards his imminent death is coupled with his awareness that he will not be remembered long, even by the poet to whom he is talking. 'Disabled' is another poem in which the notion that 'manliness' can only be seen in the well-muscled and sporty is treated ironically. The Scot's war wounds have left him with a paralysed back and amputated limbs. Men who had cheered his goals and women who had admired his physique ignore him. This formerly virile young man who would once have 'bedded' women is now pathetically dependent on women to put him to bed: 'How cold and late it is! Why don't they come / And put him to bed? Why don't they come?'

But it is not only an extreme of masculinity that has been taken up and stereotyped by society. Although homosexuality has been consistently suppressed until relatively recently, bohemian homosexual artists such as Swinburne and Wilde were given some licence to treat sexually *outré* behaviour, such as sado-masochism, as a theme for poetry. Recent criticism of Owen, especially since Paul Fussell brought to our attention the note of homoeroticism in Owen's poetry,[12] has tended to pigeon-hole Owen in this category. But, although Owen read both Swinburne and Wilde, met and read the work of Charles Scott Moncrieff and Philip Bainbrigge, as well as making literary friendships with Siegfried Sassoon and Robert Ross, this does not necessarily mean that he was part of or wrote from the same homosexual subculture.

Yet a few critics have steadily encouraged us to read some of Owen's poetry as a reflection of homoerotic love. Moreover, since many of the critical responses to Owen's work recently have been based on relating Owen's life to his work, correlations between assumptions about Owen's sexual orientation and his poems have been sought. Thus, for example, Jon Stallworthy assumes in relation to the sonnet 'To —' which is dated 'May 10, 1916. London': 'This is almost certainly a recollection of a day with the de la Touche boys'.[13] Yet, if we must read it biographically, this sonnet is much more likely to have been addressed by Owen to his two brothers, with himself as the third in the poem. My amended biographical inference here might be interesting, but it hardly explains this poem about boyhood, nor does it indicate anything about Owen's sexual preferences.

Dominic Hibberd goes so far as to assert that Owen's developing consciousness of his own sexuality emerges in his 1918 poem about Eros:

'Who is the god of Canongate' seems to be about the secret world of 'rent boys', well known to Wilde, Ross and Scott Moncrieff, its subject being a 'little god' who walks the pavements barefoot (a street boy or Eros) and is visited in his room by barefoot men (pilgrims to the shrine who need to be secret) .... The god of love, who had been hopelessly out of reach in 'To Eros' ... is no longer for Owen an inaccessible deity.[14]

Again, the biographical critic has gone over the top. In fact, through his two imaginary speakers in 'Who is the god of Canongate?', the narrator and the 'god', Owen is exploring stereotypes about love and lust in relation to both male *and* female prostitution. This poem is not a personal statement about Owen's feelings in regard to his sexual orientation, but rather it is an objective presentation of a way of looking at heterosexual and homosexual eroticism as a commodity which can be bought and sold, with the implications of this for both buyer and seller. To read this poem as a representation of the actual author's emergent sexuality and not as an imagined narrator's account of sexual behaviour is to reduce poetry to crude mimesis. Which is not to say, of course, that Owen was heterosexual or homosexual or indeed bisexual. We cannot read facts about an author's life in his poetry, although sometimes biographical facts might illumine an aspect of an author's work; for example, details about Owen's war service are necessary for putting his war poems in context. In any case, facts about Owen's sexual relationships, even whether he had any sexual coition before his death, are practically non-existent. Any inferences about Owen's sexual behaviour are based on rumours such as Hibberd's account of Charles Scott Moncrieff, or on guesses about what Owen withheld from his mother and sister in his letters to them about, for instance, his flirtation with Madame Léger.

A reconstruction of Owen's personality remains a construct, even if based only on documented facts. And recent critiques of methods of analysing texts have shown us that using the texts to reconstruct the author as an entity is irrelevant or even misleading:

> An author may embody in a work ideas, beliefs, emotions, other than or even quite opposed to those he has in real life; he may also embody different ideas, beliefs, and emotions in different works . . . . Distinct from the real author, the implied author differs from the narrator.[15]

Thus the implied author of 'A terre', for example, is not Owen but an idealized author, and the narrator is neither the real author nor the implied author. Neither Owen nor the implied author shares the narrator's point of view as a soldier dying from wounds, nor do they share the narrator's revised 'macho' outlook. And the narrator of 'Disabled', who explores the double standards of social attitudes to sexuality *vis-à-vis* disablement, is not Owen himself but a postulated detached observer.

But, as my implied reader (if he or she exists) might say, Owen must be assumed to have written his own letters in his own voice. But which persona did he assume for each letter? Son, brother, cousin, friend? Adolescent poseur? Young man about town? Embryo poet? Accomplished poet? And so on. In reading letters, we must also take into account contemporaneous conventions of letter-writing as well as an awareness of the intended recipient of the letter. Both factors will explain much of what is said and left unsaid by the letter-writer. Thus, in Owen's case, what might seem excessive use of epithets such as 'darling mother' to Susan Owen was more acceptable at the beginning of this century than it is now. Moreover, Owen was not likely to confide to his mother any accounts of his sexual relationships, although he referred obliquely to this subject a number of times. Owen's letters to Mary Owen are slightly more open about his friendships with young women than are his letters to his mother. The existence of only a few letters to his father might suggest that his mother dominated the parent–child relationships within the family, at least in the case of Wilfred; it certainly indicates that his mother's interest in the arts appealed to Wilfred Owen more as an apposite quality in a recipient of letters which were always partly intended for posterity. Owen, especially in his letters about his war experiences, implied that half-consciously he anticipated a wider readership than his mother and her friends and relations. In fact, he informed his sister that some of his war letters were as objectively 'truthful' about war as some of Sassoon's poems were.

Yet what is 'truth'? Even historical reconstructions of the society in which an author lived and wrote are prone to ideological biases and misinterpretations of facts. Perhaps only a certain kind of art can penetrate and subvert ideological biases and reveal 'truths'. David Craig and Michael Egan describe how 'remarkable literature' arises in a given period and reflects the spirit of that period:

> we are not saying only that history – by which we mean reality in process of evolving – gives writers their subject matter, which they then interpret according to their temperaments, upbringing, class etc. They interpret it also according to their culture or – in specific literary terms – by means of the forms which they invent or adapt, innovating upon what comes to them via the media in use in their society.[16]

But, in my view, rather than merely interpreting 'reality', 'remarkable literature' also stimulates the reader to question the status quo and its accepted stereotypes of behaviour, which serve to hedge in or coerce sections of society; for example, few readers of William Blake's *Songs of Experience* (1794) can resist responding to Blake's challenge to institutionalized Christianity and the state to care for its children properly. Similarly, readers of Owen's war poetry, if they throw off the restrictive practices of traditional 'lit. crit.', cannot but appreciate his radical exposure of a dehumanizing patriarchy in church and state as well as in private lives.

Owen's poetry will be read in the next century as an exposé of the 'false creeds' of patriarchal rule in which, among other things, young men were at first pressured and then conscripted into an army whose generals ordered many of them to a useless death or physical and spiritual mutilation. Ironically, Owen's poetry also celebrates the 'love' of life which those soldiers experienced; the 'greater love' in Owen's terms, however, was ironically their society's love of death, which consumed their valiant comradeship. Certainly, Owen's poetry of 1917–18 about war comprises an anti-romance, if we take into account his ironic inversion of images of 'romance', whether of secular or Christian origin. Moreover, his poetry warns us of the ill-effects of the misuse of scientific technology on man and the natural world. But Owen's exposure through his prose and poetry of received ideologies about how men and women should live has up to now been deradicalized by literary critics in their attempts to place Owen in a tradition which is merely a construct invented to provide some sort of artificial order in literary studies. Safe, but barren.

NOTES TO THE CRITICAL COMMENTARY

1 T. S. Eliot, 'Tradition and the individual talent' (1919); repr. in *Selected Prose*, ed. John Hayward, Harmondsworth, Penguin, 1953, p. 23.
2 F. R. Leavis, *New Bearings in English Poetry*, London, Chatto & Windus, 1932; repr. with 'Retrospect' 1950; Harmondsworth, Penguin, 1972, pp. 57–8.
3 A. Alvarez, *The Savage God: A Study of Suicide*, London, Weidenfeld & Nicolson, 1971, p. 201.
4 C. K. Stead, *The New Poetic: Yeats to Eliot*, London, Hutchinson, 1964, pp. 92–3.
5 Virginia Woolf, *Women and Writing*, with introduction by Michèle Barrett, London, The Women's Press, 1979, p. 2.
6 Kate Millett, *Sexual Politics*, London, Rupert Hart-Davis, 1971; repr. London, Virago, 1977, p. 25.

7 Mark Sinfield, 'Wilfred Owen's "Mental cases": source and structure', *Notes & Queries*, 29 (August 1982), p. 339.

8 Jessie Pope, *War Poems*, London, Grant Richards, 1915; repr. in Catherine Reilly (ed.), *Scars upon my Heart: Women's Poetry and Verses of the First World War*, London, Virago, 1981, p. 88.

9 Helen Hamilton, 'The jingo-woman', in Reilly (ed.), op. cit., pp. 47–9.

10 John H. Johnston, *English Poetry of the First World War: A Study in the Evolution of Lyric and Narrative Form*, Princeton, NJ, Princeton University Press, 1964, p. 207.

11 Judith Kazantis, Preface to Reilly (ed.), op. cit., p. xviii.

12 Paul Fussell, *The Great War and Modern Memory*, London, OUP, 1976, pp. 286–9.

13 Jon Stallworthy, *Wilfred Owen: A Biography*, London, OUP and Chatto & Windus, 1974, pp. 138–9.

14 Dominic Hibberd, *Owen the Poet*, London, Macmillan, 1986, p. 156.

15 Shlomith Rimmon-Kenan, *Narrative Fiction: Contemporary Poetics*, London, Methuen, 1983, p. 87.

16 David Craig and Michael Egan, 'Historicist criticism', in Peter Widdowson (ed.), *Re-Reading English*, London, Methuen, 1982, p. 217.

Reading list

Bäckman, Sven, *Tradition Transformed: Studies in the Poetry of Wilfred Owen*, Lund Studies in English 54, Lund, C. W. K. Gleerup, 1979.

Beauvoir, Simone de, *The Second Sex* (1949), trans. H. M. Parshley, London, Jonathan Cape, 1953; Harmondsworth, Penguin, 1972; repr. 1986.

Blunden, Edmund, *War Poets 1914–18*, Writers and their Work 100, London, Longman, 1958; rev. 1959.

Breen, Jennifer, 'Wilfred Owen: "Greater love" and late Romanticism', *English Literature in Transition*, 17, 3 (1974), pp. 173–83.

—— 'The dating and sources of Wilfred Owen's "Miners"', *Notes & Queries*, 21 (October 1974), pp. 366–70.

—— 'Wilfred Owen's recovery from "shell-shock"', *Notes & Queries*, 23 (July 1976), pp. 301–5.

Craig, David, and Egan, Michael, 'Historicist criticism', in Peter Widdowson (ed.), *Re-Reading English*, London, Methuen, 1982.

Culler, Jonathan, *On Deconstruction: Theory and Criticism after Structuralism*, London, Routledge & Kegan Paul, 1983.

Eliot, T. S., *Selected Prose*, ed. John Hayward, Harmondsworth, Penguin, 1953.

Fussell, Paul, *The Great War and Modern Memory*, London, OUP, 1976.

Glover, Jon, 'Whose Owen?', *Stand*, 22, 3 (1981), pp. 29–31.

Graham, Desmond, *The Truth of War: Owen, Blunden and Rosenberg*, Manchester, Carcanet, 1984.

Hibberd, Dominic, *Wilfred Owen*, Writers and their Work 246, London, British Council & Longman, 1975.

—— 'Wilfred Owen and the Georgians', *Review of English Studies*, 30 (February 1979), pp. 28–40.

—— 'Silkin on Owen: some other war', *Stand*, 21, 3 (1980), pp. 29–32.

—— (ed.), *Poetry of the First World War: A Casebook*, London, Macmillan, 1981.

—— 'Wilfred Owen's letters: some additions, amendments and notes', *Library*, 4 (September 1982), pp. 273–87.

—— *Owen the Poet*, London, Macmillan, 1986.

Kamester, Margaret, and Vellacott, Jo, *Militarism versus Feminism: Writings on Women and War*, London, Virago, 1987.

Leavis, F. R., *New Bearings in English Poetry*, London, Chatto & Windus, 1932; repr. with 'Retrospect' 1950; Harmondsworth, Penguin, 1972.

Macherey, Pierre, *A Theory of Literary Production* (1966), trans. Geoffrey Wall, London, Routledge & Kegan Paul, 1978.

Millett, Kate, *Sexual Politics*, London, Rupert Hart-Davis, 1971; repr. London, Virago, 1977.

Owen, Harold, *Journey from Obscurity: Wilfred Owen 1893–1918*, 3 vols, London, OUP, 1963–5.

Reilly, Catherine (ed.), *Scars upon my Heart: Women's Poetry and Verses of the First World War*, London, Virago, 1981.

Riffaterre, Michael, *Semiotics of Poetry*, Indiana University Press, 1978.

Rimmon-Kenan, Shlomith, *Narrative Fiction: Contemporary Poetics*, London, Methuen, 1983.

Sassoon, Siegfried, *Siegfried's Journey 1916–20*, London, Faber, 1945.

Silkin, Jon, 'Owen, elegist, satirist, or neither; a reply to Dominic Hibberd', *Stand*, 21, 3 (1980), pp. 33–6.

Sinfield, Mark, 'Wilfred Owen's "Mental cases": source and structure', *Notes & Queries*, 29 (August 1982), pp. 339–41.

Sitwell, Osbert, *Noble Essences or Courteous Revelations: An Autobiography*, vol. 5, London, Macmillan, 1950.

Stallworthy, Jon, *Wilfred Owen: A Biography*, London, OUP and Chatto & Windus, 1974.

Stead, C. K., *The New Poetic: Yeats to Eliot*, London, Hutchinson, 1964.

Todorov, Tzvetan, *Introduction to Poetics*, Brighton, Harvester, 1981.

Tompkins, Jane P., 'The reader in history: the changing shape of literary response', in J. P. Tompkins (ed.), *Reader-Response Criticism: From Formalism to Post-Structuralism*, Baltimore, Md, Johns Hopkins University Press, 1980, pp. 201–32.

Welland, Dennis S. R., *Wilfred Owen: A Critical Study*, London, Chatto & Windus, 1960; repr. with 'Postscript' 1978.

Notes

8   Keats's tombstone in Rome: *Here lies one whose name was writ in water.*

12–14   WO commented in a holiday letter from Torquay: 'I went to Teignmouth on Friday. Perhaps it was a good thing that the soft buffeting sheets and misty drifts of Devonshire rain renewed themselves almost the whole day, since Keats's letters from here are full of objurgations against the climate' (WO to SO, 25 April 1911, *CL*, p. 69).

Date   WO began this sonnet at Torquay and finished it at his home in Shrewsbury soon afterwards.

IMPRESSIONIST

WO humorously parodies Harold Monro's 'Impressions' (*Before Dawn*, 1911) by creating a philistine character who makes 'impressions' on others. This poem, which mocks the folly of a materialistic outlook on life, is an early example of WO's skill at satire.

Date   The date of this poem is surmised from the fact that it is drafted on paper which is similar to that used for other poems written between November 1911 and May 1912.

199

This poem is based on Hans Christian Andersen's fairy-tale, *Little Claus and Big Claus*. WO's use of blank verse shows a similarity of form to Keats's narratives such as *Endymion* (1818). Despite his archaisms, this early work indicates WO's control over an extended narrative in blank verse, and exemplifies his subversive sense of grim humour.

4   *wight* person.
43   *reck* pay heed to.
103   *mage ... Evil One* can your magician summon the devil?
143   *lurdane* worthless.
163   *bushel* an 8-gallon measure for corn, etc.
167   *ebon* ebony, i.e. black.
252   *corse* corpse.
303   *ween* think, suppose.
315   *kine* cows.
Date   This poem was begun in about March 1912, since a number of drafts are written on paper which is similar to that used for other poems of that period. WO commented in a letter to SO: 'I have finished a story from Andersen in Blank Verse' (15 May 1912, *CL*, p. 136).

LINES WRITTEN ON MY NINETEENTH BIRTHDAY: MARCH 18, 1912

WO wrote from Dunsden Vicarage to SO: 'on my birthday morning I was awakened by the unrelenting gnawings [pains] within, and took a bit of toast for breakfast. The couch from the passage was then brought down for me, and thereon I lay all day .... To ease me, I employed my time upon the "lines", which you have, with the ink, as it were, still wet upon them' (19 March 1912, *CL*, p. 125).

24   *clay* an image that WO used elsewhere for the human body – for example, in 'Futility'.
51–8   Ordinary recovery from physical pain is sweeter than any other bliss.

WO is not necessarily alluding to Keats's unfinished 'Eve of St Mark', since the themes of these two poems are different; he might be indicating that he composed this poem on that saint's eve (24 April). WO here tries out an 'impressionist' treatment of the 1890s motif of a maiden's 'ripening' beauty.

THE UNRETURNING

The 'unreturning' are the dead.

11   WO's use of a similar metaphor about men dying in the early hours of the morning occurs in a letter to MO in January 1912 and in the poem 'Insensibility'.

13   *Wing*   death.

Date   The MS of the 1917 or 1918 fair copy which EB used has disappeared. But in 1920 SS transcribed a fair copy of this undated sonnet into 'his copy of the 1st edn. [which] contains 15 poems transcribed from the unpublished MSS' (DSRW, 'Sassoon on Owen', *TLS*, 31 May 1974, pp. 589–90). On the verso of one of the earliest drafts (OEF) WO has drafted a letter to the Vicar of Dunsden (late 1912 or early 1913) expressing criticisms of 'the Christian life'.

STUNNED BY THEIR LIFE'S EXPLOSION INTO LOVE

This untitled sonnet is a plea for recognition of the paramount importance of poetry. The occasional grammatical inversions are characteristic of Owen's early style, in which meaning is sometimes subordinated to the exigencies of rhyme and metre.

Date   One rough draft cannot be dated, but, judging from its style, is much earlier than the fair copy, which was probably made between November 1917 and January 1918.

THE SLEEPING BEAUTY

This sonnet represents another of WO's early attempts to idealize an event in Keatsian language.

14	The poet refers to the possibility of sexually arousing a young girl, but realizes that it is *too soon* to succumb to the *part* of the prince who awakens the sleeping beauty in the fairy-tale. Nénette Léger, the 11-year-old daughter of his friends at Bagnères-de-Bigorre, is possibly one of the sources of this poem, although he was also friendly with other pre-pubescent or pubescent girls, such as the 13-year-old Millie Montague at Dunsden.
Date	WO composed this sonnet from July 1914 to October 1915. He made a fair copy between approximately November 1917 and January 1918.

1914

WO wrote this sonnet not long after the outbreak of war, originally entitling it '1915', '1914', 'The seed', and finally '1914'. The voice in this poem reflects its time: the war is part of nature's cycle, and stands for an inevitable destruction leading to the regeneration of civilization. This assumption was common on both sides until the enormity of deaths and casualties during the first battle of the Somme in 1916.

14	This final line implies that war is a sacrificial action which will bring forth new growth.
Date	WO's first draft was probably written in 1914–15. He made a subsequent fair copy at Craiglockhart between July and August 1917, and two further fair copies between November 1917 and January 1918. Although by August 1917 WO had begun to write his subversive war poems such as 'The dead-beat' and 'The show', which exposed and satirized popular ideologies about the purpose of the First World War, he left '1914' substantially as he had composed it before his enlistment.

MAUNDY THURSDAY

WO attended a Good Friday service in the French Roman Catholic church at Mérignac on 1 April 1915, where he might have witnessed the ceremony of the 'veneration of the Cross', which left him 'unchanged' (*CL*, p. 329). By ironically entitling his poem 'Maundy Thursday', and somewhat artificially subverting a Good Friday 'veneration of the Cross', WO seems to be invoking a 'new commandment' of human affection to replace the *mandatum novum* (from whence originates the word 'Maundy') of the Eucharist (the transubstantiation of the body and blood of Christ into bread and wine) which is said to have been instituted on Maundy Thursday.

14   The protagonist's kissing of the hand of the server is a spontaneous action which contrasts with the rest of the congregation's conformist observance of this dead rite.

Date This sonnet probably dates from May 1915, although the sole extant fair copy was made between November 1917 and January 1918.

NOCTURNE

A nocturne means either a ritualistic set of night prayers, or any musical composition which suggests the romantic beauty of night. WO's piece, however, draws from Keats's diction and Shelley's social ideals to provide an unromantic portrayal of night fears about dehumanizing work.

SONNET AUTUMNAL

The first extant draft of this sonnet (BL 43721, 44v) is entitled 'Autumnal'. The poet compares harbingers of autumn – frost, death of summer, *dissolution of one rose* – with intimations of the death of feelings of love, eventually culminating in the prospect of *a drear and mighty storm*.

5–10 These lines melodramatize romantic stereotypes.

Date Although WO revised this sonnet between July 1917 and January 1918, he might, judging by this Verlaine-like treatment of nature in a sonnet form, have drafted it in France in 1915.

THE ONE REMAINS

WO alludes, in one early draft, to the source of his title: 'The One remains; the many change & pass' (Shelley, *Adonais*, l. 459). Is WO extrapolating, from Shelley's postulate of an ideal beauty in the elegy on the death of Keats, a fantasy in which he also suggests a living representation of beauty?

1   *pale perfect faces*   an echo of E. B. Browning's 'pale passionate face' (*Aurora Leigh*, 1856, VI, 606).

12   *would cease my heart*   an archaism which meets the demands of metre and rhyme; WO leaves an alternative, 'would choke my song', but 'song' does not rhyme with *part*.

Date   The initial drafts of this sonnet cannot be dated, but its diction owes something to E. B. Browning's poetry which WO first mentioned in a letter of May 1914. Monsieur Léger, WO's host at Bagnères-de-Bigorre in August 1914, had met E. B. Browning. The sole extant fair copy was written between November 1917 and January 1918.

ON A DREAM

This 'dream' contains heterosexual fantasies along the lines of Madeleine's dream of Porphyro in Keats's *Eve of St Agnes*.

Date   The sole extant fair copy of this sonnet was probably written between November 1917 and January 1918, but this poem was drafted much earlier, perhaps in 1915.

WHEREAS MOST WOMEN LIVE THIS DIFFICULT LIFE

In this sonnet, an impersonal voice compares stereotypes about maternal and narcissistic women.

11   *nard*   aromatic healing or soothing ointment.

Date   This poem exists only in the form of a transcript that ELG made in 1920. JS suggests that WO wrote it in 1915 (pp. 81 and 222).

FROM MY DIARY, JULY 1914

One of the sources of this poem is probably WO's working holiday with the Léger family in the Pyrenees. He arrived there on 31 July 1914, and perhaps the use of this date in his title can be read as reflecting the end of an era of peace.

Date Although the sole extant draft was probably written between November 1917 and January 1918, this poem possibly originated in late 1914 or 1915, since, despite its use of half-rhyme, its content and diction show little of the originality of the war poems that he wrote in those months.

TO EROS

Eros has been the god or symbol of erotic love from the time of ancient Greece up to the present. Initially, this sonnet was entitled 'The end'; it is representative of a number of WO's sonnets which take up the theme of the mythical Eros with a nineties romantic relentlessness.

Date Although the fair copy was probably written between November 1917 and January 1918, this sonnet was possibly drafted in 1916 or earlier.

TO —

The narrative voice in this sonnet – which might or might not be that of an idealized WO – reflects on feelings of emotional change during pre-pubescence and pubescence. One of the sources of this poem is probably WO's own maturing in relation to his brothers, HO and CO. This sonnet implies a recognition of sexuality and loss of innocence, which are linked to becoming an adult.

11–13 The narrative voice, presumably that of a boy on the verge of adolescence, implies that acquiring knowledge of adulthood might be resisted.

14 *sand* suggests malleability and transience in human feelings.

THE END

The general theme of this sonnet is similar to that of 'The unreturning', except that in this poem the Earth's metaphorical reply almost seems to preclude the possibility of life after death.

WO wrote to SO: 'Leslie tells me that Miss Joergens considers my Sonnet on "The End" the finest of the lot. Naturally, because it is, intentionally, in her style' (12 February 1917, *CL*, p. 434). ELG, WO, and Olwen Joergens occasionally wrote poems on the same agreed topic such as 'Golden hair' or 'Happiness'.

1–4   Note WO's effective use of military metaphors.

5–6   SO's inscription on WO's headstone in Ors, France, reads: SHALL LIFE RENEW THESE BODIES? OF A TRUTH / ALL DEATH WILL HE ANNUL. By deleting the phrase with question mark after 'will he annul . . . ?', SO altered a sceptical couplet into an affirmative religious belief.

Date   This sonnet was roughly drafted in approximately September 1916, and a revised draft was made in May 1918 prior to a fair copy which cannot be dated.

STORM

This hyperbolic metaphor, which compares beauty's impact on the narrator to a cloud striking a tree with lightning, appears to be a parody in half-mocking imitation of Shelley, whose pantheism WO was later to satirize effectively in 'A terre'.

12–13   *cry aloud . . . bleak faces*   SS wrote these alternative words above WO's 'cry out' and 'their faces'.

Date   Although WO dated this poem 'October 1916', the sole extant fair copy was written at Craiglockhart between August and October 1917.

HAPPINESS

This sonnet is the first poem that WO wrote after experiencing battle at the front, but is another set piece: 'I am settling down to a little verse once more, and tonight I want to do Leslie's "Golden Hair" and OAJ's "Happiness"' (letter to SO, [12] February 1917, *CL*, p. 434).

5–6   WO wrote to SO: 'My "Happiness" is dedicated to you. It contains perhaps two good lines. Between you an' me the sentiment is all bilge' (25 February 1917, *CL*, p. 437).

12–14   WO wrote to SO: 'Tennyson, it seems, was always a great child. So should I have been, but for Beaumont Hamel [where WO experienced heavy fighting]. (Not before January 1917 did I write the *only lines* of mine that carry the stamp of maturity: these: "But the old happiness is unreturning. / Boys have no grief so grievous as youth's yearning; / Boys have no sadness sadder than our hope.")' ([7 August 1917]).

Date   WO wrote a first draft in February 1917, worked on the poem again between July and August 1917, but did not complete all his revisions. This text is my reading of his final draft (BL 43721, 25).

WITH AN IDENTITY DISC

Previous editors, except JS, published titles from earlier drafts: EB and CDL, 'To my friend (with an identity disc)', and DH, 'Sonnet to my friend: with an identity disc'. Three identity discs, which each British soldier wore around his neck, carried his name and number: if a soldier was killed, one disc was sent to his next-of-kin. WO had from memory copied Shakespeare's sonnet 'To me, fair friend, you never can be old' into the notebook in which he drafted his own sonnet tentatively addressed to his brother, CO (BL 43721, 157).

4–8   Previous editors, except JS, print an earlier version of these lines.

11   *Let my inscription be this soldier's disc* Like EB, CDL, and DH, I use SS's words, which he wrote as an alternative to WO's 'But let my death be memoried on this disc' (BL 43720, 87v).

13   *may* SS wrote this word above WO's 'let'.

14   *blurred* SS wrote this word above WO's 'vague'.

Date   An early draft of this sonnet was sent to CO on 14 March 1917 in a letter. SS's revisions were probably written on WO's final draft at Craiglockhart between August and October 1917.

The speaker refers to two conventional notions of 'fate': more time alive, or entrance to eternity.

1–2   *Fortune, Chance, Necessity, or Death*   The poet personifies these abstractions as *informers* who determine one's fate.

5–8   If the speaker strays from *fatal ordnance* – i.e. tries to quit the battlefield with its death-dealing (*fatal*) cannons and guns – then even his *trustiest friends* might hold him to that duty. All previous editors have altered WO's *ordnance* to 'ordinance', but, in so doing, they misread the extended metaphor of this sonnet which concerns not a civilian law ('ordinance') but the possible results of participating in or avoiding warfare.

9–14   The *Escape* lies in seeking *Beauty*, a stock Romantic 'gospel' which WO begins to subvert in his major poems a few weeks later.

SONG OF SONGS

This title is probably an allusion to the biblical Song of Solomon which is commonly known as the Song of Songs ('The song of songs, which is Solomon's' (Solomon 1:1). The Song of Solomon is much more vigorously sensual in its use of metaphors about love than is WO's, which echoes the Pre-Raphaelite group in its attenuated use of poetic diction.

SIX O'CLOCK IN PRINCES STREET

Princes Street is one of Edinburgh's main streets which WO mentioned in a letter to SO: 'I ... do a bit of a dash down Princes Street' ([7 August 1917] *CL*, p. 471).

6   *Following gleams*   perhaps the poetic gleams of Romanticism. WO later parodied Tennyson's *Merlin and the Gleam* (ll. 7–10) in a letter to SS (27 November 1917).

7–8   The voice of the poet contrasts the pursuit of Romanticism – *tiring after beauty* – with identification of himself with the common man as epitomized by the newsboy who brings the news about nations at war. In this poem, WO is perhaps drawing on his understanding of Keats's notion of 'Negative Capability', in that he imagines empathizing with the newsboy in the way that Keats saw himself losing his identity in even the existence of a sparrow: 'if a Sparrow come before my Window I take part in its existince [sic] and pick about the Gravel' (letter to Benjamin Bailey, 22 November 1817, *Letters of John Keats*, ed. Robert Gittings, London, OUP, 1970, repr. 1975, p. 38).

THE DEAD-BEAT

WO wrote this satirical narrative shortly after introducing himself to Siegfried Sassoon at Craiglockhart War Hospital. This meeting seems to have acted as the final catalyst to WO's imagination in his creation of war poetry. (See WO's letter to ELG, 22 August 1917, in which he tells his cousin that 'The dead-beat' is 'in Sassoon's style', and cites his first version of this poem.)

9–14   See WO's letter to ELG, 22 August 1917, for his initial version of these lines. In his final draft, WO has discarded the facetious alliteration of 'Where ministers smile ministerially' (an echo of an earlier letter of 2 August 1915). Instead he sets the soldier's collapse and death in a dramatic form by creating another character who comments sympathetically on the soldier's plight. *Blighty* England, home, after foreign service.

15   *sent him down*   sent him back from the front line for medical treatment at a casualty station.

19   WO emphasized to ELG that his poem was based on an actual incident by annotating the final lines, '*Those* are the very words!' The actual cause of death is left open.

AT A CALVARY NEAR THE ANCRE

A calvary – a statue of Christ on the Cross situated near the French river Ancre – is the subject of this poem. WO was stationed at Beaumont Hamel near this river early in 1917 (*CL*, p. 421).

2   The replica of the crucified Christ has been war-damaged.

3   *His disciples hide apart* satiric irony at the expense of modern church leaders, an irony which is developed in the second stanza.

4   *bear with Him* The ordinary soldiers metaphorically carry Christ's cross.

5   *Golgotha* 'place of skulls'; the Hebrew name for Calvary, the site of the Crucifixion.

5–8   The priests – army chaplains, and perhaps even more the war-supporting bishops and other clerics at home who propagate war fever – have been *flesh-marked* by the devil: 'If any man worship the beast and his image, and receive *his* mark in his forehead, or in his hand, the same shall drink of the wine of the wrath of god' (Revelation 9:10).

9   *scribes* journalists.

11–12 Any soldiers and other people who sacrifice their lives for others and do not hate are Christ's true followers.

Date   No MS exists, except one in SO's handwriting, so it is not possible to date this poem, except to estimate that it was probably composed after WO had met SS at Craiglockhart in August 1917, since its satire relates to some of SS's poems in that vein, such as ' "They" ' (31 October 1916).

INSPECTION

An earlier draft of this poem is entitled 'Dirt' (OEF, 244). The first-person speaker is an officer inspecting his platoon.

1–4   WO's use of soldiers' vernacular in dialogue probably owes something to the influence of SS and Kipling.

6–8   The poet, through the reported speech of the soldier, alludes ironically to Lady Macbeth's attempt to wash away her 'damned spot' of guilty blood (*Macbeth*, V.i.35).

15   *white-washed* an ironic reference to the pallor associated with the loss of blood from a fatal wound, as well

as both to an army method of cleaning up by white-
washing in order to prepare for an official inspection,
and to high officials' covering up the truth about the
causes and effects of the war.

This sonnet, which was initially entitled 'Sonnet to beauty' (*CL*,
p. 494), is one of the exercises that he wrote on set themes with
ELG and Olwen Joergens. Beauty is personified as a lover in an
extended analogy between the lover's *hand* and a *hermitage*.

9–12   The imagery in these lines echoes E. B. Browning's
        'close hand of love' which protects the beloved from the
        world's pain (*Sonnets from the Portuguese*, 1850, XXIV).
Date   WO dated one early draft 'Aug. 29–30 1917' and wrote
        a fair copy between January and February 1918.

ANTHEM FOR DOOMED YOUTH

WO's initial title for this sonnet was 'Anthem for dead youth',
which he altered at the suggestion of SS, who helped him to
revise this poem.

2–4   WO employs the noises of warfare ironically in that the
        sounds of battle are made to represent the music of a
        secular requiem for dead soldiers.
5–7   The *wailing shells* are metaphorically a dissonant and
        irreligious choir of mourning.
9–13   In the sestet, WO no longer inverts and parodies the
        performance of traditional burial rites, and consequently
        his imagery and diction embody some of the stereotypes
        which at that time might be associated with a household
        mourning the death of a family member: *holy glimmers*,
        pallor of girls' brows, and *Their flowers the tenderness of
        patient minds*.
13   *patient* SS altered WO's 'silent' to *patient*. In the con-
        text, either adjective tends to romanticize the sentiment.
14   The metaphor of 'each dusk' representing the drawing-
        down of blinds in a household that is mourning a dead

loved one effectively dramatizes the daily mortality rate
of soldiers.

THE NEXT WAR

In this title, WO is referring to the war that he never lived to
fight – that is, the humanitarian struggle to provide better conditions of life for everyone in peacetime. In the poem, an imaginary soldier–narrator scoffs defiantly at the dangers of death
in battle, then prophesies a future in which human beings will
fight *greater wars* against poverty and illness. On 31 August 1918,
however, WO in a letter to SS expressed pessimism about the
outcome of the 'more hopeless' peacetime struggle for better
conditions of life.

Epi-graph	The final couplet of SS's 'A letter home' (to Robert Graves). SS implies that his 'dream' of romanticized friendship reduces the terrors of warfare.
2	*eaten with him* JS reads 'ate beside him'.
7	*when* JS reads 'if'.
11	*his* JS reads 'His'.
13–14	JS reads 'And greater wars: when every fighter brags / He fights on Death, for lives; not men, for flags.' Unlike previous editors, JS is following BL 43720, 48, because WO wrote this fair copy in July 1918 (see JS, pp. 165 and 549). I follow *The Hydra* on the grounds that WO, as editor, approved this published version. On 2 October 1917 he told SO: 'I included my "Next War" in *The Hydra* in order to strike a note.'
Date	WO wrote and published this poem during September 1917; he considered but did not confirm some revision of it in July 1918.

WINTER SONG

The first stanza of this lyric describes the change from autumn to
winter; the second stanza refers metaphorically to the 'autumn'
years of an ageing adult. JS (p. 101) suggests that WO addressed
this poem to 7-year-old Arthur Newboult, but the imagery

relates more to an admired older person. WO wrote to SO after her visit to him in Edinburgh, 'But without the veil I saw better the supremer beauty [in your face] of the ashes of all your Sacrifices' (30 July 1917 *CL*, p. 479).

8   *spiritual glinter*   the features of the addressee will, despite the loss of physical beauty, show forth the spiritual life within.

9–10   The poet implies that white hair and the pallor of age have their own intrinsic beauty.

DULCE ET DECORUM EST

WO explained his title and the thrust of his satire in this poem: 'The famous Latin tag [from Horace] means of course "*It is sweet and meet to die for one's country*"! *Sweet*! And *decorous*' (?16 October 1917). Earlier drafts of this poem had an epigraph, 'To Jessie Pope *etc.*' or 'To a Certain Poetess'. Jessie Pope published many jingles in *Punch*, the *Daily Mail*, and the *Daily Express* during the war. (See, for example, 'The call', reprinted in part in my Critical commentary. 'The call' and 'War girls' are reprinted in Catherine Reilly (ed.), *Scars upon my Heart: Women's Poetry and Verse of the First World War*, London, Virago, 1981.) WO's poem is an ironic response to the fervid militarism of people like Jessie Pope.

1–8   The narrator sets the scene, presenting us with soldiers who are *like old beggars*, and not vigorous young heroes.

8   SS/ES and EB read 'Of gas-shells dropping softly behind'. WO did not finish this line: BL 43720, 21, has *tired, outstripped Five-Nines* deleted. But the somewhat unsatisfactory scansion in this deleted line seems preferable to the introduction of gas-shells here which pre-empts the dramatic surprise of *Gas! GAS!* at the beginning of the next section. In this text, I follow CDL, DH, and JS.

           Five-Nines   5.9-calibre explosive shells.

10   *helmets*   gas-masks, which resemble divers' masks with snorkels.

13–14   The narrator, like a deep-sea diver, has now put on his gas-mask and is observing through its *panes* a soldier who is being gassed because he is not wearing a mask.

19–24 The narrator specifies the effects of mustard-gas on the body of the gas-poisoned soldier.

25 *My friend* The narrator implicates any reader who glorifies death in war.

DISABLED

The narrator describes a badly mutilated Scottish soldier in a wheelchair outside the institution in which he survives but scarcely lives. On 14 October 1917 WO wrote to SO: 'when they [SS and Robert Graves] were together [SS] showed him my longish war-piece "Disabled" (you haven't seen it) & it seems Graves was mightily impressed, and considers me a kind of *Find*!!'

14 His handsome appearance attracted not only young women but also an artist who was infatuated with his looks and wanted to paint his portrait.

16 *his back will never brace* his injury to his back is permanent.

17 *lost his colour* This phrase implies pallor associated with loss of blood as well as the loss of the regimental 'colour', i.e. the flag of the regiment.

20 The narrator ironically associates the haemorrhage of blood from his near-fatal thigh wound with sexual ejaculation in this formerly virile young man.

21 The relatively petty but exaggerated aggression in football is contrasted with the intense violence of war. The army often recruited at football matches.

23–8 An innocent narcissism and a projection of this self-love on to young women seem to have prompted his enlistment.

25 *god in kilts* a catchphrase for a strong, handsome soldier of a Highland regiment.

27 *giddy jilts* In Scotland, this is a flippant term for a girl or young woman.

29 He pretended to be over 18 in order to be allowed to enlist in the army.

30–1 The soldier was unaware of the political causes or pretexts for this war. WO is not here expressing his own opinion about the causes of the war, but he is ironically indicating the political milieu of his imagined protagonist just before he joined up.

37–44 The soldier, who had once been a star footballer, and who had joined up with the illusion that he would enjoy combat, is now totally disabled, and ironically has become an object of pious interrogation and institutionalized charity. No longer are *women's eyes* attracted to him. Sean O'Casey, in his play, *The Silver Tassie* (1928), similarly presents the plight of a disabled war hero who is abandoned by his lover, family, and friends.

45–6 Ironically, he is now dependent on women to *put him to bed*, in contrast with his pre-war virile manhood when he could expect to take women to bed.

THE SENTRY

On 22 September 1918, WO sent a fair copy of this poem enclosed with a letter and part of another poem, 'Spring offensive', to SS. The title, 'The blind', is deleted, and 'The sentry' substituted on the left-hand margin in WO's handwriting. In the right-hand margin is a note, 'Please confer title if worthy', in WO's script. Perhaps he wanted SS to decide between the two titles. In a letter of 16 January 1917, WO had given an account of a sentry being blinded. In that prose account, WO described graphically his own actions and feelings just after the event, whereas in his later narrative poem he brought out the moral significance of the blinding of the sentry, and used the circumstances of this blinding as a metaphor for society's loss of moral vision.

3 *Hammered* JS reads 'Lit full' from the copy that WO sent to SS, which JS claims supersedes BL 43720, 23r and v. But on BL 43720, 23r, WO deleted 'Lit full' and substituted 'Hammered' – which shows that the BL MS is later than the SS MS. Also, this BL fair copy is entitled 'The sentry' without any reference to his earlier title, 'The blind'.

17 *him* JS reads 'it'.

21	*he'd* JS reads 'they'd'.

21   *he'd*   JS reads 'they'd'.

32   *broken*   JS reads 'shivered'.

36   *died*   JS reads 'gone'. This final line of the narrative has an ironic ambiguity: the sentry, in a hallucination, perhaps near the point of death, seems momentarily to believe he has recovered his sight, or to imagine that he is having a vision of an afterlife. But the rest of the platoon, who are literally in darkness, have also lost their insight into events, as perhaps their warmongering society can be said to have done.

Date   WO probably began drafting this poem in October 1917 and worked on it up to September 1918.

THE CHANCES

The *chances* are five different possible outcomes for soldiers who fought in a battle in the First World War. WO's use of soldiers' vernacular in this poem suggests the influence not only of SS but also of Kipling. WO had helped students to translate some of Kipling's poetry into French (*CL*, p. 250).

4   Previous editors, except JS, give two additional lines here: ' "Over the top to-morrer; boys, we're for it. / First wave we are, first ruddy wave; that's tore it!" ' These editors were following an earlier draft, BL 43720, 29, but, judging from WO's deletions and substitutions, BL 43721, 42, is the last extant draft.

5   *knocked out*   killed.
       cushy   easy, comfortable (Anglo-Indian), i.e. not badly wounded.

6   *Scuppered*   in this context, taken prisoner.
       mushy   emotionally overwrought.

9–10   The soldier ironically implies that one would be more fortunate to be taken prisoner by the Germans (Fritz) than to be killed or badly wounded or even left fully fit to fight another battle.

12   *a blighty*   a flesh wound that necessitates a return to England.

SOLDIER'S DREAM

This satire of the major churches' endorsement of militarism opens with a soldier's wishful thinking, which echoes the fantasies in the folksong, 'The Big Rock Candy Mountains'.

3   *Mausers and Colts* German and American types of revolver.

6   *pikel* hayfork or pitchfork (*OED*).

7–8   An implicit criticism of both established Christianity and authoritarianism, since Christ's message of healing is contrasted with God the Father's and the Archangel Michael's martial approach. An earlier draft (CDL, p. 84) indicates that the assisting archangel might refer to the intervention by the United States in the war.

GREATER LOVE

The title is partly an ironic allusion to the New Testament, 'Greater love hath no man than this, that a man lay down his life – for a friend.' WO expanded on this quotation (John 15:13) to SO, 'Is it spoken in English only and French? I do not believe so. Thus you see how pure Christianity will not fit in with pure patriotism' ([?26] May 1917). Other 'greater loves' that are treated ironically in this poem are romantic love between sweethearts, patriotic love of country, and God's love for mankind. By revealing the soldiers' love as consisting of 'carrying the cross' for everyone else, the poet ironically exposes conventional ideologies that underpin sexual romance, patriotism, and Christian practice, as well as the languages of those ideologies. The soldiers' 'greater love' ironically leads them to kill others, even if it is in self-defence, and to sacrifice their own lives on behalf of a public who cannot know the extremity of the soldiers' experiences and feelings.

In both content and form, 'Greater love' parodies Swinburne's 'Before the mirror':

    White rose in red rose-garden
      Is not so white;

Snowdrops that plead for pardon
  And pine for fright
Because the hard East blows
Over their maiden rows
  Grow not as this face grows from pale to bright.

In 'Greater love' WO mocks Swinburne's romanticized aestheticism by showing up its effeteness and trivializing quality. (See Jennifer Breen, 'Wilfred Owen: "Greater love" and late Romanticism', *English Literature in Transition*, 17, 3 (1974), pp. 173–83).

1–2   In this conceit, the poet ironically links a symbol of romantic passion, *Red lips*, with stones bloodied by dying soldiers, and, by means of parody, exposes the falseness of the assumptions underlying the nature of aesthetic–decadent literature such as Swinburne's.

7   *slender attitude* The poet implies both women's playing up to romantic stereotypes, and the political and social attitudinizing of war patriots.

9–12   The *rolling* of the soldiers in agonizing death has an ironic counterpart in sexual coition, but the soldiers' *fierce love* results only in death.

23   The soldier's rifle is ironically identified with the Christian cross, implying that society has betrayed Christian ideals by engaging in warfare. The Christian emblem, the *cross*, also suggests that the soldiers are suffering for the sins of mankind, that is, they are true Christs. Are their deaths shown to be attributable either to their 'greater love' of self-sacrifice, or to society's perverse love of death?

24   This final line contains an allusion to Christ's words to Mary Magdalene after the Resurrection, when He asks why she is weeping, and then warns her, 'Touch me not, for I am not yet ascended to my Father' (John 20: 15–17). Like Mary Magdalene, who did not understand the significance of Christ's Crucifixion, European society did not understand the tragedy or foresee the consequences of bringing about the deaths of so many of its young men.

Date   Early drafts of 'Greater love' are written on the reverse
        of some of WO's early sonnets. On 7 September 1917,
        WO asked SO to forward his early poems to him at
        Craiglockhart, where he made minor revisions in copy-
        ing some of the early poems. Thus he probably drafted
        'Greater love' in October 1917 on the reverse of some
        of those early MSS, and revised this poem up to July
        1918.

CONSCIOUS

This poem describes a soldier-patient who is trying to regain
consciousness in hospital.

3   WO had used this image to his sister, MO, from the
        13th Casualty Clearing Station, France: 'I have superb
        weather, socially-possible friends, great blue bowls of
        yellow Mayflower' (8 May 1917).
7   SS/ES, EB, CDL, and DH have conflated different
        drafts; for example, CDL's line here reads, 'Why are
        they laughing? / What's inside that jug?'
12–16   The soldier-patient is hallucinated, in that memories of
        being shell-shocked are intermingled with his hospital
        experience.

THE SHOW

A 'show' usually means an entertaining display, but during the
Great War 'a show' was slang for 'a battle'. WO's initial title was
'Vision'. The poem gives a bird's-eye view of a fantastic and
grotesque battle scene, and thus the title, 'The show', alludes
ironically to the action as both a display and a battlefield. In his
epigraph WO misquotes, with a certain black humour, Yeats's
'burnished' as *tarnished* from Forgael's lines in Yeats's poetic
drama, *The Shadowy Waters* (1906). WO thus implies that the
war has 'tarnished' romantic mythologies about beauty and
eternity. WO's systematic use of half-rhyme – and here he uses it
for perhaps the first time in his war poetry – also subverts the
conventions of rhymed lyric poetry.

1–3	The narrator is looking down from the sky to the battle-field of the Western Front in the Great War; he is accompanied on high by the spirit of Death.
4–5	The battle scene resembles the cratered surface of the moon as well as a human face *pitted with great pocks and scabs of plagues*. In letters of 19 January 1917 and 14 May 1917, WO used imagery in prose which is similar to that in this first section.
6	*horror of harsh wire* Both Allied and German sides barricaded themselves behind coils of barbed wire which stretched right along the battlefront between the two enemies' lines of trenches.
7	*caterpillars* platoons of soldiers advancing in single file.
9	*ditches* trenches.
17	*Brown* khaki. *Brown* and *grey* signify the Allied and German uniforms respectively.
	bristling spines the spikes on German helmets.
23–9	The narrator seems to descend with the figure of Death at the moment when the officer's soul leaves his decapitated body. The final identification of the narrator with the officer, who is the head of the worm which is his platoon, is an effective resolution of the grotesque fantasy within the poem; it is also almost a macabre premonition, since WO was shot while leading his platoon across the Sambre Canal.

ASLEEP

Initially, this poem was entitled 'Lines on a soldier whom shrapnel killed asleep' and 'Killed asleep by shrapnel'. WO described this lyric to ELG as coming from 'Winchester Downs, as I crossed the long backs of the downs after leaving you. It is written *as from* the trenches. I could almost see the dead lying about in the hollows of the downs' (16 November 1917).

5	*There was a quaking* JS reads 'There heaved a quaking'. He preferred an earlier MS which WO sent in his letter to ELG.
9	*intrusive lead* a piece of shrapnel.
18	JS reads 'Of finished fields, and wire-scrags rusty old'.

The title means 'apology for my poetry' or 'why I write what I write'. WO originally wrote 'Apologia pro poema mea', but in the 1920 edn SS or ES corrected his Latin grammar. Although warfare for the participants is *absurd* and *the sorrowful dark of hell*, the poet emphasizes that he writes in order to show the irony of the extraordinary antithesis to that absurd *hell*: the soldiers' brave *passion of oblation* in their self-sacrifice. The reader might question, however, whether such 'passion' is engendered by a death-wish in society, on behalf of which the soldiers are dying.

17–21 The poet repudiates romantic illusions about sexual love, in favour of the reality of spiritual companionship achieved through the endurance of suffering together.

22 *wound with war's hard wire* The pun on *wound* indicates the irony of how the barbed-wire barriers in No Man's Land metaphorically represent comradeship between fellow soldiers.

25–8 Stereotypes about the nature of *beauty*, *oaths*, *music*, and *peace* are inverted.

29–36 In these final two stanzas, the poet implies that the popular concept of a 'God' of battle, which is inverted in the first stanza of this poem, must be the Antichrist, since war is the *dark of hell*. The only compassionate response to this perversion of ideals and destruction of men is to identify with the soldiers' sorrows: only then can we understand their ironic laughter and the poet's subversion of established beliefs.

I SAW HIS ROUND MOUTH'S CRIMSON DEEPEN AS IT FELL

This poem is untitled. In this brief lyric, the death of a man from a fatal wound is compared with a receding sunset.

LE CHRISTIANISME

By using the French for 'Christianity', WO sets this poem in France. The sole extant fair copy is annotated 'Quivières', the French town where WO was stationed in April 1917 (*CL*, p. 453).

In the first stanza, the poet alludes to the ineffectuality of the church militant – the *packed-up saints* – in facing the *trouble* of war. In the second, the trite formulae and totems (plaster madonnas) of Christianity are mocked. But it is the popular representation of Christianity that is satirized in this poem, and not the principles of the New Testament.

7   *old tin hat*   A soldier had placed an army helmet on the statue.

8   *piece of hell*   shrapnel. This phrase works also as a pun on 'peace of God'.

WHO IS THE GOD OF CANONGATE?

This untitled poem in rhyming couplets consists of a dialogue between an unspecified interlocutor and Eros, the god of erotic love; the poet tries in this rather artificial structure to encapsulate the implications of sexual experience both as a commercial transaction and as a free exchange.

1–4   The *god of Canongate* and of the *heart of London* is Eros, the mythical god of erotic love, known commonly as 'Cupid'. Canongate in Edinburgh was frequented by prostitutes in the First World War, which suggests Eros is here seen ironically by the poet as the god of lust and prostitution.

13–14 This couplet marks a change of tone in the poem, since from here onwards the poet explores sexual love as a creative force.

CRAMPED IN THAT FUNNELLED HOLE

This poem is possibly a spin-off from 'Exposure', since a broken line from that poem heads the MS (BL 43720, 30): 'successive [*sic*] of bullets streak the silence'. In 'Cramped in that funnelled hole' the imagery has something in common with the following passage from Fitzwater Wray's translation of Henri Barbusse's war novel, *Le Feu* (1917), which WO read at Craiglockhart: 'In the distance he saw the night as *they* would pass it – cramped up, trembling with vigilance in the deep darkness, at the bottom of the listening-hole whose ragged jaws showed in black outline all around whenever a gun hurled its dawn into the sky' (p. 126).

5   'And they remembered Hell has many mouths' is an alternative line.

5–9   Compare these lines with Tennyson's 'The Charge of the Light Brigade' (1854):

> While horse and hero fell,
> They that had fought so well
> Came thro' the jaws of Death,
> Back from the mouth of Hell,
> All that was left of them.
> Left of six hundred.

The poet both parodies and inverts Tennyson's conventional war imagery, while echoing his rhyme, so that the metaphors about 'death's jaws' and 'Hell's mouth' signify the specific conditions and emotions of men in a shell-hole at the front.

8   Previous editors read 'Under the mud where long ago they fell'.

EXPOSURE

The title refers not only to the soldiers lying out in the snow but also to the 'exposure' – questioning – of the implicit ideological assumptions that these soldiers are sacrificing themselves in a defence and renewal of the civilized world. In letters to SO on 4 February and 25 April 1917, WO describes two experiences of lying out exposed in snow and cold at the front. This is probably the second war poem in which WO consistently employs half-rhyme to achieve an effect of ironic dissonance; for example, *knive us/nervous* and *silent/salient* in the first stanza.

1   Note the inversion of Keats's opening lines in 'Ode to a nightingale': 'My heart aches and a drowsy numbness pains / My sense'.

3   *confuse our memory of the salient*   The soldiers are confused about which point of territory they are defending against attack.

14   *grey*   the colour of the German uniforms as well as the winter storm clouds.

22–9   The poet creates in the soldiers' minds a fantasy which echoes Keats's 'Ode to a nightingale', in which the narrator escapes mentally from the 'weariness, the fever and the fret' to an unreal world of unusual beauty: 'I cannot see what flowers are at my feet, / Nor what soft incense hangs upon the boughs' (ll. 40–1). The poet reverts briefly in the sixth stanza from half-rhyme to nearly full rhyme in order to emphasize the image of the peaceful sanctuary of home. The soldiers, like the narrator in 'Ode to a nightingale', finally return to the nightmare of reality.

26   *glozed*   'To gloze' means both 'to shine brightly' and 'to veil with specious comments' (*OED*). Although the coals seem to glow brightly, they are a deceptive or a specious image – in fact, almost a hallucination.

33–5   Do soldiers die because they love or fear God, and were born to provide the sacrificial seed for His invincible spring, i.e. the rebirth of civilization? WO is subverting this ideological assumption. His ambiguity suggests that they die because God's love for them seems to be on the wane; or, ironically, that they have been made willing victims of society's 'dead' concepts of God's love and His 'invincible spring'.

34   *not loath*   quite willingly.

36   *this frost*   SS/ES, EB, and CDL read 'His frost', but WO wrote *this* in his final draft, thus dropping any further speculative irony about God, but instead asserting the malevolent predominance of mankind's perverse relationship with nature.

36–40   This specific conclusion corresponds with Barbusse's less subtle *Le Feu* (1917), in which one of the characters avers, 'I don't believe in God because of the cold. I've seen men become corpses bit by bit, just simply with cold' (p. 204).

Date   Despite the fact that WO appeared to date 'Exposure' 'February 1916', this poem was probably first begun in late November or early December 1917, when WO read

Le Feu, and was revised during 1918. The final draft which all editors have followed can be dated almost conclusively September 1918, because it is written on paper which is similar to that used for a draft of 'Elegy in April and September' (September 1918). WO probably revised 'Exposure' up to the time of his death. And 'February 1916' was probably a slip of the pen for 1918, or the '6' is an unfinished '8'. Also, see DH, 'The date of Wilfred Owen's "Exposure"', *Notes & Queries*, 23 (July 1976), pp. 305–8.

INSENSIBILITY

The title of this Pindaric ode refers to the various types of insensibility of feeling that soldiers might experience and which are recorded in the poem. In a letter of 4 January 1917, WO described his initial perception of the effects of war on the faces of officers – 'harassed' – and on the ordinary soldiers – 'expressionless lumps'. In the poem are revealed some of the reasons for anxiety or lack of expression.

3   *fleers* mocks. Some soldiers quell their humane feelings and therefore are not mocked by feeling compassion for the men they see killed.

5   *the alleys cobbled with their brothers*   WO used a similar phrasing in a letter to MO: 'They are dying again at Beaumont Hamel, which already in 1916 was cobbled with skulls' ([?25 March 1918], *CL*, p. 542).

27   The poet suggests that those soldiers who *lose imagination* (l. 19) are metaphorically unable to enlarge their hearts with concern for the dying.

32–3   WO had used a similar image previously in 'The unreturning': 'The weak-limned hour when sick men's sighs are drained.' He quoted its source indirectly in a letter of January 1912, 'You know that at 3 a.m. our life ebbs at its lowest; that is "the hour when sick men die"' (Sir Lewis Morris, *The Epic of Hades*, in *CL*, p. 106). But in this war poem the men's *sighs are drained*, i.e. they die in a dawn attack.

225

40–9   Unlike a poet–philosopher, the ordinary soldier is not at
         the mercy of thought. A confusion here between im-
         aginative and intellectual dullness implies inaccurately
         that the uneducated live in a state of blankness.

55   *moans*   SS/ES, CDL, and DH read 'mourns', although
         in BL 43720, 20, WO has deleted 'mourns' and sub-
         stituted *moans*. EB and JS read 'moans'.

50–8   This final stanza refers to civilians whom the poet repre-
         sents as having deliberately shut their minds to the plight
         of the soldiers.

STRANGE MEETING

This title might be an allusion to Shelley's *The Revolt of Islam*:

> And one whose spear had pierced me, leaned beside,
>   With quivering lips and humid eyes; – and all
> Seemed like some brothers on a journey wide
>   Gone forth, whom now strange meeting did befall
>   In a strange land.   (V, 1828–32)

But, by contrast with WO's 'Strange meeting', in Shelley's poem
the two warriors are reconciled in life, not death.

For this poem, WO probably also drew on his reading of Sir
Lewis Morris's *Epic of Hades* (1877), which contains brief poems
about encounters in hell, as well as on his knowledge of the Rev.
H. F. Cary's translation of Dante's *The Vision, or Hell, Purgatory,
and Paradise*. And 'Strange meeting', with its encounter after
death between killed and killer, has echoes of folk and literary
legends about the *Doppelgänger* motif (an apparition, or wraith-
like 'double' of oneself, which might be seen in dreams as a pre-
monition of death, or seen of someone else after that person's
death). (See also DSRW, pp. 100–3.)

But 'Strange meeting' is more than a reflection of the literary
and psychological stereotypes of the 'double' or 'alter ego' –
which are, after all, merely instances of self-indulgence in the
paranormal or of self-referential narcissism. WO uses these conventions in order to reveal 'the truth untold, the pity of war'
through his nightmare vision of the dead killer listening to his
victim's elegy on their deaths.

2   *profound dull tunnel*   a mental journey into the uncon-
       scious of the narrator; a literal descent into a deep under-
       ground trench at the front; and the hell or underworld
       of classical mythology.
3   *groined*   built with groins, i.e. an arch formed with
       intersecting vaults.
4   *encumbered sleepers*   sufferers in hell.
13   *flues*   ducts for conveying smoke as from a deep dug-
       out; here, presumably smoke from the fires of hell.
36   This line echoes Wordsworth's 'Thoughts that do often
       lie too deep for tears' ('Intimations of immortality from
       recollections of early childhood', l. 207). WO means
       that not all ideals have been corrupted in war.
39   In this line the poet implies that the spiritual suffering of
       men of imagination and thought can be as harrowing
       and as Christ-like as suffering from physical wounds.
40   WO substituted this line for the more specific, and there-
       fore less universal, 'I was a German conscript and your
       friend'.
Date   WO probably drafted some lines of this poem in Novem-
       ber 1917, and the major part of it between January and
       February 1918.

SONNET: ON SEEING A PIECE OF OUR HEAVY ARTILLERY BROUGHT INTO ACTION

The mode in the octet of this sonnet is that of mock-prayer,
in which the poet adopts the mask of a modern warrior who is
worshipping his god of mechanized warfare and damning the
enemy for their 'sins'. This parody of prayer is directed partly at
clerics and laymen who prayed for victory over Germany, but
more specifically at ecclesiastics who blessed new guns before
they went into action against the enemy.

   In the sestet the poet reverts to genuine, if bitter, prayer, cursing not the enemy, but the piece of artillery as a symbol of the
war machine itself.

5   *Arrogance*   The poet ironically reflects the popular belief
       that this term applied only to the Kaiser's industrially
       successful Germany.

9   *malison*   curse.

11–14   a synecdoche in which the big gun stands for all military
        hardware in the poet's prayer for disarmament.

S.I.W.

Self-inflicted wounds were either minor wounds inflicted by a
soldier on himself in order to be sent home, or suicide. In his
epigraph, WO gives an ironic meaning to a line from Yeats's
play, *The King's Threshold* (1904) – 'For that man there has set
his teeth to die' – in that the soldier shoots himself between his
teeth. 'S.I.W.' is a parody of an epic poem: the prologue, which
is usually a brief introduction that sets the scene, is here four
times longer than the action. The poet thus establishes that the
soldier's anguish – which is built up in the prologue – is in its
prolongation the source of the soldier's suicide.

10   *YM hut*   Young Men's Christian Association Recrea-
        tion hut.

15   *Reckless with ague*   shaking with fever.

17   *trench foot*   feet badly affected by much standing in
        water.

20   *this world's Powers*   the major warring nations, especial-
        ly Britain, France, and Germany.

28   *English ball*   a solid, non-explosive missile from a rifle
        or pistol on his own side.

31   *insuperable*   Previous editors read 'and blind', but BL
        43720, 32r, supports my reading.

36   *kissed*   an inversion of the erotic connotation of this
        word; here a sign of affection is ironically associated
        with a violent, self-inflicted death – shooting oneself
        with one's own rifle.

37   *'Tim died smiling.'*   His smile is the grotesque effect of
        being shot through the mouth, and is not the happiness
        of release through death.

HOSPITAL BARGE

WO was himself conveyed in a steam-tug when he was a shell-
shock patient at the 13th Casualty Clearing Station: 'I sailed in a

steam-tug about 6 miles down the Canal with another "inmate" .... Just as in the Winter when I woke up lying on the burning cold snow I fancied I must have died & been pitch-forked into the Wrong Place, so, yesterday, it was not more difficult to imagine that my dusky barge was wending up to Avalon, and the peace of Arthur, and where Lancelot heals him of his grievous wound' (10 May 1917).

12–14   An allusion to these lines from Tennyson's *Morte d'Arthur*:

> Then saw they how there hove a dusky barge,
> Dark as a funeral scarf from stem to stern,
> Beneath them; and descending they were ware
> That all the decks were dense with stately forms
> Black-stoled, black-hooded, like a dream – by these
> Three Queens with crowns of gold – and from them rose
> A cry that shiver'd to the tingling stars,
> And, as it were one voice an agony
> Of lamentation, like a wind, that shrills
> All night in a waste land, where no one comes,
> Or hath come, since the making of the world.
> (ll. 360–71)

The poet contrasts the wounded soldiers of mechanized warfare with the heroes of the Arthurian legend: pathos blends with irony.

14   *Merlin*   magician at the court of King Arthur.

A TERRE

This poem is a dramatic monologue by an officer dying of wounds. *A terre* is French for 'to earth'. WO is alluding to Genesis 3:19: 'In the sweat of thy face shalt thou eat bread, till thou return unto the ground, for out of it wast thou taken: for dust thou art, and unto dust shalt thou return.' 'A terre' is an expanded version of an earlier poem, 'Wild with all regrets', which WO had dedicated to SS; its title alludes to one of Tennyson's songs, 'Tears, idle tears', from *The Princess*, in which the narrator recalls the past:

Dear as remember'd kisses after death,
And sweet as those by hopeless fancy feign'd
On lips that are for others: deep as love
Deep as first love, and wild with all regret;
O Death in Life, the days that are no more.

Unlike his final title, 'A terre', his earlier title, 'Wild with all re-grets', in relation to Tennyson's Romanticism here, is not charac-teristically ironic.

1	*three parts shell*	The officer has been badly wounded from shell-fire.
5	*peg out soldierly*	die bravely in battle.

7–8 Coins used to be placed on the eyelids of corpses in order to keep their eyes shut (DH, p. 129). The poet uses this metaphor to suggest that the bandages on the soldier's eyes remind him of his coming death, and that the medals which he won in battle are of no use to him, but ironically have become a sign of what has brought about his early death.

10 *(That's for your poetry book.)* The dying soldier is talk-ing to a poet who will record his story for him. This device serves to convince us of the authenticity of the narrative, in that, although we might think at first that the soldier's vivid metaphors are not appropriate for the voice of a war-weary, mutilated officer, we now realize that he is supposedly devising them to suit his listener, a poet, who is a fictional character, and not necessarily WO himself.

12–14 These lines are a reference to SS's satire of patriotic majors in 'Base details' (1917); WO's soldier-narrator would prefer any life, even that of SS's abhorred stereo-typical majors, rather than death.

16–18 The officer-narrator anticipates that *the arts of hurting* perhaps should not, in his poet-listener's view, be taught to boys. Through his narrator and listener, WO implicit-ly queries stereotypes about masculinity that are inevita-bly associated with power and violence.

24 *grow me legs* The officer's legs have been shot off and/or amputated.

27   *mummy-case*   He is so wrapped in bandages that he resembles an Egyptian mummy, i.e. a corpse embalmed for burial.

30–5   These lines embody one of the central themes of the poem: that social prejudices against humble occupations or dirty kinds of work are foolish in the face of each person's final end as dust in the earth.

35   *Must I be his load?*   Must my mutilated body be a muckman's 'load'? The officer sardonically considers the jobs of dustman and undertaker as similar in relation to his own death.

36   *dug-out rat*   Rats flourished on the Western Front, especially on the corpses of soldiers.

37   *lives*   Previous editors, except JS, preferred 'existences' which WO deleted and replaced with *lives* in his final MS.

44–7   These lines allude to a passage in *Adonais*, Shelley's elegy on the death of Keats:

> He is made one with Nature …
> He is a presence to be felt and known
> In darkness and in light, from herb and stone.
> (ll. 370–4)

Thus the poet represents the narrator as mocking Shelley's pantheism in that even the *dullest Tommy* now takes Shelley with literal reductiveness: 'pushing up daisies', i.e. fertilizing the plants, was a cynical catchphrase for the extent of the dead soldier's afterlife.

49–50   The poet, through his narrator, mocks the commonly believed piece of British propaganda that the Germans (*the Boche*) in the First War boiled down their prisoners in order to make soap. The narrator with black humour explodes this rumour, with his ribald question about whether Germans will turn into cannibals.

52–5   The officer is resigned to the physical dissolution of his body in the earth after death.

58–63   As for his *soul* or *spirit*: the dying soldier thinks that at first he will be remembered in spirit by his friends, then not at all.

231

64–5	All that the soldier requires is spiritual support in the act of dying: *weaned* implies that the soldier's need is similar to that of the baby dependent on its mother.

MINERS

EB quotes a letter, which is no longer extant, from WO to SO: 'Wrote a poem on the Colliery Disaster: but I get mixed up with the War at the end. It is short, but oh! sour!' ([?14 January 1918]). This 'Colliery Disaster', in which 155 miners were killed at Halmerend on 12 January 1918, was reported in the *Daily News* on 14 January: 'A sad feature of the disaster is that most of the missing are young men and boys. Half a dozen boys of between 14 and 15 were doing their first week's work in the pit, and there were about 50 youths who only started work last year.' But in 'Miners' WO has universalized this documentary material.

8	*fawns* more usually spelt 'fauns', a class of 'rural deities' (*OED*).
19	For this line, JS reads 'Many the muscled bodies charred' from BL 43720, 78. But WO had checked the proof of 'Miners' just prior to its appearance in *The Nation*, and I print this version on the grounds that WO had approved it.
21–4	Coal miners were recruited specifically for tunnelling companies during the war and were employed in tactical mining under the German lines. *Worked dark pits* implies the hell-like atmosphere of battle as well as tactical military mining; but this phrase also symbolizes the work of all ordinary soldiers at war. *Peace* is used ironically in that, first, it is the lot of those soldiers who will cease being at war only when they die in war; and, secondly, the political leaders pontificated that peace would result from war.
34	For this line, JS reads 'Left in the ground', because he prefers WO's 'original' line and not the version that WO approved for *The Nation*.

EB and CDL called this poem 'Bold Horatius'. WO crossed out his initial title 'Schoolmistress', without substituting another one. JS restores this deleted title.

1–4   An allusion to Thomas Babington Macaulay's poem 'Horatius', in *The Lays of Ancient Rome* (1842).

5–10   The poet satirically pricks the notion of romance by implying that, although the schoolteacher had responded to Macaulay's inflated narrative about the legendary Roman warrior, she is too snobbish to return the down-to-earth greetings of modern soldiers.

THE LETTER

This poem, in soldiers' vernacular, is an imaginary letter being written at the front by an ordinary soldier to his wife in England. The 'letter' is interpolated with bracketed comments by the letter-writer to his friends around him.

1   *B.E.F.* British Expeditionary Force.

5   *square-'eaded 'Uns* A reference to the Germans by the shape of their helmets.

15   *VRACH!* the sound of an exploding shell.

17   *When me and you* Ironically, at the point of planning some intimacy with his wife, the soldier has to break off his letter in order to get ready for battle, and is killed. His friend, Jim, will thus have to write the opposite of what the soldier was about to tell his wife in relation to their reunion.

THE LAST LAUGH

WO commented, in reference to 'Last words', an early version of this poem, that there 'is a point where prayer is indistinguishable from blasphemy. There is a point where blasphemy is indistinguishable from prayer' (letter to SO, 18 February 1918). But, in 'The last laugh', this observation is employed to show how war has undermined the received ideology of Christianity: it is immaterial whether the dying soldier takes the name of Jesus in vain or not because the noise of bullets asserts that all is *vain*. In the second stanza, the institution of the family is mocked: the dying soldier sighs for his parents, but is ridiculed by weapons as a *fool* and is represented as *childlike* in death. In the third stanza, the weaponry mocks a dying soldier's memory of his lover: the language of Romantic poetry is inverted, in that the soldier's *whole face kissed the mud* in death. Although WO used regular rhyme in his first version, 'Last words', he subsequently in later drafts of 'The last word' and 'The last laugh' sought the discordant effects of half-rhyme, which seems to add to the dissidence of the text: war is not stopped by Christian, familial, or Romantic ideologies, but instead the viciousness of war appears to be a corruption of these beliefs.

Date   WO drafted the first version of this poem, 'Last words', in January–February 1918; he finished his second version, 'The last word', by March 1918; and he completed his final version, 'The last laugh', by July 1918.

THE SEND-OFF

This poem was initially entitled 'Inostensibility' and 'The draft'.

4–5   The poet ironically mocks women's sentimental farewells to departing soldiers; he compares the flowers they give to those laid on corpses at funerals.

19   *village wells* SS/ES, CDL, DH read 'still village wells'. In BL 43720, 18, which is WO's final version, he deleted 'still', 'strange', and 'silent', in that order, and, although he might have intended to substitute an alternative adjective, he did not do so.

ARMS AND THE BOY

This title might contain an implicit reference to G. B. Shaw's play, *Arms and the Man* (1894), an anti-romantic drama about militarism. 'Arms and the boy' tends to idealize the innocence of youth in the face of the brutality of war.

2   *keen with hunger of blood* This image echoes Shelley's poem, *The Mask of Anarchy* (stanza 77):

> *Let the fixed bayonet*
> *Gleam with sharp desire to wet*
> *Its bright point in English blood*
> *Looking keen as one for food.*

3   *like a madman's flash* This simile suggests the frenetic manner in which a bayonet is used, as well as the shine of its steel.

6   *nuzzle* to burrow with the nose, or to nestle (*OED*). In this context, *nuzzle* has ironic overtones in that this word is associated both with infantile pleasure and with adult sexuality.

9   In a letter to SO, WO commented on the innocence of some of the boys he helped to train for war: 'one of the underage came to me with an offering of apples!! Poor penniless schoolboy! But you must not think there was anything but ingenuousness. These Lancashires are extraordinarily open, honest, and incapable of strategy' (3 July 1916).

11–12 Despite his training in the weaponry of war, the 'boy' cannot be transformed into a devil.

FUTILITY

In an early draft, this lyric was entitled 'Frustration' (OEF, VH).

9   *clays of a cold star* a metaphorical reference to the sun's power to renew life on earth or, with poetic licence, on a *star*.

12   *Was it . . . clay grew tall?* Humans evolved as intelligent upright beings, so why end one such life abruptly?

13–14 This rhetorical question suggests that, if life can be so casually destroyed, then what is the purpose of creation?

THE CALLS

A stereotyped mode of noting sounds which metaphorically indicate *calls* to duty or to a vocation including finally the poet's own vocation to write about the *distress* of men at war.

18–19 The poet mocks the war-profiteers, who, obeying government injunctions to eat less bread as a wartime device to conserve food supplies, ate instead more luxurious food which they could well afford. WO did not complete this stanza, crossing out both attempts: 'I've had my fill' and 'Here I've no rime: that's proper/decent'.

23 This line is incomplete. WO's alternative attempts are: 'And I remember – last December' and 'No rime again Thank Heaven', which suggests that he did not take this poem very seriously.

24–7 Although the narrator of 'The calls' is not necessarily WO, he commented, on about 10 August 1918, on his own role as poet of war, 'I shall be better able to cry my outcry, playing my part' (letter to SO).

TRAINING

9 *crown* in the context of this poem, more likely to mean an emblem of victory than of martyrdom – though evidently with a facetiously ironic implication.

MENTAL CASES

In an early draft, WO entitled this poem, 'The deranged' (letter to SO, 25 May 1918); the fair copy has the title 'Mental cases', which WO altered momentarily to 'The aliens', but then changed back to 'Mental cases' (BL 43720, 12, 13, and 14).

1–9 An interlocutor asks an extended question about the nature of the place in which he and his companion walk; it could be any long-stay mental hospital, but to the speaker it seems like hell.

10–28 His companion replies that these are men who have fought in battle and suffered psychically from witnessing the murder of many men. This speaker indicts both himself and his questioner, and, indirectly, society, who *dealt them war and madness*.

28 *madness* Although this poem is an imaginary account

of how war brought about the psychic destruction of man, WO in writing it inevitably drew on not only what he saw as a patient at the Craiglockhart War Hospital for officers with nervous disorders, but also on what he himself felt as a patient there.

THE PARABLE OF THE OLD MAN AND THE YOUNG

The title indicates that this poem is a parody of the story from Genesis (22:1–19) about Abraham, who has acquiesced in God's demand that he sacrifice his son. But when the angel appears, suggesting that Abraham sacrifice instead 'a ram caught in a thicket by his horns', he spares his son.

1   *Abram*   metonymy for politicians and war-profiteers.
5   *fire and iron*   implies images of armaments.
7   *belts and straps*   suggests the soldiers' uniforms and equipment.
8   *parapets and trenches*   a reference to the front lines.
12–14   Previous editors, except JS, follow BL 43720, 15, a fair copy in which these three lines vary slightly from the OS fair copy, which I use.
14   *Ram of Pride*   the nationalisms of warring nations.
15–16   The poet deftly and ironically reverses the biblical story in order to reveal the barbarism of supposedly Christian leaders sacrificing their young men, i.e. *half the seed of Europe*.
Date   WO made fair copies of this poem in approximately July 1918, but it was probably drafted earlier.

THE KIND GHOSTS

WO's provisional title for this poem was probably 'Britannia', since the latter title appears on one of WO's lists of poems and there is no other poem that fits this title (BL 43721, 43v).

1   *She*   Britannia, 'a poetic name for Britain personified as female' (*OED*); also, the allegorical emblem of Death who is often personified in medieval iconography as a falsely seductive female.

11   *her terraces, their hecatombs* Britain has become symbolically the place of 'great public sacrifices' (*OED*).

SPRING OFFENSIVE

This 'offensive', or battle initiated by the protagonists of the poem, takes place in 'spring'. In another sense, the poet represents the natural world – the 'spring' – as metaphorically offering a warning to, then conducting an 'offensive' against, the soldiers. This poem might in part be an ironic response to Julian Grenfell's 'Into battle' (1915), in which the 'spring' is metaphorically shown as reassuring to the soldiers.

2–3   *and lying easy ... knees* JS reads 'and eased of pack-loads, were at ease; / And leaning on the nearest chest or knees'.

12   *glass* The sky mirrors a warning in its flashes from explosions, gunfire, and shell-bursts; the criss-cross of shells against its glassy background signifies war in the same way that lightning signifies a thunderstorm; and *glass* can also mean a barometer, so that metaphorically nature is predicting a storm.

14   *buttercup* JS reads 'buttercups'.

18   *All their strange day* Previous editors, except JS, delete this phrase because WO crossed it out without substituting any other.

21   *battle* WO deleted this word, without making any substitution.

27–32   WO described in prose an experience of himself and his battalion 'going over the top' (see letter to SO, 25 April 1917, and letter to CO, 14 May 1917). These letters reflect his immediate and personal feelings about an offensive, whereas in the poem he examines the universal significance of such battles.

30–1   *sudden cups ... their blood* The *buttercup* (l. 14), which had appeared to bless the men, now metaphorically act as sacrificial vessels catching the blood of the soldiers.

34   This line is unfinished. JS quotes DSRW's textual note (reproduced in CDL) as the source of his reading: 'My

impression is that Owen changed l. 34 as follows: (a) *unseen* was cancelled and *surf of* substituted above; (b) he then cancelled *Leapt to the unseen* and substituted above *Breasted the shrieking*; (c) next he cancelled *the shrieking*, put in another *the* before it and *even rapture of bullets* after it, and then cancelled *Breasted*. The best alternative to EB I can suggest is *Breasted the surf of bullets, or went up.*'

39   *drave* drove (*OED*).

45   *cool and peaceful air* Previous editors read 'cool peaceful air', although WO wrote an abbreviated *and* after *cool* (see CDL's note).

Date   WO revised this poem between July and September 1918, but he did not complete his revisions. It is not possible to estimate the date of his first composition of 'Spring offensive', but JS claims that an undated MS forwarded separately with a letter to SS by WO on 22 September 1918 was written subsequent to the BL MS (43720 27, 28r and v) that I and other previous editors follow. Deletions and substitutions in this BL MS, however, confirm that WO made them after sending his part-draft to SS.

SMILE, SMILE, SMILE

'Smile, smile, smile' is the final line of the refrain of a popular song of that period, 'Pack up your troubles . . .'. WO is satirizing not only those people who are taken in by soliders' smiles in the face of adversity, but also the glibness of the popular song.

4–6   The *Daily Mail*, which WO read, referred on 19 September 1918 to 'the decent and comfortable homes society owes returning soldiers'.

9–17 WO is alluding to speeches by the British Minister for Labour and the French Premier, Clemenceau: 'Did you see what the Minister of Labour said in the *Mail* the other day? "The first instincts of the men *after the cessation of* hostilities will be to return home." and again – "All classes *acknowledge* their indebtedness to the soldiers & sailors . . ." About the same day, Clemenceau is re-

239

ported by the *Times* as saying: "All are worthy ... yet we should be untrue to ourselves if we forgot that the *greatest* glory will be to the splendid poilus, who, etc."' (letter to SS, 22 September 1918). Clemenceau's speech included the following rhetoric: 'We should be unworthy of the great destiny that is allotted to us if we were to sacrifice any people, great or small, to the appetites and fury of implacable domination which is still lurking behind the latest falsehoods of barbarism .... Our dead have given their blood in token of our acceptance of this the greatest challenge to the laws of civilized man' (*The Times*, 19 September 1918, p. 5). WO in his poem satirizes such rhetoric.

12   *solidly indemnified*   The victorious nations, Britain and France, must keep fighting until the enemy agrees to pay extensive war damages.

17   *nation in integrity*   Ironically, the *integrity* of the *nation*'s warmongering rhetoric is maintained at the cost of the literal breaking-up of the *nation* through loss of life.

23   *save under France*   those soldiers who are now buried in France.

26   *poor things*   This patronizing epithet, which WO satirizes, is normally used in reference to the disabled, mentally ill, children, or the recently dead.

PREFACE

In mid-1918, WO drafted this Preface for a proposed collection of poems to which he tentatively gave the title, *Disabled and Other Poems* (OEF 348). But he finished neither this Preface nor the preparation for his book.

TO SUSAN OWEN, 2 APRIL 1911

WO, who was a pupil-teacher for a few months at the Wyle Cop School in Shrewsbury, was approaching his London matriculation examination, and was trying to find a way of pursuing further study as well as earning his living.

3	*Mr Robson* the Rev. Herbert Eric Robson (1877–1917), vicar at Kidmore End, Reading (1906–16).
6	*Mr Edwards* a teacher at Shrewsbury Technical School, where WO had been a pupil since the age of 13.
6	*Mr Lightbourne* headmaster at Wyle Cop School, Shrewsbury.
9	*P.T.'s* pupil-teachers.
14	*June ... terrors* WO is alluding to his matriculation examination in June.
15–19	*It is a flaw ... (Keats)* 'Epistle to J. H. Reynolds'.
25–8	*But let me ... this view* WO means that he can justify Keats's *attitude to knowledge* because he is modelling his ideas on those of Keats.
31	*Woodruff* white-flowered plant (*OED*).

TO SUSAN OWEN, 18 JUNE 1911

Alpenrose, Kidmore End, Reading, where WO was staying, was the home of John Gunston, who married Emma Shaw, SO's elder sister. They had four children – Gordon, Vera, Dorothy, Leslie. WO was particularly friendly with Leslie.

19–21	*'Wiggan of Dunsden' ... with ours* The Rev. Herbert Wigan (1862–1947) was vicar at Dunsden, near Reading, from 1904 to 1917. WO worked as his assistant from October 1911 to January 1913. The Rev. H. Cutler, a former vicar of Dunsden Parish Church, notes that several elderly parishioners commented on the instability of the Rev. Wigan's religious allegiances (letter from the Rev. H. Cutler, 16 June 1972). While WO was at Dunsden, Mr Wigan seemed to have already abandoned his High Church stance and was in the thick of Protestant evangelical fervour.
33	*Churchman* founded in 1897.
42	*E.Q.* Edward Quayle, a tinplate broker in Liverpool, who married Tom Owen's eldest sister, May. After her death, he married May's and Tom's sister, Emma (*CL*, p. 17).
68–74	*Am I then to avoid ... length of time* *Pitch*, a black dis-

tillation of tar or turpentine, was used by Mr Robson as a metaphor for the undesirability of becoming an elementary schoolteacher. WO was already teaching as a pupil-teacher, so that, in order not to be *defiled* in Mr Robson's view, he must give up this teaching.

78–9   *Uriconium . . . Mr Colyer*   Mr Colyer was assistant curator at Reading Public Museum and Art Gallery. Uriconium was the Roman city at Wroxeter on the Severn, east of Shrewsbury; it had first been excavated in 1859–61. WO was very interested in Roman remains, and wrote a poem, 'Uriconium', on that city (JS, pp. 65–8).

TO MARY OWEN, 7 NOVEMBER 1911

Mary Owen was WO's younger sister. SO was staying with her Gunston relations in order to visit WO at Dunsden vicarage where he had taken up the post of vicar's assistant after his hopes of a scholarship to university had been dashed by his receiving only a pass in his matriculation examination.

16   *Mr Kemp*   Alfred Saxelby Kemp was the other lay assistant at Dunsden vicarage; unlike WO, he subsequently became a clergyman.

17   *Bishop Ingham*   The Rev. Ernest Graham Ingham (1851–1926) was Home Secretary of the Church Missionary Society between 1904 and 1912.

TO SUSAN OWEN [4 JANUARY 1913]

This is one of the letters which WO's younger brother, HO, who later assisted in the editing of *CL*, partly and, so far, irretrievably censored.

1–3   *The furore . . . a year ago*   JS suggests the following interpretation: 'Could the furore have been caused by Wigan [the vicar] finding Vivian Rampton [a young protégé of WO's] smuggled into the vicarage? Wilfred, it would appear, had "discovered" him something *under* a year before, but this was hardly a moment for chronological exactitude' (*Wilfred Owen*, London, OUP and Chatto & Windus, 1974, p. 83). More probably, however, WO 'discovered' (i.e. found out) the vicar to be a philistine and religious bigot much earlier, but their mutual antipathy, for reasons which would have been obvious in the missing parts of this letter, had come to a head in January 1913.

2   *Mnemosyne*   the mother, by Zeus, of the nine Muses; the name means 'memory'.

6–8   *I have ... Tracts!*   Mr Wigan had interviewed WO and recommended him to read *Tracts* i.e. pamphlets on religious subjects.

13   *hotbed of religion*   WO was referring to the vicar's attraction towards, and embracing of, low-church evangelism.

15–17   *'Westward Ho!' ... England*   Charles Kingsley's novel, *Westward Ho!* (1855), in which Jesuit priests are prominent, is set at the time of the Spanish Armada.

20   *thunder and lightning*   his phrase recurs as a metaphor in Owen's sonnet, 'Storm'.

25–6   *flight ... from overbearing elders*   another theme that is central in 'Storm'.

52   *E.W.M.'s pamphlet*   the Rev. E. W. Moore's pamphlet, which apparently SO had advised WO to read. He dismissed such moralistic tracts as *quite beside the mark for me* (ll. 53–4).

DRAFT OF A LETTER TO THE REV. WIGAN, [? FEBRUARY 1913]

WO might not have sent a fair copy of this letter to Mr Wigan.

TO ALEC PATON, NOVEMBER 1913

WO left Dunsden in February 1913 and was ill for some months. Partly on the recommendation of his doctor, he travelled in mid-September 1913 to Bordeaux in order to work as a teacher of English language at the Berlitz School of Languages. Alec Paton was a friend from his schooldays at Birkenhead Institute, Liverpool.

36–7   *kindness ... in Wales*   WO had holidayed in Wales in
1903 and 1905 as a guest of Alec Paton and his family.

8–10   *the countess ... 'heart trouble'*   WO implied that he had
not 'fallen in love'.

22–5   *All women ... I ought*   WO's claim here that he disliked
women seemed to be directed at women who impor-
tuned him sexually, especially prostitutes (*mercenaries*).
He seems to be reassuring his mother.

27–33   *And if ... pale*   DH restored the missing words that
HO had attempted to delete (see DH, 'Wilfred Owen's
letters: some additions, amendments and notes', *Library*,
4 (September 1982), p. 280).

30   *revelations*   WO implied that his mother had not en-
lightened him about sexuality.

21   *crise de nerfs*   In the months after he left Dunsden, he
had suffered an illness which was partly psychogenic in
origin, because he had experienced a sense of failure in
his first work away from home.

38   *first public examination*   at Shrewsbury Technical School.

42–4   *Is any scene ... paragraph*   This scene occurs in George
Eliot's novel, *Romola* (1863).

99   *Miss Martin*   an art teacher at the Birkenhead Institute.

117   *Aunt Emily Owen*   Edward Quayle's second wife.

127–35 *The true artist ... allowances for him*   Bernard Shaw,
Man and Superman, I (1903).

WO was holidaying in the Pyrenees with Monsieur and Madame
Léger and their 11-year-old daughter, Nénette, partly as a guest
but also partly in order to give Madame Léger and Nénette les-

sons in English. Madame Léger had been one of his pupils at the Berlitz School.

6–7   *a doctor of Bagnères*   The villa was owned by Dr Cazalas.

6–17   *Mademoiselle Levallois* a professional violinist.

21   *the Stretton brotherhood* the Stretton hills near Shrewsbury.

58   *tant pis* what a pity!

68   *Some of her writings are astonishing* Nénette later published three novels (DH, *Owen the Poet*, London, Macmillan, 1986, p. 193).

72   *Marche Funèbre* WO drew on this music when writing the fragment 'An imperial elegy' (JS, pp. 453–4).

77   *War* The First World War began on 4 August 1914.

98   *villégiature* stay in the the country; out-of-town holiday.

TO HAROLD OWEN, WEDNESDAY, 23 SEPTEMBER [1914]

WO stayed with Monsieur and Madame Léger at their home in Bordeaux from 17 September to 7 October 1914.

2–3   *Safe at home* HO, a Fourth Officer on *La Esmeraldas*, was on leave at his home in Shrewsbury.

23   *Escoula* Jean Escoula (1851–1911).

47   Tailhade Laurent Tailhade (1854–1919), a poet whom WO met through the Légers.

68   *Zouave* member of French light-infantry corps.

TO SUSAN OWEN, 5 MARCH 1915

WO was now employed at Mérignac, near Bordeaux, as tutor to the four de la Touche boys who had been unable to return to Downside School in England because of disruption of shipping in the Channel. He drafted this letter on Saturday, 6 February 1915 (*CL*, pp. 319–20). Although we do not know how many of WO's letters were drafted and revised in this way, the revisions in this letter suggest that WO thought carefully about how he expressed himself in letters.

3–4   *three pages missing*   DH suggests that three pages are
       missing, and that these pages might concern 'money and
       his rich uncle' (DH, 'Wilfred Owen's letters', p. 282).
       Probably they also relate the episode of his caning two
       of the de la Touche boys, since this account forms part
       of the earlier draft.
7   *Rich Uncle*   Edward Quayle.
34–5   *the fullest . . . a Poet*   WO romanticized about leading
       the life of a poet.
43   *to a Call*   WO meant that he was still open to a Call
       from God, but any notion of his having a religious voca-
       tion had been dissipated at Dunsden vicarage.
62–4   *That tide . . . flood*   WO was alluding to a passage from
       Julius Caesar, IV.3: 'There is a tide in the affairs of men /
       Which, taken at the flood, leads on to fortune'.

TO SUSAN OWEN, [*c.*20] JUNE 1915

WO had travelled to London via Paris in order to execute a business commission for the perfumier, Monsieur Peyronnet. He
had left Mérignac and on his return from London he had taken
new lodgings in Bordeaux. Nevertheless, he still travelled to
Mérignac to teach the de la Touche boys and continued his other
private tutoring in Bordeaux.

16–37 *I told him . . . shooter ready by then*   WO's visit to London
       had touched off his desire to enlist.
37   *Lloyd George*   then Minister for War. He was Prime
       Minister between 1916 and 1922.
48   *Dr Loughrey*   He married SO's youngest sister, Mary.

TO SUSAN OWEN, SATURDAY [POSTMARK 10 JULY 1915]

2   *without address*   WO did not wait for his mother to send
       the full address of the Artists' Rifles Regiment.

TO SUSAN OWEN, THURSDAY MNG. [21 OCTOBER 1915]

WO returned to England on 14 September 1915, accompanying
the de la Touche boys on their journey back to Downside School.

He then joined the Artists' Rifles Regiment in order to obtain a commission as an officer.

3   *Headquarters*   i.e. of the Artists' Rifles, Dukes Road, Euston Road, WC1.

35–6   *I am the British Army*   This is either a slip of the pen or humorous hyperbole.

56   *Poetry Bookshop*   Harold Monro opened this shop for the sale of books and fostering of interest in poetry at 35 Devonshire Street in 1913.

TO SUSAN OWEN, SATURDAY [4 MARCH 1916]

WO was writing from a Young Men's Christian Association recreation hut at Romford where he was a cadet officer. He had just been returned abruptly from a ten days' training course in London, where he had lodged privately in rooms above Harold Monro's Poetry Bookshop.

20–7   *I thought ... what 'modern'*   WO had sought Harold Monro's advice on his writing of sonnets. Monro had founded *The Poetry Review*, which WO had read as well as his books of poems, *Before Dawn* (1911) and *Children of Love* (1914). Monro had also published *Strange Meetings* in 1917. Monro, via his *Review* and the Poetry Bookshop, fostered 'Georgian' poetry, i.e. an early twentieth-century school of poetry which is now noted for its continuity with the late Victorian 'Romantic' or 1890s 'decadent' conventions about nature, love, beauty, and so on.

28–9   *the 'Little Books of Georgian Verse'*   a series of new poetry by individual authors, published by Erskine MacDonald. These authors have mostly been forgotten. Olwen Joergens, who wrote poems with WO and ELG on specified topics, published *The Woman and the Sage* (1917) in this series.

30   *Prof. Morley*   Edith Morley was Professor of English at the University of Reading (1907–40). She had taught WO Old English at the end of his time at Dunsden vicarage, and later she encouraged him to sit for a scholar-

ship to Reading University which he did not win. He had sent her 'The little mermaid' and some other poems for her critical comments.

38   *Swiss Housekeeper*   Alida Klemantski, who was also interested in poetry. She became Harold Monro's second wife in 1920.

TO SUSAN OWEN, TUESDAY [15 AUGUST 1916]

WO was on a training course in marksmanship at Mytchett Musketry Camp near Aldershot. He had been commissioned into the 5th Battalion Manchester Regiment on 4 June 1916, but he spent another six months in the 3/5th (Reserve) Battalion Manchester Regiment in musketry training at Aldershot, Farnborough, Oswestry, Southport, and Fleetwood.

TO SUSAN OWEN, 1 JANUARY 1917

At the end of 1916, WO travelled to France, where he was drafted into the 2nd Battalion Manchester Regiment, which was a regular battalion, and not one drawn up especially for the war. He joined his battalion, which was stationed near Beaumont Hamel, France, on 1 or 2 January 1917. During that harshly cold January, WO was engaged with his battalion in capturing German observation posts in preparation for the Battles of Arras, which took place in April that year (*History of the Great War Based on Official Documents*, comp. Cyril Falls, 1940, p. 73).

26–8   *If on my Field Post Card … the Front*   WO intended to befuddle the censor by making a code from the alternative items on an official field postcard. He was not supposed to indicate when or where he was actually fighting.

TO SUSAN OWEN, 4 JANUARY 1917

At the front from 4 to 12 January, WO reconnoitred the part of the line that he and his platoon were to occupy.

18   *Sir Percy Cunynghame*   Cunynghame (1867–1941) was

248

a Lieutenant-Colonel in the Manchester Regiment.

45   *Bairnsfather*   Bruce Bairnsfather drew war cartoons for the popular press.

52   *'Daily Mail' map*   The map showed the Saint-Quentin front and the British line on the Somme.

59   *Mistletoe*   This is a code word by which WO indicated to SO that he was about to reveal the name of the area or village where he was stationed. The second letter of each handwritten line after *Mistletoe* would make up the name of the place, in this instance, 'Somme' (see DH, 'Concealed messages in Wilfred Owen's trench letters', *Notes & Queries*, 27 (December 1980), p. 531). SO could also have discovered this fact from WO's reference to the *Daily Mail* map.

TO SUSAN OWEN, SUNDAY, 7 JANUARY 1917

The Manchester Battalion left Halloy on 6 January, marching to Beauval, and then motoring to Bertrancourt.

4   *redoubtable*   formidable.

14   *the Guns*   large guns such as howitzers.

15   *sublimity*   inspiring awe or wonder.

21–2   *I have had to censor . . . inspiring reading*   One of the duties of officers was to censor private soldiers' letters in order to ensure that information about the progress of the war was not sent home. WO implied that the letters he read showed pessimism about the war.

23   *reading Trench Standing Orders*   He had been telling the men in his platoon the rules that operated when they were in the trenches.

24   *Verb. Sap.*   A wise reader would not need to ask any more. In other words, his men had been disobeying some of these rules, and WO had to remind them about the standing orders.

TO SUSAN OWEN [9 JANUARY 1917]

WO's battalion was now at Bertrancourt.

6   *Gehenna*   hell.

19   *ear-defenders*   ear-muffs or ear-plugs which were worn
      to cut out noise.
20   *pharmacopoeia*   stock of drugs.
21   *HQ*   headquarters

TO SUSAN OWEN, 10 JANUARY 1917

WO was in the vicinity of Beaumont Hamel.

5   *concussion*   violent shaking.
23   *Company Commander*   Captain H. R. Crichton Green
      (1892–1963).
25   *Heydon*   Second Lieutenant A. Heydon, who was killed
      in April 1917.
33–4 *Whale Oil*   sperm of the whale; used for conditioning
      the soldiers' feet so that they could march each day.
36   *Lice-ntious*   a pun on the words 'lice' and 'licentious',
      implying that the men who catch lice are also inclined to
      catch pubic lice because of their lascivious behaviour.
44   *Cromwellian Troopers*   WO suggested that in his leg-
      gings and gauntlets he looked like a soldier in Crom-
      well's army.
49   *Mistletoe*   According to DH, the code word for this
      place is Serre.
53   *Chloride of Lime*   used in purifying water.
55   *Perrier*   bottled water.
60   *boracic powder*   white powder used as a weak antiseptic
      for the eye.
67   *annoy . . . , for*   Words are omitted in order not to offend
      the people to whom WO referred.

TO SUSAN OWEN, TUES: 16 JANUARY 1917

WO was engaged with his platoon in reconnoitring the area
around Beaumont Hamel.

7   *seventh hell*   an inversion of 'seventh heaven', which
      means a state of bliss or extreme felicity (*OED*).

52–3　*one lad ... blinded*　WO's poem, 'The sentry', is partly based on this incident of blinding.

65–6　*distinguished countryman*　Lloyd George, at that time Prime Minister. WO was referring to the Owen family's Welsh origins.

TO SUSAN OWEN, FRIDAY, 19 JANUARY 1917

WO was still somewhere behind the front line at Beaumont Hamel.

11　*G A S*　Different kinds of poisonous gases were dropped by shell on the soldiers.

35　*parvenus*　upstarts, meaning the ruling politicians, who have gained wealth or position.

39–40　*Slough of Despond*　a place of despair which Christian passes through on his pilgrimage from the City of Destruction: 'As the sinner is awakened about his lost condition, there arise in his soul many fears and doubts, and discouraging apprehensions which all of them get together, and settle in this place' (John Bunyan, *Pilgrim's Progress*, 1678).

41　*fires of Sodom and Gomorrah*　two places mentioned in the Old Testament which God punished with fire and brimstone for their wickedness (Genesis 19:24).

42　*Babylon the Fallen*　Babylon was also destroyed by God because of the sinfulness of its people (Isaiah 20:9).

43–4　*It is pock-marked ... cancer*　WO repeated these images in his poem, 'The show'.

46–7　*'Somme Pictures'*　unrealistic photographs that were distributed by the army to the press in order to reassure the public.

49–51　*No Man's Land ... madness*　These images also appear in 'The show'.

53　*Krupp*　This family owned the monopoly of German arms manufacture during the First World War.

54　*Chlorina-Phosgena*　*Chlorina* is a heavy, yellow-green, poisonous gas which was used to gas soldiers on the front lines. *Phosgena* is a colourless poisonous gas. WO joined the two chemical names into a black parody of a girl's name.

TO SUSAN OWEN, SUNDAY, 4 FEBRUARY 1917

WO had been transferred from the front line to Abbeville, so that he could undertake a month's course in learning transport duties, i.e. methods of bringing supplies to the front lines.

10–42   *I have no mind . . . scenting carrion*   WO drew on this experience when writing 'Exposure'.

10   *Tour*   The battalion continued in its attempt at reconnaissance of the German lines, which involved exposing themselves to German gun- and shell-fire, while trying to gain information about the position of the enemy. WO also used the word *tour* ironically, implying a sightseeing tour.

53   *Me in Transports?*   WO is punning on this word, which can also mean 'delight'. His first experience of the front line has dashed his earlier enthusiasm.

59   *young Scotch Officer*   WO later centred his poem, 'Disabled', on the experience of a Scottish officer.

61   *riding*   Much of the transport work was done on horseback.

86   *Quite 10 years ago*   WO had holidayed in France with his father in 1908 and 1909.

91–102 *I suppose . . . 'soldierly spirit'*   These lines exemplify how already in prose WO had discovered appropriate imagery, although he had not yet begun to do so in poetry.

104   *Tankerville Street*   in Shrewsbury.

117–18 *All the brothers . . . college there*   The four de la Touche boys, whom WO had tutored at Mérignac, near Bordeaux, were at school (Stonyhurst College) in Lancashire.

118–19 *Miss de la Touche . . . Belgian Hospital*   The boys' aunt then ran a hospital for refugees from Beligum.

[? TO SUSAN OWEN], 14 MARCH 1917

On 1 March 1917, WO had returned from the Advanced Horse
Transport Depot to the front, where his battalion was stationed
in the French part of the line at Beaumont Hamel. Subsequently
he fell down a cellar at Le Quesnoy-en-Santerre. The remainder
of this letter has been lost, but EB printed this portion of it in his
'Memoir' in the 1931 edition.

TO SUSAN OWEN, SUNDAY, [18] MARCH [1917]

WO was sent to the 13th Casualty Clearing Station at Gailly,
where patients with 'shell-shock' and other kinds of nervous disorders were treated.

11	*shanty*	Military Hospital at Nesle.
16	*smooth away trouble*	WO was quoting ironically from Rupert Brooke's 'The great lover', ll. 35–6.
32	*Pte. Heath*	WO's batman or servant.
36	*six lines missing*	The missing six lines have been scored out indecipherably by HO.

TO SUSAN OWEN, 4 APRIL 1917

WO returned to his battalion on the outskirts of Saint-Quentin,
a cathedral town, when he had recovered at the 13th Casualty
Clearing Station.

6	*something great*	The battalion had attacked Savy Wood on 2 April.
27	*town*	Saint-Quentin. The battles referred to by WO formed part of the larger offensive – the Battles of Arras – which took place throughout April 1917 (*History of the Great War Based on Official Documents*, comp. Cyril Falls, 1940, pp. 170–1).
39	*this bit of paper*	WO's final page was written on the reverse of an army amendment about training.

2   *'in rest'*   The battalion had been withdrawn to Beauvois.

12–17   *We stuck ... wet snow*   WO probably drew on this experience also when writing 'Exposure'.

19   *Town*   Saint-Quentin.

TO SUSAN OWEN, 25 APRIL 1917

WO's battalion returned from Beauvois to Savy Wood in order to assist the French in another attack on Saint-Quentin. Subsequently they moved back behind the front line to Quivières.

7   *bayonet work*   killing the enemy with bayonets in hand-to-hand fighting.

10   *village*   Fayet.

11–12   *Never before ... in the open*   Thirty men were killed. This attack is probably one of the sources of WO's poem 'Spring offensive'.

27   *Gaukroger*   Second Lieutenant Gaukroger, Manchester Regiment. WO's experience of being blown into the air by a shell, as well as grief about Gaukroger's death, especially the manner of it, led to WO's nervous breakdown and subsequent invaliding back to Great Britain for treatment.

TO SUSAN OWEN, 2 MAY 1917

WO has been returned to the 13th Casualty Clearing Station.

6   *Neurasthenia*   This was the then current medical term for neuroses and various disorders of the nervous system, including those associated with 'shell-shock', i.e. the effects of explosives and other elements of technological warfare.

13   *none of woman born*   WO suggested that, like Macbeth, he thinks that none 'of woman born' can harm him (*Macbeth*, V.viii).

32   *Blighty*   a wound that ensured a return to England (Army slang).

34   *a Blight*   possibly an allusion to venereal disease.

62   *a Casual*   a casualty. WO did not want friends or rela-
        tions to know that he was back in hospital.

TO COLIN OWEN, 14 MAY 1917

7–24   *The sensations . . . the Barrage*   WO was describing the
        action he was involved in at Fayet.

21–2   *the ground . . . wounded bodies*   WO used this image
        again in 'The show'.

TO SUSAN OWEN, [?26] MAY 1917

The 13th Casualty Clearing Station had been restaffed and re-
named the 41st Stationary Hospital.

3   *Great Shadow*   CO will face conscription at 18.

6   *fantasy*   I omitted WO's parody, based on biblical re-
        ferences, from his letter to CO, 14 May 1917.

30–1   *Frederick & Arthur Wood*   These brothers were travel-
        ling evangelists who, according to WO, were avoiding
        joining the armed forces, not by claiming conscientious
        objection, but by asserting that their services in spiri-
        tual healing were needed by the community. Frederick
        seemed to have denied the German origin of his name.

52–3   *Greater love . . . friend*   WO is quoting from John 15:13.

58   *Wells' Book*   H. G. Wells, *The Invisible King* (1917).

61   *The Passionate Friends*   H. G. Wells's *The Passionate
        Friends* (1913) is concerned with prostitution.

71   *O. Henry*   William Sydney Porter, an American writer
        of short stories.

73   *the next Evacuation*   WO meant that he would be re-
        turned to England because he had not yet recovered
        from his nervous disorder.

TO LESLIE GUNSTON, WEDNESDAY [25] JULY 1917

WO has been sent, via the Welsh Military Hospital at Netley,
Southampton, to Craiglockhart War Hospital, near Edinburgh.

This military hospital specialized in treating officers with neurological complaints, whether of physical or psychogenic origin. Craiglockhart was formerly a hydro which provided residents with a regime of hydropathic therapy, i.e. the internal and external application of mineral spring water. WO was under the care of the psychiatrist Dr Arthur Brock, whose methods of treatment included social and occupational therapy.

4–8   'Field Club' ... learned society   WO was referring to his boyhood 'Astronomical, Geological, and Botanical Society', which he had formed with Leslie (Black Moth) and Vera Gunston. WO was now one of the founders of the Craiglockhart Field Club.

13   our Mag.   The Hydra was the Craiglockhart magazine which WO edited.

19–24 How Earth ... his eyes   JS printed the remainder of 'The wrestlers', pp. 520–5.

26   Locke's Usurper   W. J. Locke, The Usurper (1901).

TO SUSAN OWEN, TUES. NIGHT [7 AUGUST 1917]

6   a boy ... M. Léger   Monsieur Léger had known E. B. Browning.

7   Flapper   a slang word for a fashionable young woman with a short hairstyle. WO implied that he was not attracted to vapid young women.

12–19 But as for misery ... Beaumont Hamel   WO compared Tennyson's 'Crossing the bar' (1896), which romanticized death, with his own experience of being near death with dead men for comforters on the Beaumont Hamel front between January and April 1917.

22–4   But the old happiness ... our hope   These are the last lines of 'Happiness'.

25   Mayes   a fellow patient.

32   Holyrood   Holyroodhouse was a former royal palace.

TO SUSAN OWEN, FRIDAY NIGHT [10 AUGUST 1917]

11–14 'Ye have heard ... the other also.'   Matthew 5:38, 39.

20   wear my star and eat my rations   i.e. retains his commission and eats army food.

27   *converted Horatio Bottomley* In a letter of 10 June 1917, WO wrote that Bottomley 'preached . . . of salvation by *death in war*' (*CL*, p. 468). Bottomley financed and wrote for the militaristic and chauvinist *John Bull*. In his use of this reference with the adjective *converted*, WO showed that he was aware of his own tendency towards tub-thumping.

30–2   *In my eye . . . in many eyes* Matthew 7:3–5.

32–6   *It is this . . . 'Kings and Christs'* WO seemed to be re-considering his letter of [?26] May 1917: that 'greater love' – the love of Christ – existed in No Man's Land. He here asserted that it is a distorted view to rational-ize battle in terms of soldiers dying for their friends. In his unfinished, rejected poem, 'Kings and Christs' (JS, pp. 500–3), he implies that a soldier dying in war might 'die as Christ'.

42   *copy* Significantly, WO uses the term which is usually applied to an article prepared for publication.

TO LESLIE GUNSTON, 22 AUGUST 1917

SS had made a statement to the effect that the war which he had entered 'as a war of defence and liberation' had become 'a war of aggression and conquest'. He had also arranged for this state-ment to be publicized through a question in Parliament, but in-stead of his being court-martialled for treason, he was sent for treatment to Craiglockhart War Hospital (SS, *Siegfried's Journey, 1916–20*, Faber, London, 1946, p. 56).

3   *Siegfried Sassoon* SS described his first meeting with WO in *Siegfried's Journey 1916–1920*, London, Faber, 1946, ch. 6.

13   '*God the Invisible King*' H. G. Wells had just published *God the Invisible King* (London, Cassell, May 1917).

16–36   This early draft of WO's first major war poem shows the impact of his reading SS's satirical war poems.

38–9   *I am going to send . . . First Publication* WO intended to give SS's first book of poetry to ELG in order to cele-brate the publication of ELG's *The Nymph and Other Poems* (London, Stockwell, November 1917).

41–2   *Georgian Anthology*   This anthology was published by
        the Poetry Bookshop.
42–4   *pointed out ... stanzas*   WO altered 'The dead-beat' in
        the light of SS's comments.
45   *Antaeus*   'The wrestlers', JS, pp. 520–5.
47   *Sing me ... Laugh*   'Song of Songs'.
66   *Morals*   J. W. Locke, *The Morals of Marcus Ordeyne*,
        London, Bodley Head, 1905.

TO TOM OWEN, 26 AUGUST 1917

2   *this work of Sassoon's*   *The Old Huntsman and Other Poems*
        (1917).
4   *Na-poo*   *Il n'y (en) a plus, (fini)*:   'There's no more of it,
        finished.' There's nothing more to be said (Army slang;
        corruption of French).

TO MARY OWEN, THURSDAY, 29 AUGUST 1917

3   *Aberystwyth*   The Owen family were holidaying in
        Wales.
15–17   *My dear ... Na-poo*   WO referred again to SS's war
        poems, and compared their truthfulness with that of
        some of his own letters about the war.
27   *a Board*   a meeting of superior officers who would re-
        ceive medical reports and assess WO's state of mental
        health in order to decide his future.

TO SUSAN OWEN, 7 SEPTEMBER 1917

5   *the Grays'*   an Edinburgh family whom WO had met
        through the offices of his psychiatrist, Dr Brock.
22   *the Slum Gardens*   These gardens were designed for
        the disadvantaged in Edinburgh. The users cultivated
        the gardens. Part of Dr Brock's method of psychothera-
        peutic treatment was to encourage his patients to foster
        their pre-war interests. At Dunsden, WO had visited
        the poor, but on this occasion he seemed to enjoy more
        his talk about literature with one of the Misses Wyer.
        He planned to send her a copy of his book of poems,
        had he survived the war.

33–4   *Alec Waugh's book 'Loom of Youth'*   published in 1917.

45   *painful war poem*   Possibly SS's poem was 'Prelude: the troops'.

70   *angels ...*   Seventeen words are omitted in order to avoid giving offence.

TO SUSAN OWEN, TUESDAY, [10] SEPTEMBER 1917

5–8   *The enclosed ... parcel*   WO was referring to some unwanted enclosure in his parcel of manuscripts.

12   *no Barrack Room Ballads*   WO meant that he had written no poems as earthy as Rudyard Kipling's in the soldier's vernacular.

48–9   *and me ...*   Six words have been omitted in order to avoid giving offence.

54   *Tomaso*   the Italian singer mentioned in WO's letter of 7 September 1917.

76   *'Purple'*   JS, p. 117.

TO SUSAN OWEN, SUNDAY, 14 OCTOBER [1917]

23   *Last poem of O.H.*   WO referred to 'A letter home: to Robert Graves'.

31   *No thanks*   WO objected to Robert Graves's patronage.

35–7   *quotation ... for himself*   SS did not use this quotation, whatever it was.

43   *neurasthenic ... neurotic*   WO was distinguishing between *neurotic* anxieties which might be troublesome but are not incapacitating, and *neurasthenia*, which is mental illness or complete nervous debility.

48   *Webby people*   WO belittled the Webb family, who were acquaintances in Shrewsbury.

TO SIEGFRIED SASSOON, 5 NOVEMBER 1917

WO had been discharged from Craiglockhart and was at his mother's home on leave for three weeks.

2–3   *your envelope ... Club Staircase*   When WO parted from SS at the Scottish Conservative Club, Edinburgh, SS gave WO £10 in a sealed envelope.

4   *a gourd, a Gothic vacuum*   WO was quoting ironically a

phrase from Alymer Strong's book of verse, *A Human Voice* (London, Elkin Mathews, 1917), which he and SS had laughed over at their last meeting: 'O is it true I have become / This gourd, this gothic vacuum?'

6   *grame*   anger, vexation; grief, sorrow (*OED*). Although this word is obsolete (except in archaic forms), WO echoes Alymer Strong's use of it in order to refer to his own feelings of vexation at having been silently given £10 by Sassoon.

22   *I love you, dispassionately*   Critics disagree about whether WO's friendship with SS was asexual. From the 1960s onwards, the word *love* has almost invariably been associated with sexual passion and has been used less and less in its platonic or Christian meanings. But in 1918 a strong *love* between men or between women or between man and woman could be construed as *dispassionate* – as WO himself here pointedly emphasizes.

33   *note from Robt. Ross*   SS gave WO a letter of introduction to Robert Ross: 'Wilfred had no literary connection in London, and during the next few months Robbie made him known to various people who were glad to welcome this new and gifted young war poet' (*Siegfried's Journey 1916–1920*, London, Faber, 1946, p. 65). Ross, a homosexual who had befriended Oscar Wilde, was the kingpin in a literary circle which included SS, Charles Scott Moncrieff, Osbert Sitwell, Robert Graves, H. G. Wells, and Arnold Bennett.

36   *Fairies & Fusiliers*   Robert Graves had just published this.

44–53   *What I most miss ... for long*   a memory of an outing with Mrs Fullerton and four boys from Tynecastle School.

TO SIEGFRIED SASSOON, 27 NOVEMBER 1917

After three weeks' leave, during which he stayed mainly at Shrewsbury with excursions to London to meet Robert Ross and other literati and to Winchester to visit his cousin ELG, WO was posted to the 5th (Reserve) Battalion Manchester Regiment at Scarborough. Officers stayed at the Queen's Hotel and Clarence Gardens Hotel, and the ordinary soldiers were quartered in barracks at nearby Burniston. WO was made Camp Commandant at the Clarence Gardens Hotel.

10–12   *I had a Third Heaven ... on Wednesday*   WO referred to his weekend in London from 9 to 11 November. On Wednesday, 14 November, he returned to London from Winchester and spent three hours at the Poetry Bookshop *en route* to Shrewsbury.

15–16   *fine book ... herewith*   WO sent SS a copy of ELG's just-published *The Nymph and Other Poems*, but SS never mentioned this book in subsequent letters to WO.

18   *R.R.*   Robert Ross, who had a flat at Half Moon Street.

33   *R. Nichols*   Second Lieutenant Robert Nichols (1893–1944) had published two books of war poems: *Invocation: War Poems and Others* (London, Elkin Mathews, 1917) and *Ardours and Endurances* (London, Chatto & Windus, 1917).

42   *R. G's book*   Robert Graves's *Fairies and Fusiliers*.

47   *Gracchus*   Robert Graves, after his character in 'The legion'.

50–1   *his Letter ... yours to him*   Graves had written 'Letter to SS from Mametz Wood', to which SS had responded with 'A letter home' addressed to Robert Graves.

54   *Mad Jack*   SS had been given this nickname because of his daredevil exploits along the front line in France.

58   *sentencience*   'sententious' and 'sentence' are amalgamated in fun by WO.

64   *subject ...*   Words are omitted to avoid giving offence.

67   *'Vision'*   'The show'.

70–1   *'Soldier's Dream' ... Cambridge*   This poem did not appear in *The Nation* or in the *Cambridge Magazine*.

90–1   *I am Owen ... the Gleam*   WO was parodying the first stanza of Tennyson's *Merlin and the Gleam*.

TO SIEGFRIED SASSOON, 6 DECEMBER 1917

8   *Vowel-Rime stunt*   WO was referring to his use of half-rhyme in 'The show' and 'Wild with all regrets', which

is an early version of 'A terre'.

9   *Flea to Soul*   WO asked whether his sudden change of tone in ll. 29–35 of 'Wild with all regrets' is effective.

11   *Theosophist*   a fellow patient at Craiglockhart.

TO LESLIE GUNSTON, 30 DECEMBER 1917

6   *Gosse's life of A.C.S.*   Edmund Gosse, *The Life of Algernon Charles Swinburne* (1917).

11   Robert Graves' letter is printed in *CL*, pp. 595–6.

26   *in your Line*   ELG could not enlist because of a mitral murmur and was working voluntarily in catering at a YMCA canteen for soldiers at Winchester.

TO SUSAN OWEN, 31 DECEMBER 1917

4   *Johnny & Bobby*   de la Touche, whom WO had taught at Mérignac, near Bordeaux.

9   *my cher ami*   Pierre Berthaud.

31–3   *a Poet . . . a poet's poet*   WO implied that his reputation is based on contemporary poets' admiration, since he has not had a book published to a wider audience.

34–5   *I am started . . . my galleon*   Compare this image of success with WO's letter to SO of 5 March 1915, ll. 62–6.

40   *shambles*   butcher's slaughter-house or scene of carnage (*OED*). WO recalled 1 January 1917, when he had first arrived in France.

TO LESLIE GUNSTON, 8 JANUARY 1918

16   *The Times . . . what it says*   the *Times Literary Supplement*'s review of ELG's *The Nymph and Other Poems* (1917) was somewhat unfavourable.

31   *Wells' 'What is coming'*   H. G. Wells, *What is Coming? A Forecast after the War*, London, Cassell, 1916.

32   *Hazlitt's 'Essays'*   William Hazlitt was an early nineteenth century critic and essayist.

33   *essays by A. K. Thompson*   *The Greek Tradition: Essays in the Reconstruction of Ancient Thought*, London, Allen & Unwin, 1915.

35   *Wells' '... Harman'* H. G. Wells, *Wife of Sir Isaac Harman*, 1914.

TO LESLIE GUNSTON, SATURDAY NIGHT [26 JANUARY 1918]

13   *Lord Rhondda* Food Controller.
14   *Max Beerbohm* author and artist.
        George Belcher artist and cartoonist.
19–21   *Max B. ... my neck* WO was referring to Beerbohm's
        cartoon style.
22   *Edward Marsh* He edited the five Georgian anthologies
        from 1912 to 1921.
26–7   *this week's 'Nation' ... poem in it* 'Miners' was pub-
        lished in *The Nation* on 26 January 1918.

TO LESLIE GUNSTON, [POSTMARK 12 FEBRUARY 1918]

4   *the Two Guineas* WO was referring to his payment
        from *The Nation* for 'Miners'.

TO SUSAN OWEN, TUESDAY [POSTMARK 12 MARCH 1918]

WO had been transferred to the Command Depot at Ripon,
Yorkshire, and had entered upon his final stage of retraining for
return to the front.

5   *Priestley* Lieutenant H. Priestley, 7th Manchester Regi-
        ment, with whom WO had become friendly at Scar-
        borough, and to whom he asked his mother to send the
        scroll, or wall poster.

TO SUSAN OWEN, EASTER SUNDAY [13 MARCH 1918]

WO had moved into a cottage at Ripon, but he wrote this letter
from the Command Headquarters.

12   *Mrs A* a friend of SO's.
13   *Bainbrigge* Philip Bainbrigge, an officer, had been a
        master at Shrewsbury Technical School between 1913
        and 1917.
34   *the present Battle* the second Somme battle in March

1918, which was the last major offensive launched by
the Germans. Losses were heavy on both sides.

44–8   *The Mystery Gun ... pretty work*   Seventy-five civilians
were killed in this German shelling of Paris. WO's dis-
like of war-profiteers engendered his ironic remark
about *unnecessary civilians.*

54–6   *God so hated ... comfortable life*   WO was parodying
John 3:16: 'For God so loved the world, that he gave his
only begotten Son, that whosoever believeth in him
should not perish, but have everlasting life.'

TO OSBERT SITWELL, JULY 1918

WO had been ordered back to the 5th (Reserve) Battalion
Manchester Regiment at Scarborough in early June.

1   Osbert Sitwell, who had met WO through Robert Ross,
had sent him an epigram satirizing Clemenceau, the
French premier, through religious imagery.

2–8   *I rehearsed ... appreciated*   WO told Sitwell that his
fellow officers would not understand his satire, but that
he would have the poem translated, since a French audience might appreciate it.

9–11   *copy out ... as Editor*   Osbert and Edith Sitwell edited
an annual anthology, *Wheels,* and had asked WO to con-
tribute some poems to the 1918 volume. Seven of WO's
war poems were published posthumously in *Wheels:
Fourth Cycle* (1919).

15–22   *teaching Christ ... Golgotha*   WO was using an extended
analogy in which he compared the soldiers to Christ
before Calvary.

24–9   *Canning ... Rigby's*   both at that time Scarborough
booksellers.

31–2   *Is the 1918 vol. ... Music Hall Tank?*   WO enquired
whether the Sitwells' 1918 anthology, *Wheels,* would
contain satires similar to SS's 'Blighters'.

38–9   *Westborough*   Scarborough's main street.

41   *G.S.*   graded as fit for service. WO was expressing
sarcasm about his father's notion that his being fit for
war service meant that he was 'normal'.

4   *draft leave*   Officers were given three weeks' home leave before being drafted to France.

6–7   *I shall be better . . . my part*   WO was alluding to an unpublished poem by SS which ended: 'O my heart / Be still; you have cried your cry, you have played your part.'

11–12   *Stiebel's job on the Stunt*   i.e. as messing officer for the battalion; WO had carried out this work during a mock attack.

20   *Siegfried . . . next week*   SS had been invalided back to England after having been wounded in the head.

31   *Hastings*   CO, who was now in the RAF, had been posted to Hastings.

32   *Portsmouth*   HO had been on a gunnery course there.

WO was drafted to France in mid-August and, after embarkation leave, travelled to base camp at Étaples, France, on 31 August 1918.

20–30   See letter to SO [10 August 1918], ll. 6–7.

6   *Lancaster Gate*   SS was in the American Women's Hospital, Lancaster Gate, Hyde Park.

9   *wage the bitterer war*   'The next war' echoes WO's notion here of social 'warfare' to alleviate poverty and pain.

3–4   *The sun . . . bright*   These are the opening lines of Shelley's 'Stanzas, written in dejection, near Naples'.

6   *Caverns & Abysmals*   metaphors for warfare.

12   *Shape*   WO specifically rejected the notion that he was interested in the schoolboy's physical appearance.

23   *only in the leg*   SS had told WO that he would stab him

in the leg – i.e. prevent him from returning to the front
– if he were to be drafted to France again.

14   *Minister of Labour*   G. H. Roberts.
21   *poilus*   ordinary soldiers.

4–5   *in action for some days*   On 1 and 2 October the Manchester battalion took part in an offensive and broke
through the Beaurevoir–Fonsomme line, taking over
200 prisoners.

22   *recommended for the Military Cross*   The citation for WO's
Military Cross read: 'For conspicuous gallantry and
devotion to duty in the attack on the Fonsomme Line on
1st/2nd October 1918. On the Company Commander
becoming a casualty, he assumed command and showed
fine leadership and resisted a heavy counter-attack. He
personally manipulated a captured enemy Machine Gun
from an isolated position and inflicted considerable
losses on the enemy. Throughout he behaved most
gallantly.'

5–6   *O.C. D Coy.*   officer in charge of D Company.
19–20   *Deceased*   WO later intended to write the truth about
these dead soldiers, but at that moment he had to send
back each of these men's letters to his next-of-kin.
23–6   *Full of confidence … 'en pamoisons'*   WO, who was
making a joke at SS's expense, either meant that the
seraphic lance corporal would have caused SS to have been
en pamoisons, i.e. in a swoon, or that the exhilaration of
capturing the machine-guns would have caused SS intense excitement.
25–6   *glorious … peace talk*   WO is parodying a 'Special Order
of the Day', which inveighs against 'dangerous peace
talk'.

30   This line came from 'Sick leave' (SS, *The War Poems*, arr. and introd. Rupert Hart-Davis, London, Faber, 1983).

32–3   *C. Attack   Counter-Attack and Other Poems* (1918).

33–4   *Adjutant ... Erskine MacD.'s 'Soldier-Poets'*   Erskine MacDonald published two books of soldiers' verse, *Soldier Poets: Songs of the Fighting Men* (ed. Galloway Kyle, 1916) and *More Songs of the Fighting Men* (1917). WO was referring to the latter collection. Second Lieutenant Murray McClymont, 2nd/10th (Scottish) KLR, the *Adjutant*, had three poems in *More Songs of the Fighting Men*.

40   *Prewett*   Frank Prewett, a Canadian, published a book of poems after the war.

41   *O'Riordan*   Conal O'Riordan wrote an account of his soldiering in 'One more fortunate', *A Martial Medley*, ed. Eric Partridge, London, Scholartis Press, 1931, pp. 357–61.

51   *exposed flanks*   WO was not eager to expose his own person to shells and bullets, nor did he want to form part of a battalion flank, i.e. the exposed left or right side of a military formation. WO probably also intended a sexual innuendo, since this letter is addressed to SS.

53   *the Ed. of 'Today'*   Holbrook Jackson.

54   *Mais*   S. B. Mais, literary reviewer for the *Evening News*.

58   *choicest of specimens*   the 'Special Order of the Day' that WO parodied in ll. 25–6.

TO LESLIE GUNSTON, 25 OCTOBER 1918

WO had moved with his battalion to Bohain and Bussigny at the rear of the front line.

3   *that Roundel*   ELG has had a roundel published in *The Nation*.

21   *against War ...*   Two sentences are omitted in order to avoid giving offence.

22–30 *There are ... kiss was*   WO had been flirting with and kissing the French mayor's two daughters, and, as he implied, he might have seduced one of them.

30   *was* ....   One sentence is omitted, in order to avoid giving offence.

TO SUSAN OWEN, THURS., 31 OCTOBER [1918] 6.15 P.M.

This is WO's last extant letter, before he was killed at Ors in an attack on the eastern bank of the Sambre–Oise Canal on 4 November 1918. WO's parents learned of his death on 11 November 1918, the day of the Armistice.